In a Queer Time and Place

SEXUAL CULTURES: New Directions from the
Center for Lesbian and Gay Studies
General Editors: José Esteban Muñoz and Ann Pellegrini

Judith Halberstam

In a Queer Time and Place

Transgender Bodies, Subcultural Lives

NEW YORK UNIVERSITY PRESS New York and London

NEW YORK UNIVERSITY PRESS
New York and London
www.nyupress.org

Library of Congress Cataloging-in-Publication Data
Halberstam, Judith, 1961–
In a queer time and place : transgender bodies, subcultural lives /
Judith Halberstam.
p. cm. — (Sexual cultures)
Includes bibliographical references and index.
ISBN 0–8147–3584–3 (cloth : alk. paper) —
ISBN 0–8147–3585–1 (pbk. : alk. paper)
1. Teena, Brandon, 1972–1993.   2. Transsexualism.
3. Gender identity.   4. Sex role.   5. Transsexuals in motion pictures.
6. Transsexuals in literature.   7. Marginality, Social.   I. Title.   II. Series.
HQ75.5.H335   2004
306.76'8—dc22   2004018151

Contents

A color insert of illustrations for chapter 5 follows page 120.

Acknowledgments

In a book about time, timing is everything, and as I finish this manuscript and begin a new project, I am also on the verge of leaving one job and taking another. Since the Literature Department at the University of California at San Diego (UCSD) has provided such an extraordinary intellectual environment for my work, I feel as regretful about leaving my colleagues in La Jolla as I am excited about my move to the University of Southern California (USC) in downtown Los Angeles. UCSD's Literature Department is far ahead of its time in terms of its conception of cultural studies, global cultures, and the future of the humanities; I have learned so much there about how to be a part of an evolving intellectual project and how to collaborate with people who may have different scholarly interests from my own. But it is time to leave there and begin something new, and as I leave, I want to thank and acknowledge the entire department. I also extend thanks for support at UCSD that ran far beyond the bounds of collegiality over the years to John D. Blanco, Michael Davidson, Page Dubois, Steven Epstein, Steve Fagin, Takashi Fujitani, Rosemary Marangoly George, Nicole King, Susan Kirkpatrick, Nayan Shah, Shelley Streeby, and Lisa Yoneyama. Lisa Lowe has been an exceptional friend and a model for how to combine an impassioned pedagogy with a principled commitment to abstract thinking. Working with her on our Perverse Modernities series has been an honor and an inspiration, and in many ways it is Lisa's vision of intellectual community that I take away with me from La Jolla. Eileen Myles and I have been victims of bad timing in that I am leaving as she settles into building an arts scene in San Diego; but I look forward to creating queer havoc with her in the larger arena of Southern California. David Roman, my new colleague at USC makes the move from UCSD to USC, exciting and worthwhile.

An incomplete list of other friends and colleagues who have supported this work across queer space and time and in a variety of locations include Lauren Berlant, Daphne Brooks, Judith Butler, George Chauncey, David Eng, Jillana Enteen, Licia Fiol-Matta, Carla Freccero, Elizabeth Freeman, Diana Fuss, Jane Gallop, Jody Greene, David Halperin, Laura A. Harris, Gil Hochberg, John Howard, George Lipsitz, Ira Livingston, Amelia Jones, Amy Kautzman, Kara Keeling, Laura Kipnis, Heather Love, Richard Meyer, Esther Newton, Marcia Ochoa, Jenni Olson, Katrin Pahl, Pratibha Parmar, Jordana Rosenberg, Gayle Rubin, James Schultz, Cherry Smyth, Gayle Wald, Patti White, and Robyn Wiegman. In Australia, I thank Vicky Crowley, Fanny Jacobsen, Annamarie Jagose, and Linnell Secomb. In Taiwan, thanks to Antonia Chao, Josephine Ho, Naifei Ding, Jiazhen Ni, and Amie Parry. Members of the Sexuality and Space research group at UCHRI—Alicia Arrizon, Tom Boellstorff, Rod Ferguson, Glen Mimura, Chandan Reddy, Jennifer Terry, and Karen Tongson—have provided me with a generative discussion space for new ideas. Karen Tongson in particular has been an excellent ally and interlocutor. I thank David Theo Goldberg and UCHRI for hosting the group. For sharing their artwork and their ideas about it with me, I thank Linda Besemer, Brian Dawn Chalkley, Silas Howard, JA Nicholls, and Del LaGrace Volcano.

José Esteban Muñoz and Ann Pellegrini have been encouraging series editors, and NYU Press's Eric Zinner has been helpful throughout. Lisa Duggan and Nicholas Mirzoeff were tough and careful readers of the manuscript, and this book is much better for their generosity and care. My appreciation to Emily Park for attending to the important details. Thanks and love finally to Gayatri Gopinath, still here through thick and thin.

Portions of this book have been previously published. A short version of chapter 2 was published in Robert J. Corber and Stephen Valocchi, eds., *Queer Studies: An Interdisciplinary Reader* (London: Blackwell, 2002), 159–70. Pieces of chapter 3 have appeared in "Queer Auto/Biographies," ed. Thomas Spear, special issue, *a/b* 15, no. 1 (Summer 2000): 62–81; and María Carla Sánchez and Linda Schlossberg, eds., *Passing: Identity and Interpretation in Sexuality, Race, and Religion* (New York: New York University Press, 2001), 13–37. A short version of chapter 4 appeared in *Screen* 42, no. 3 (Autumn 2001): 294–98. Chapter 6 appeared in "Men and Lesbianism," special issue, *GLQ* 7, no. 3 (2001): 425–52. A section of chapter 7 was published in *International Journal of Cultural Studies* 6, no. 3 (September 2003): 235–54.

1

Queer Temporality and Postmodern Geographies

> How can a relational system be reached through sexual practices? Is it possible to create a homosexual mode of life? . . . To be "gay," I think, is not to identify with the psychological traits and the visible masks of the homosexual, but to try to define and develop a way of life.
>
> —Michel Foucault, "Friendship as a Way of Life"

> There is never one geography of authority and there is never one geography of resistance. Further, the map of resistance is not simply the underside of the map of domination—if only because each is a lie to the other, and each gives the lie to the other.
>
> —Steve Pile, "Opposition, Political Identities, and Spaces of Resistance"

This book makes the perhaps overly ambitious claim that there is such a thing as "queer time" and "queer space." Queer uses of time and space develop, at least in part, in opposition to the institutions of family, heterosexuality, and reproduction. They also develop according to other logics of location, movement, and identification. If we try to think about queerness as an outcome of strange temporalities, imaginative life schedules, and eccentric economic practices, we detach queerness from sexual identity and come closer to understanding Foucault's comment in "Friendship as a Way of Life" that "homosexuality threatens people as a 'way of life' rather than as a way of having sex" (310). In Foucault's radical formulation, queer friendships, queer networks, and the existence of these relations in space and in relation to the use of time mark out the particularity and indeed the perceived menace of homosexual life. In this book, the queer "way of life" will encompass subcultural practices, alternative methods of alliance, forms of transgender embodiment, and those forms of representation dedicated to capturing these willfully eccentric modes of being. Obviously not all gay, lesbian, and transgender people live their lives in radically different ways from their heterosexual counterparts, but part of what has made queerness compelling as a form of self-description in the past decade or so has to do with the way it has the potential to open up new life narratives and alternative relations to time and space.

Queer time perhaps emerges most spectacularly, at the end of the twentieth century, from within those gay communities whose horizons of possibility have been severely diminished by the AIDS epidemic. In his memoir of his lover's death from AIDS, poet Mark Doty writes: "All my life I've lived with a future which constantly diminishes but never vanishes" (Doty 1996, 4). The constantly diminishing future creates a new emphasis on the here, the present, the now, and while the threat of no future hovers overhead like a storm cloud, the urgency of being also expands the potential of the moment and, as Doty explores, squeezes new possibilities out of the time at hand. In his poem "In Time of Plague," Thom Gunn explores the erotics of compressed time and impending mortality: "My thoughts are crowded with death / and it draws so oddly on the sexual / that I am confused/confused to be attracted / by, in effect, my own annihilation" (Gunn 1993, 59). Queer time, as it flashes into view in the heart of a crisis, exploits the potential of what Charles-Pierre Baudelaire called in relation to modernism "The transient, the fleeting, the contingent." Some gay men have responded to the threat of AIDS, for example, by rethinking the conventional emphasis on longevity and futurity, and by making community in relation to risk, disease, infection, and death (Bersani 1996; Edelman 1998). And yet queer time, even as it emerges from the AIDS crisis, is not only about compression and annihilation; it is also about the potentiality of a life unscripted by the conventions of family, inheritance, and child rearing. In the sections on subcultures in this book, I will examine the queer temporalities that are proper to subcultural activities, and will propose that we rethink the adult/youth binary in relation to an "epistemology of youth" that disrupts conventional accounts of youth culture, adulthood, and maturity.[1] Queer subcultures produce alternative temporalities by allowing their participants to believe that their futures can be imagined according to logics that lie outside of those paradigmatic markers of life experience—namely, birth, marriage, reproduction, and death.

These new temporal logics, again, have emerged most obviously in the literatures produced in relation to the AIDS epidemic. For example, in *The Hours,* Michael Cunningham's beautiful rewriting of Virginia Woolf's *Mrs. Dalloway,* Cunningham takes the temporal frame of Woolf's novel (life in a day) and emphasizes its new, but also queer rendering of time and space. Indeed, Cunningham rationalizes Woolf's authorial decision to have the young Clarissa Dalloway "love another girl" in terms of queer temporality. He explains: "Clarissa Dalloway in her first youth, will love another girl, Virginia thinks; Clarissa will believe that a rich, riotous future is opening before her, but eventually (how, exactly, will the change be accomplished?) she will come to her senses, as young women do and marry a suitable man" (Cunningham 1998, 81–82). The "riotous future," which emerges in Woolf's novel from a lesbian kiss in Clarissa's youth, becomes, in Cunningham's skillful rewrite, a queer time that is both realized and ultimately disappointing in its own narrative arc. Cunningham tracks Woolf's autobiographical story of a descent into madness and suicide alongside a contemporary narrative of Clarissa Vaughn, who has refused to "come to her senses" and lives with a woman named Sally while caring for her best friend, Richard, a writer dying of AIDS. Cunningham's elegant formulation of queer temporality opens up the possibility of a "rich, riotous future" and closes it down in the same aesthetic gesture. While Woolf, following Sigmund Freud, knows that Clarissa must come to her senses (and like Freud, Woolf cannot imagine "how the change [will] be accomplished"), Cunningham turns Clarissa away from the seemingly inexorable march of narrative time toward marriage (death) and uses not consummation but the kiss as the gateway to alternative outcomes. For Woolf, the kiss constituted one of those "moments of being" that her writing struggled to encounter and inhabit; for Cunningham, the kiss is a place where, as Carolyn Dinshaw terms it in *Getting Medieval,* different histories "touch" or brush up against each other, creating temporal havoc in the key of desire (Dinshaw 1999).

While there is now a wealth of excellent work focused on the temporality of lives lived in direct relation to the HIV virus (Edelman 1998), we find far less work on the other part of Cunningham's equation: those lives lived in the "shadow of an epidemic," the lives of women, transgenders, and queers who partake of this temporal shift in less obvious ways. Furthermore, the experience of HIV for heterosexual and queer people of color does not necessarily offer the same kind of hopeful reinvention of conventional understandings of time. As Cathy Cohen's work in *The Boundaries of Blackness: AIDS and the Breakdown of Black Politics* shows, some bodies are simply considered "expendable," both in mainstream and marginal communities, and the abbreviated life spans of black queers or poor drug users, say, does not inspire the same kind of metaphysical speculation on curtailed futures, intensified presents, or reformulated histories; rather, the premature deaths of poor people and people of color in a nation that pumps drugs into impoverished urban communities and withholds basic health care privileges, is simply business as usual (Cohen 1999). Samuel Delany articulates beautifully the difficulty in connecting radical political practice to exploited populations when he claims, "We must remember that it is only those workers—usually urban artists (a realization Marx did come to)—whose money comes from several different social class sources, up and down the social ladder, who can afford to entertain a truly radical political practice" (Reid-Pharr 2001, xii). And yet, as Robert Reid-Pharr argues in *Black Gay Man,* the book that Delany's essay introduces, the relation between the universal and the particular that allows for the elevation of white male experience (gay or straight) to the level of generality and the reduction of, say, black gay experience to the status of the individual, can only come undone through a consideration of the counterlogics that emerge from "the humdrum perversities of our existence" (12). *In a Queer Time and Place* seeks to unravel precisely those claims made on the universal from and on behalf of white male subjects theorizing postmodern temporality and geography.

Queer time and space are useful frameworks for assessing political and cultural change in the late twentieth and early twenty-first centuries (both what has changed and what must change). The critical languages that we have developed to try to assess the obstacles to social change have a way of both stymieing our political agendas and alienating nonacademic constituencies. I try here to make queer time and queer space into useful terms for academic and nonacademic considerations of life, location, and transformation. To give an example of the way in which critical languages can sometimes weigh us down, consider the fact that we have become adept within postmodernism at talking about "normativity," but far less adept at describing in rich detail the practices and structures that both oppose and sustain conventional forms of association, belonging, and identification. I try to use the concept of queer time to make clear how respectability, and notions of the normal on which it depends, may be upheld by a middle-class logic of reproductive temporality. And so, in Western cultures, we chart the emergence of the adult from the dangerous and unruly period of adolescence as a desired process of maturation; and we create longevity as the most desirable future, applaud the pursuit of long life (under any circumstances), and pathologize modes of living that show little or no concern for longevity. Within the life cycle of the Western human subject, long periods of stability are considered to be desirable, and people who live in rapid bursts (drug addicts, for example) are characterized as immature and even dangerous. But the ludic temporality created by drugs (captured by Salvador Dalí as a melting clock and by William Burroughs as "junk time") reveals the artificiality of our privileged constructions of time and activity. In the works of queer postmodern writers like Lynn Breedlove (*Godspeed*), Eileen Myles (*Chelsea Girls*), and others, speed itself (the drug as well as the motion) becomes the motor of an alternative history as their queer heroes rewrite completely narratives of female rebellion (Myles 1994; Breedlove 2002).

The time of reproduction is ruled by a biological clock for women and by strict bourgeois rules of respectability and scheduling for married couples. Obviously, not all people who have children keep or even are able to keep reproductive time, but many and possibly most people believe that the scheduling of repro-time is natural and desirable. Family time refers to the normative scheduling of daily life (early to bed, early to rise) that accompanies the practice of child rearing. This timetable is governed by an imagined set of children's needs, and it relates to beliefs about children's health and healthful environments for child rearing. The time of inheritance refers to an overview of generational time within which values, wealth, goods, and morals are passed through family ties from one generation to the next. It also connects the family to the historical past of the nation, and glances ahead to connect the family to the future of both familial and national stability. In this category we can include the kinds of hypothetical temporality—the time of "what if"—that demands protection in the way of insurance policies, health care, and wills.

In queer renderings of postmodern geography, the notion of a body-centered identity gives way to a model that locates sexual subjectivities within and between embodiment, place, and practice. But queer work on sexuality and space, like queer work on sexuality and time, has had to respond to canonical work on "postmodern geography" by Edward Soja, Fredric Jameson, David Harvey, and others that has actively excluded sexuality as a category for analysis precisely because desire has been cast by neo-Marxists as part of a ludic body politics that obstructs the "real" work of activism (Soja 1989; Harvey 1990; Jameson 1997). This foundational exclusion, which assigned sexuality to body/local/personal and took class/global/political as its proper frame of reference, has made it difficult to introduce questions of sexuality and space into the more general conversations about globalization and transnational capitalism. Both Anna Tsing and Steve Pile refer this problem as the issue of "scale." Pile, for example, rejects the notion that certain

5

political arenas of struggle (say, class) are more important than others (say, sexuality), and instead he offers that we rethink these seemingly competing struggles in terms of scale by recognizing that while we tend to view local struggles as less significant than global ones, ultimately "the local and the global are not natural scales, but formed precisely out of the struggles that seemingly they only contain" (Pile 1997, 13).

A "queer" adjustment in the way in which we think about time, in fact, requires and produces new conceptions of space. And in fact, much of the contemporary theory seeking to disconnect queerness from an essential definition of homosexual embodiment has focused on queer space and queer practices. By articulating and elaborating a concept of queer time, I suggest new ways of understanding the nonnormative behaviors that have clear but not essential relations to gay and lesbian subjects. For the purpose of this book, "queer" refers to nonnormative logics and organizations of community, sexual identity, embodiment, and activity in space and time. "Queer time" is a term for those specific models of temporality that emerge within postmodernism once one leaves the temporal frames of bourgeois reproduction and family, longevity, risk/safety, and inheritance. "Queer space" refers to the place-making practices within postmodernism in which queer people engage and it also describes the new understandings of space enabled by the production of queer counterpublics. Meanwhile, "postmodernism" in this project takes on meaning in relation to new forms of cultural production that emerge both in sync with and running counter to what Jameson has called the "logic" of late capitalism in his book *Postmodernism* (1997). I see postmodernism as simultaneously a crisis and an opportunity—a crisis in the stability of form and meaning, and an opportunity to rethink the practice of cultural production, its hierarchies and power dynamics, its tendency to resist or capitulate. In his work on postmodern geography, Pile also locates postmodernism in terms of the changing relationship between opposition and authority; he reminds us, crucially, that "the map of resistance is not simply the underside of the map of domination" (6).

In *The Condition of Postmodernity*, Harvey demonstrates that our conceptions of space and time are social constructions forged out of vibrant and volatile social relations (Harvey 1990). Harvey's analysis of postmodern time and space is worth examining in detail both because he energetically deconstructs the naturalization of modes of temporality and because he does so with no awareness of having instituted and presumed a normative framework for his alternative understanding of time. Furthermore, Harvey's concept of "time/space compression" and his accounts of the role of culture in late capitalism have become hegemonic in academic contexts. Harvey asserts that because we experience time as some form of natural progression, we fail to realize or notice its construction. Accordingly, we have concepts like "industrial" time and "family" time, time of "progress," "austerity" versus "instant" gratification, "postponement" versus "immediacy." And to all of these different kinds of temporality, we assign value and meaning. Time, Harvey explains, is organized according to the logic of capital accumulation, but those who benefit from capitalism in particular experience this logic as inevitable, and they are therefore able to ignore, repress, or erase the demands made on them and others by an unjust system. We like to imagine, Harvey implies, both that our time is our own and, as the cliché goes, "there is a time and a place for everything." These formulaic responses to time and temporal logics produce emotional and even physical responses to different kinds of time: thus people feel guilty about leisure, frustrated by waiting, satisfied by punctuality, and so on. These emotional responses add to our sense of time as "natural."

Samuel Beckett's famous play *Waiting for Godot* can be read, for example, as a defamiliarization of time spent: a treatise on the feeling of time wasted, of inertia or time outside of capitalist propulsion. Waiting, in this play, seems to be a form of postponement until it becomes clear that nothing has been postponed and nothing will be resumed. In Beckett's play, the future does not simply become diminished, it actually begins to weigh on the present as a burden. If poetry, according to W. H. Auden, "makes nothing happen," the absurdist drama makes the audience wait for nothing to happen, and the experience of duration makes visible the formlessness of time. Since Beckett's clowns go nowhere while waiting, we also see the usually invisible fault lines between time and space as temporal stasis is figured as immobility.

The different forms of time management that Harvey mentions and highlights are all adjusted to the schedule of normativity without ever being discussed as such. In fact, we could say that normativity, as it has been defined and theorized within queer studies, is the big word missing from almost all the discussions of postmodern geography within a Marxist tradition. Since most of these discussions are dependent on the work of Foucault and since normativity was Foucault's primary understanding of the function of modern power, this is a huge oversight, and one with consequences for the discussion of sexuality in relation to time and space. Harvey's concept of time/space compressions, for instance, explains that all of the time cycles that we have naturalized and internalized (leisure, inertia, recreation, work/industrial, family/domesticity) are also spatial practices, but again, Harvey misses the opportunity to deconstruct the meaning of naturalization with regard to specific normalized ways of being. The meaning of space, Harvey asserts, undergoes a double process of naturalization: first, it is naturalized in relation to use values (we presume that our use of space is the only and inevitable use of space—private property, for example); but second, we naturalize space by subordinating it to time. The construction of spatial practices, in other words, is obscured by the naturalization of both time and space. Harvey argues for multiple conceptions of time and space, but he does not adequately describe how time/space becomes naturalized, on the one hand, and how hegemonic constructions of time and space are uniquely gendered and sexualized, on the other. His is an avowedly materialist analysis of time/space dedicated understandably to uncovering the processes of capitalism, but it lacks a simultaneous desire to uncover the processes of heteronormativity, racism, and sexism.

We need, for example, a much more rigorous understanding of the gendering of domestic space. Harvey could have pointed to the work within feminist history on the creation of separate spheres, for one, to show where and how the time/space continuum breaks down under the weight of critical scrutiny (Cott 1977; Smith-Rosenberg 1985). Feminist historians have claimed for some thirty years that in the eighteenth and nineteenth centuries, as the European bourgeoisie assumed class dominance over the aristocracy and proletariat, a separation of spheres graphically represented the gendered logic of the public/private binary and annexed middle-class women to the home, leaving the realm of politics and commerce to white men (McHugh 1999; Duggan 2000). Furthermore, as work by Paul Gilroy and Joseph Roach has shown, histories of racialization cannot avoid spatial conceptions of time, conflict, or political economy (Gilroy 1993; Roach 1996). Indeed, the histories of racialized peoples have been histories of immigration, diaspora, and forced migration. Only a single-minded focus on the history of the white working class and an abstract concept of capital can give rise to the kind of neat scheme that Harvey establishes whereby time dominates critical consciousness and suppresses an understanding of spatiality.

Lindon Barrett's *Blackness and Value: Seeing Double* provides one good antidote to Harvey's clean rendering of Enlightenment divisions of space and time (Barrett 1999). According to the account that Barrett gives in his book, Western philosophy can be historically located as a discourse that accompanies capitalism, and works to justify and rationalize a patently brutal and unjust system as inevitably scientific and organic. So seamlessly has capitalism been rationalized over the last two hundred years, in fact, that we no longer see the fault lines that divide black from white, work from play, subject from object. In true deconstructive form and with painstaking care, Barrett restores the original foundations of Western thought that were used to designate black as inhuman and white as human, black in association with idleness, perverse sexuality, and lack of self-consciousness, and white in association with diligence, legibility, the normal, the domestic, restraint, and self-awareness. By tracing this philosophical history, Barrett is able to explain the meaning of blackness in different historical periods in opposition to the seemingly inevitable, transparent, and neutral rhetorics of time and space that govern those periods.

Tsing also criticizes Harvey for making the breaks between space and time, modern and postmodern, economics and culture so clean and so distinct. She theorizes global capitalism much more precisely in relation to new eras of speed and connection, travel, movement, and communication; she lays out the contradictory results of global capitalism in terms of what it enables as well as what forms of oppression it enacts: Tsing reminds us that globalization makes a transnational politics (environmentalism, human rights, feminism) possible even as it consolidates U.S. hegemony. Harvey can only describe the condition of postmodernism in terms of new forms of domination and, like Jameson, can only think about cultural production as a channel for U.S. hegemony. Tsing, an anthropologist, is in many ways an unlikely defender of the nonsymmetrical relationship of cultural production to economic production, but her most important critique of Harvey concerns his characterization of postmodern culture as "a mirror of economic realities" (Tsing 2002, 466). Harvey's analysis, according to Tsing, suffers first from a simplistic mode of taking cultural shifts and then mapping them onto economic shifts; second, she claims that Harvey makes all of his assumptions about globalization without using an ethnographic research base. Finally, he overgeneralizes the "postmodern condition" on the basis of a flawed understanding of the role of culture, and then allows culture to stand in for all kinds of other evidence of the effects of globalization.

In relation to gender, race, and alternative or subcultural production, therefore, Harvey's grand theory of "the experience of space and time" in postmodernity leaves the power structures of biased differentiation intact, and presumes that, in Pile's formulation, opposition can only be an "echo of domination" (Pile 1997, 13). But while Harvey, like Soja and Jameson, can be counted on at least to nod to the racialization and gendering of postmodern space, also like Soja and Jameson, he has nothing to say about sexuality and space. Both Soja and Harvey claim that it was Foucault's interviews on space and published lecture notes on "heterotopia" that, as Soja puts it, created the conditions for a postmodern geography. The Foucault who inspires the post-modern Marxist geographers is clearly the Foucault of *Discipline and Punish*, but not that of *The History of Sexuality*. Indeed, Harvey misses several obvious opportunities to discuss the naturalization of time and space in relation to sexuality. Reproductive time and family time are, above all, heteronormative time/space constructs. But while Harvey hints at the gender politics of these forms of time/space, he does not mention the possibility that all kinds of people, especially in postmodernity, will and do opt to live outside of repro-ductive and familial time as well as on the edges of logics of labor and pro-duction. By doing so, they also often live outside the logic of capital accu-mulation: here we could consider ravers, club kids, HIV-positive barebackers, rent boys, sex workers, homeless people, drug dealers, and the unemployed. Perhaps such people could productively be called "queer subjects" in terms of the ways they live (deliberately, accidentally, or of necessity) during the hours when others sleep and in the spaces (physical, metaphysical, and eco-nomic) that others have abandoned, and in terms of the ways they might work in the domains that other people assign to privacy and family. Finally, as I will trace in this book, for some queer subjects, time and space are limned by risks they are willing to take: the transgender person who risks his life by passing in a small town, the subcultural musicians who risk their livelihoods by immersing themselves in nonlucrative practices, the queer performers who destabilize the normative values that make everyone else feel safe and secure; but also those people who live without financial safety nets, without homes, without steady jobs, outside the organizations of time and space that have been established for the purposes of protecting the rich few from every-one else.

Using the Foucault of *The History of Sexuality*, we can return to the con-cepts of time that Harvey takes for granted and expose their hidden but im-plicit logics (Foucault 1986). Stephen M. Barber and David L. Clark, in their introduction to a book of essays on Eve Kosofsky Sedgwick, present perhaps the most compelling reading to date of a queer temporality that emerges from Foucault's formulation of modernity as "an attitude rather than as a pe-riod of history" (Barber 2002, 304). Barber and Clark locate Foucault's comments on modernity alongside Sedgwick's comments on queerness in order to define queerness as a temporality—"a 'moment,' it is also then a force; or rather it is a crossing of temporality with force" (8). In Sedgwick, Barber and Clark identify an elaboration of the relation between temporality and writing; in Foucault, they find a model for the relation between temporality and ways of being. They summarize these currents in terms of a "moment," a "persistent present," or "a queer temporality that is at once indefinite and virtual but also forceful, resilient, and undeniable" (2). It is this model of time, the model that emerges between Foucault and Sedgwick, that is lost to and overlooked by Marxist geographers for whom the past represents the logic for the present, and the future represents the fruition of this logic.

Postmodern geography, indeed, has built on Foucault's speculative but powerful essay on heterotopia and on Foucault's claim in this essay that "the present epoch will be above all an epoch of space" (Foucault 1986, 22). Based on this insight, Soja and Harvey argue that critical theory has privileged time/history over space/geography with many different implications. But for both Harvey in *The Condition of Postmodernity* and Jameson in "The Cultural Logic of Postmodernism," postmodernism is a strange and even bewildering confusion of time and space where history has lost its (materialist) meaning, time has become a perpetual present, and space has flattened out in the face of creeping globalization. Both theorists evince a palpable nostalgia for modernism with its apparent oppositional logics and its clear articulations of both alienation and revolution; and both theorists oppose the politics of the local within "an epoch of space" to the politics of the global—a global capitalism opposed by some kind of utopian global socialism, and no politics outside this framework registers as meaningful. Predictably, then, the "local" for postmodern geographers becomes the debased term in the binary, and their focus on the global, the abstract, and even the universal is opposed to the local with its associations with the concrete, the specific, the narrow, the empirical, and even the bodily. As Tsing puts it, the local becomes just a "stopping place for the global" in Marxist accounts, and all too often the local represents place, while the global represents circulation, travel, and migration. By refusing to set local/global up in a dialectical relation, Tsing allows for a logic of diversity: diverse locals, globals, capitalisms, temporalities (Tsing 2002).

Stuart Hall also reminds us in his essay on "The Global and the Local" that "the more we understand about the development of Capital itself, the more we understand that it is only part of the story" (Hall 1997). And as Doreen

Massey says of Harvey's exclusive focus on capital, "In Harvey's account, capital always wins, and it seems capital can only win" (Massey 1994, 140). Massey suggests that alternatives are rarely suggested by those theorists of the dominant; we are always already trapped, and the more we find evidence of alternatives in local contexts, the more the local becomes mistrusted as "place bound," reactionary, and even fascist. Work on sexuality and space offers a far more complicated picture of globalization and the relationships between the global and the local than Harvey or Soja allow. Indeed, queer studies of sexuality and space present the opportunity for a developed understanding of the local, the nonmetropolitan (not the same thing, I know), and the situated. And while work on globalization will inevitably skim the surface of local variations and perhaps even reproduce the homogenizing effects of globalization in the process of attempting to offer a critique, queer studies of space, sexuality, and embodiment explore the postmodern politics of place in all of its contradiction, and in the process, they expose the contours of what I call in chapter 2 "metronormativity."

One theorist who has accounted for the possibility of "the end of capitalism" is J. K. Gibson-Graham, the collaborative moniker for the joint theories of Julie Graham and Katherine Gibson. In the original and inspirational call for an anticapitalist imaginary, Gibson-Graham argues that "it is the way capitalism has been 'thought' that has made it so difficult for people to imagine its supersession" (Gibson-Graham 1996, 5). Drawing on feminist studies and queer theory, Gibson-Graham contends that capitalism has been unnecessarily stabilized within Marxist representations as a totalizing force and a unitary entity. If we destabilize the meaning of capitalism using poststructuralist critiques of identity and signification, then we can begin to see the multiplicity of noncapitalist forms that constitute, supplement, and abridge global capitalism, but we can also begin to imagine, by beginning to see, the alternatives to capitalism that already exist and are presently under construction. Gibson-Graham calls for the "querying" of globalization through a wide-ranging recognition of its incomplete status, its discontinuities, instabilities, and vulnerabilities. Gibson-Graham proposes "the severing of globalization from a fixed capitalist identity, a breaking apart of the monolithic significations of capitalism (market/commodity/capital) and a liberation of different economic beings and practices" (146).

The literature on sexuality and space is growing rapidly, but it tends to focus on gay men, and it is often comparative only to the extent that it takes white gay male sexual communities as a highly evolved model that other sexual cultures try to imitate and reproduce. One of the best studies of sexual space that does still focus on gay men, but recognizes the fault lines of class, race, and gender in the construction of sexual communities is Samuel R. Delany's *Times Square Red, Times Square Blue*. Delany's book breaks the mold in the genre of gay male accounts of space that often take the form of travelogues and then compare the author's sexual experiences with gay men in a variety of global locations, only to argue for a kind of universal homosexuality within which fluidity and flexibility are the order of the day (Browning 1996). In Delany's book, the geo-specific sexual practices he describes belong to the interactions between men of different classes and races in New York's porn shops and triple-X theaters. These practices develop and are assigned meaning only in the context of the porn theater, and their meanings shift and change when the men leave the darkened theater and reemerge into the city. Delany's study illustrates a few of the claims I have been making here about queer time and space: first, that oppositional cultures, or in Pile's terms, "geographies of resistance," are not symmetrical to the authority they oppose; second, that the relations between sexuality and time and space provide immense insight into the flows of power and subversion within postmodernism; and finally, that queers use space and time in ways that challenge conventional logics of development, maturity, adulthood, and responsibility (Delany 1999).

Delany's groundbreaking analysis of the destruction of sexual subcultures during the corporate development of New York City's Times Square allows him to take issue with the notion that increasing public safety was the main motivation behind the area's face-lift. While developers claimed that the sex industries in Times Square rendered the area wholly unsafe for women and families especially, Delany argues that there is no particular relationship between street safety and the presence or absence of sex workers. He states unequivocally: "What I see lurking behind the positive foregrounding of 'family values' (along with, in the name of such values, the violent suppression of urban social structures, economic, social and sexual) is a wholly provincial and absolutely small-town terror of cross-class contact" (153). While I want to return to this notion of the small-town terror of contact with otherness in my chapters on Brandon Teena, here I am interested in Delany's insights about urban sex cultures and their understandings of space and time.

Delany divides his book into two sections, as the title suggests, and while the first half provides an ethnographic account of the denizens of porn theaters, dotted with anecdotes of Delany's encounters with various men, the second half articulates a theory of space, intimacy, and bodily contact in postmodernism. In this latter section, Delany makes some big claims. First, he proposes that "given the mode of capitalism under which we live, life is at its most rewarding, productive, and pleasant when large numbers of people understand, appreciate and seek out interclass contact and communication conducted in a mode of good will" (111). The encounters between men in the sex cinemas of midtown Manhattan are one of the few remaining zones of pleasurable interclass contact, according to Delany, and by razing this area, the urban planners of the new Times Square are deploying a logic of "safety" to justify the destruction of an intricate subcultural system. In its place, the corporate developers will construct a street mall guaranteed to make the tourists who visit Times Square feel safe enough to spend their money there. The second proposal made by Delany redefines class struggle for a postmodern politics. He argues that class war works silently against the social practices through which interclass contact can take place. In other words, what we understand in this day and age as "class war" is not simply owners exploiting labor or labor rebelling against managers but a struggle between those who value interclass contact and work hard to maintain those arenas in which it can occur, and those who fear it and work to create sterile spaces free of class mixing.

In order to create and maintain new spaces for interclass contact, Delany asserts that we need to be able, first, to imagine such spaces; we have to find out where they are, and how they can be sustained and supported. Second, we need to theorize the new spaces. It is not enough simply to point to new sites for interclass contact but as Delany has done here, we have to create a complex discourse around them through narrative and the meticulous work of archiving. Third, we have to avoid nostalgia for what was and what has disappeared while creating a new formulation for future spaces and architectures. Finally, Delany urges us to narrate an account of the invisible institutions that prop up counterpublics, but also to tell the story of the new technologies that want to eradicate them through a moral campaign about cleaning up the city. Delany repeatedly claims in *Times Square Red* that small towns in the United States are (if measured in terms of the number of crimes per capita) far more violent than big cities and that the structure of violence, particularly violence against queers, say, in each location is quite different. In a small town, the violence tends to be predictable, he claims, since locals often initiate violence against strangers or outsiders; but in the city, violence is random and unpredictable. Delany suggests that we break away from the cozy fantasies of small-town safety and big-city danger, and reconsider the actual risks of different locations in terms of the different populations that inhabit them. Specifically, he recommends that we not design urban areas to suit suburban visitors, and that we start to consider the problem of small-town violence in terms of the lack of cross-class, cross-race, or cross-sexual contact in small towns and rural areas.

Women are tellingly absent from Delany's smart, engaging, and even revolutionary account of sexual subcultures, and one is led to conclude by the end of the book that as of now, there is no role for women in this subterranean world of public sex. While it is not my project here to discuss the possibilities for women to develop venues for public sex, I do want to address the absence of gender as a category of analysis in much of the work on sexuality and space by shifting the terms of discussion from the global to the local in relation to postmodern geographies; and by shifting the focus from urban to rural in relation to queer geographies. I will also argue for a new conception of space and sexuality—what I call a "technotopic" understanding of space in chapter 5—that opens up in queer art making.

The division between urban and rural or urban and small town has had a major impact on the ways in which queer community has been formed and perceived in the United States. Until recently, small towns were considered hostile to queers and urban areas were cast as the queer's natural environment. In contemporary debates about urban life, affluent gay populations are often described as part of a "creative class" that enhances the city's cultural life and cultural capital, and this class of gays are then cast in opposition to the small-town family life and values of midwestern Americans (Florida 2002). While there is plenty of truth to this division between urban and small-town life, between hetero-familial cultures and queer creative and sexual cultures, the division also occludes the lives of nonurban queers. *In a Queer Time and Place* both confirms that queer subcultures thrive in urban areas *and* contests the essential characterizations of queer life as urban. In an extended consideration of the life and death of Brandon Teena, a young transgender man who was murdered in small-town Nebraska, I look at how the transgender body functions in relation to time and space as a rich site for fantasies of futurity and anachronism, and I ask here why transgenderism holds so much significance in postmodernism.

The first half of the book considers the sudden visibility of the transgender body in the late twentieth century against the backdrop of changing conceptions of space and identity. This book actually began as a study of the tragic 1993 murder of Brandon. After passing as a man and dating local girls in Nebraska, Brandon died a brutal death at the hands of two local boys who felt threatened by his masculinity. In death, Brandon became a hero, a martyr, and a fallen friend to hundreds of viewers and readers who would have shown little to no interest in his plight had he been killed in a traffic accident or died of disease. Chapters 2 and 3 explore the case of Brandon Teena in detail, and I return to the questions raised there about space, place, and identity later in my reading of Kimberly Peirce's feature film made about Brandon in 1999: *Boys Don't Cry*. I had originally planned a study of the Brandon case along the lines of some of the books that have been written about the murder of Matthew Shepard in Wyoming (Loffreda 2002). But as the "Brandon industry" grew, and as films, videos, novels, true-crime mysteries and other accounts of the case were released, I felt ambivalent about simply contributing to the growing fascination with this young transgender man among urban gays and lesbians. In the hopes of steering clear of the representational and emotional vortex that surrounded Brandon, I decided to study the construction of Brandon in terms of some of the questions about time and space raised by queer studies. And so, I look at Brandon as a figure who represents both anachronism (an earlier model of gay identity as gender inversion) and dislocatedness (a person who chooses the rural over the urban as his theater for staging his gender); Brandon is literally and figuratively out of time and out of place.

Mark Seltzer claims in his work on America's "wound culture" that we live in a society so preoccupied with scenes of violence and violation that trauma has become "an effect in search of a cause" (Seltzer 1998, 257). Seltzer's formulation of the psychological experience of trauma as a belated or retrospective construction of the physical experience of violation describes perfectly the kind of attention directed at a Brandon Teena or a Matthew Shepard; such figures are made to stand in for the hurts and the indignities that are so often rendered invisible by the peculiar closet structure of homophobia. A generous reading of this process, by which a community selects a violated member to represent otherwise unrepresentable damage, would see a transformation of a personal affront into a political one. A less generous reading might argue that the process of selecting (white and young) martyrs within urban queer activism allows for an increasingly empowered urban middle-class gay and lesbian community to disavow its growing access to privilege in order to demand new forms of state recognition, and to find new ways of accessing respectability and its rewards. Many of the gays and lesbians who attended candlelit vigils for Brandon, and even more so for Matthew Shepard, were indeed people who would otherwise never involve themselves in political activism, and who certainly would not be organizing on behalf of gender-variant queers or queers of color. The varied responses to the tragic murders of these two young, white, rural queers have much to tell us about selective memorialization and political activism, space and sexual identity, and the mobilization of trauma. While the first chapters of *In a Queer Time and Place* focus specifically on the Brandon Teena case, the middle section of this book takes the thematics raised by this case to other arenas of representation, and traces the interactive relations between dominant and alternative genders in twentieth-century visual cultures.

Chapter 4 on queer film and the transgender look, chapter 5 on queer visual culture and figurations of ambiguous embodiment, and to a certain extent chapter 6 on mainstream appropriations of gender ambiguity all examine the circuits of influence that allow for the emergence of the transgender body as simultaneously a symbol for postmodern flexibility and a legible form of embodied subjectivity. At times, I look at the depiction of transgenderism separate from transgender subjects; at others, I explore self-representations of and by transgender subjects. Several chapters in this book try to account for the relations between different levels of cultural production. In chapter 5, I take up debates in art history about the relationships between avant-gardes and subcultures, and I apply them to contemporary queer visual art. In chapter 6, I try to track the barely discernible imprint of influence that transgender subcultures have had on mainstream representations of gender. As my earlier book on female masculinity showed, representations of the gender-ambiguous female body have rarely produced the same interest that their male counterparts (sissy boys, drag queens, transvestites) inspire (Halberstam 1998). And the masculine woman in the past has rarely been depicted as an interesting phenomenon—usually, she has been portrayed as the outcome of failed femininity, or as the result of pathetic and unsuccessful male mimicry. Chapter 6 examines recent comedies about English masculinity like *The Full Monty* and *Austin Powers*. Each of these texts humorously foregrounds the relationship between alternative and dominant masculinities, and surprisingly credits alternative masculinities with the reconstruction of the terms of masculine embodiment. This chapter will ask how and why the genre of comedy allows for an acknowledgment of the influence of minority masculinities. In the case of *Austin Powers*, in particular,

I will propose that the success of the male parody that the film undertakes depends on an appropriation of drag king strategies of male impersonation. Chapter 7 builds on the set of questions I asked in the *Austin Powers* chapter about influence, the circulation of cultural texts, male parody, and subcultural intensity, and the questions in chapter 5 about the avant-garde's appropriation of subcultural material, and explores dyke subcultures as one site for the development of queer counterpublics and queer temporalities. I end this chapter and the book with a specific case history, the musical career of Ferron, through which to analyze the theme of generational conflict and queer time.

Throughout this book, I return to the transgender body as a contradictory site in postmodernism. The gender-ambiguous individual today represents a very different set of assumptions about gender than the gender-inverted subject of the early twentieth century; and as a model of gender inversion recedes into anachronism, the transgender body has emerged as futurity itself, a kind of heroic fulfillment of postmodern promises of gender flexibility. Why has gender flexibility become a site of both fascination and promise in the late twentieth century and what did this new flexibility have to do with other economies of flexibility within postmodernism? As Emily Martin's book *Flexible Bodies* shows in relation to historically variable conceptions of the immune system, flexibility has become "one of our new taken-for-granted virtues for persons and their bodies" (Martin 1995). She continues, "Flexibility has also become a powerful commodity, something scarce and highly valued, that can be used to discriminate against some people" (xvii). While we have become used to thinking in terms of "flexible citizenship" and "flexible accumulation" as some of the sinister sides of this new "virtue," the contemporary interest in flexible genders, from talk shows to blockbuster movies, may also be a part of the conceptualization of a new global elite (Ong 1999).

Because bodily flexibility has become both a commodity (in the case of cosmetic surgeries for example) and a form of commodification, it is not enough in this "age of flexibility" to celebrate gender flexibility as simply another sign of progress and liberation. Promoting flexibility at the level of identity and personal choices may sound like a postmodern or even a queer program for social change. But it as easily describes the advertising strategies of huge corporations like the Gap, who sell their products by casting their consumers as simultaneously all the same and all different. Indeed, the new popularity of "stretch" fabrics accommodates precisely this model of bodily fluidity by creating apparel that can stretch to meet the demands of the unique and individual body that fills it. Advertising by other companies, like Dr Pepper, whose ads exhort the consumer to "be you!" and who sell transgression *as* individualism, also play with what could be called a "bad" reading of postmodern gender. Postmodern gender theory has largely been (wrongly) interpreted as both a description of and a call for greater degrees of flexibility and fluidity. Many young gays and lesbians think of themselves as part of a "post-gender" world and for them the idea of "labeling" becomes a sign of an oppression they have happily cast off in order to move into a pluralistic world of infinite diversity. In other words, it has become commonplace and even clichéd for young urban (white) gays and lesbians to claim that they do not like "labels" and do not want to be "pigeon holed" by identity categories, even as those same identity categories represent the activist labors of previous generations that brought us to the brink of "liberation" in the first place. Many urban gays and lesbians of different age groups also express a humanistic sense that their uniqueness cannot be captured by the application of a blanket term. The emergence of this liberal, indeed neo-liberal, notion of "uniqueness as radical style" in hip queer urban settings must be considered alongside the transmutations of capitalism in late postmodernity. As Lisa Duggan claims: "new neoliberal sexual politics . . . might be termed the new homonormativity—it is a politics that does not contest dominant heteronormative assumptions and institutions, but upholds and sustains them, while promising the possibility of a semobilized gay constituency and a privatized, depoliticized gay culture anchored in domesticity and consumption" (Duggan 2003).

Harvey has characterized late capitalism in terms of "flexibility with respect to labour processes, labour markets, products and patterns of consumption" (Harvey 1990, 147). Increased flexibility, as we now know, leads to increased opportunities for the exploitation by transnational corporations of cheap labor markets in Third World nations and in immigrant communities in the First World. The local and inter-subjective forms of flexibility may be said to contribute to what Anna Tsing calls the "charisma of globalization" by incorporating a seemingly radical ethic of flexibility into understandings of selfhood. In queer communities, what I will define as "transgressive exceptionalism" can be seen as a by-product of local translations of neo-liberalism.

As many Marxist critics in particular seem to be fond of pointing out, identity politics in the late twentieth century has mutated in some cases from a necessary and strategic critique of universalism into a stymied and myopic politics of self. There are few case studies in the critiques of identity politics, however, and too often one particular theorist (usually a very prominent and sophisticated queer theorist) will stand in for projects that may be characterized as bound and limited to identity claims. Many important theoretical projects have been dismissed as "identity politics" because writers remain fuzzy about the meaning of this term and in many ways, identity politics has become the new "essentialism," a marker, in other words, of some combination of naiveté and narrowness that supposedly blocks more expansive and sophisticated projects. Too often in academia "identity politics" will be used as an accusation of "interestedness," and the accuser will seek to return discussion to a more detached project with supposedly great validity and broader applications.

In a very useful essay on "Taking Identity Politics Seriously," anthropologist James Clifford warns that the blanket dismissal of identity politics by intellectuals on the Left runs the risk of missing the "complex volatility, ambivalent potential, and historical necessity of contemporary social movements" (Clifford 2000, 95). Building on the work of Stuart Hall, Clifford argues that we cannot dismiss the methods used by various communities to "make 'room' for themselves in a crowded world"; instead, he and Hall separately call for sustained analysis of the ways in which "human beings become agents." Clifford believes that "historically informed ethnography" must be central to a "comparative understanding of the politics of identity" (103). While the work I do in this book cannot by any stretch of the imagination be called "ethnography," it does try to make sense of the ways that new gender communities make "room" for themselves, by piecing together a story of emergence from a set of representations produced and circulated within postmodernism.

Often, identity politics becomes far more of a problem outside than inside academia. In mainstream gay, lesbian, and trans communities in the United States, battles rage about what group occupies the more transgressive or aggrieved position, and only rarely are such debates framed in terms of larger discussions about capitalism, class, or economics. In this context then, "transgressive exceptionalism" refers to the practice of taking the moral high ground by claiming to be more oppressed and more extraordinary than others. The rehearsal of identity-bound debates outside the academy speaks not simply to a lack of sophistication in such debates, but suggests that academics have failed to take their ideas beyond the university and have not made necessary interventions in public intellectual venues. In transgender contexts, for example, as sociologist Henry Rubin reports, transgender and transsexual subjects have articulated deep suspicions of academic researchers and this has made it very difficult for academics to either conduct extensive ethnographies or intervene in community debates about the meaning of multiple forms of gender ambiguity (Rubin 2003). Surprisingly, transgenders and transsexuals seem not to have quite the same suspicion of social service workers and so they have made the inroads that academic researchers could not into trans communities (Valentine 2000). Indeed, in recent years, the term "transgender" has circulated and taken on meaning often in relation to social service provider interventions into youth groups and sex worker communities.

In the hope that a productive and generative project can be successfully wrested from a deep consideration of the meaning of transgenderism in relation to postmodern understandings of time and space, I offer in the next two sections some alternative ways of accounting for and sustaining the imaginative leap that transgenderism actually represents within queer theory and queer communities. I hope that the essays collected here can begin a dialogue about the meaning of gender variance in queer communities that moves beyond claims of either uniqueness or unilateral oppression, and beyond the binary division of flexibility or rigidity. Steve Pile warns against the premature stabilization of this binary, arguing that "the subjects of resistance are neither fixed nor fluid, but both and more. And this 'more' involves a sense that resistance is resistance to both fixity and to fluidity" (1997, 30). At a moment when the U.S. economic interests in the Middle East are covered over by rhetoric about freedom and liberty, it is important to study the form and structure of the many contradictions of transnational capital at local as well as global levels. Transgenderism, with its promise of gender liberation and its patina of transgression, its promise of flexibility and its reality of a committed rigidity, could be the successful outcome of years of gender activism; or, just as easily, it could be the sign of the reincorporation of a radical subculture back into the flexible economy of postmodern culture. This book tries to keep transgenderism alive as a meaningful designator of unpredictable gender identities and practices, and it locates the transgender figure as a central player in numerous postmodern debates about space and sexuality, subcultural production, rural gender roles, art and gender ambiguity, the politics of biography, historical conceptions of manhood, gender and genre, and the local as opposed to the global.

2

The Brandon Archive

The road was straight, the country was level as a lake, and other cars were
seldom sighted. This was "out there"—or getting near it.
—Truman Capote, *In Cold Blood*

Out There

Our relations to place, like our relations to people, are studded with bias,
riven with contradictions, and complicated by opaque emotional responses.
I am one of those people for whom lonely rural landscapes feel laden with
menace, and for many years nonurban areas were simply "out there," strange
and distant horizons populated by hostile populations. It is still true that a
densely packed urban street or a metallic skyline can release a surge of ex-
citement for me while a vast open landscape fills me with dread. In December 1993, I remember reading a short story in the newspaper about an exe-
cution-style killing in rural Nebraska. The story seemed unremarkable except
for one small detail buried in the heart of the report: one of the murder victims was a young female-bodied person who had been passing as a man. The
murder of this young transgender person sent shock waves through queer
communities in the United States, and created fierce identitarian battles between transsexual activists and gay and lesbian activists, with each group trying to claim Brandon Teena as one of their own. The struggles over the legacy
of Brandon represented much more than a local skirmish over the naming or
classification of fallen brethren; indeed, they testified to the political complexities of an activism sparked by murder and energized by the work of me-
morializing individuals. The fascination with murder and mayhem that
characterizes U.S. popular culture has led some theorists to point to the emergence of a wound culture. It is easy to explain why homophobic violence
might generate such fierce activist responses; it is harder to mobilize such responses for purposes that extend beyond demands for protection and recognition from the state. My purpose here is to build on the flashes of insight af-
forded by violent encounters between "normal" guys and gender-variant
people in order to theorize the meaning of gender transitivity in late capitalism. Here I will use the notions of relays of influence between dominant and

minority masculinities to consider the place and space of the masculine transgender subject.

The tragic facts in the case of the murder of Brandon Teena and his two friends are as follows: on December 31, 1993, three young people were shot to death, execution style, in Falls City in rural Nebraska. Ordinarily, this story would have evoked only mild interest from mainstream America and a few questions about the specific brutalities of rural America; one of the three victims, however, was a young white person who had been born a woman, but who was living as a man and had been dating local girls. The other two victims, Brandon's friend Lisa Lambert, and her friend Philip DeVine, a disabled African American man, appeared to have been killed because they were in the wrong place at the wrong time, although this too is debatable.

This chapter relates, explores, and maps the shape and the meaning of the remarkable archive that has developed in the aftermath of the slaying of Brandon Teena, Lisa, and Philip; the archive has created a new "Brandon." This new Brandon is the name that we now give to a set of comforting fictions about queer life in small-town America. The Brandon archive is simultaneously a resource, a productive narrative, a set of representations, a history, a memorial, and a time capsule. It literally records a moment in the history of twentieth-century struggles around the meaning of gender categories and it becomes a guide to future resolutions. So, while in my next chapter I will examine the "politics of transgender biography" and the difficulties involved in telling stories about people who have created specific life narratives, here I want to lay out the geopolitical ramifications of Brandon's murder by imagining the Brandon archive as made up of the insights and revelations allowed by a careful consideration of the many lives and social formations that Brandon's life and death sheds light on. If we think of the murder of Brandon as less of a personal tragedy that has been broadened out to create a symbolic event and more of a constructed memorial to the violence directed at queer and transgender lives, we will be better equipped to approach the geographic and class specificities of rural Nebraska.

The execution of Brandon, Lisa, and Philip was in fact more like an earthquake or a five-alarm fire than an individualized event: its eruption damaged more than just the three who died and the two who killed; it actually devastated the whole town, and brought a flood of reporters, cameras, and journalists into the area to pick through the debris and size up the import of the disaster. That media rush, in many ways, transformed the Brandon murders from a circumscribed event to an ever evolving narrative. As we will see in the next chapter, among the magazine articles, talk shows, and other media that covered the case, an Oscar-winning feature film, *Boys Don't Cry*, was released about Brandon's death. This film, more than any other representation of the case, has determined the legacy of the murders. In a later chapter, "The Transgender Look," I will explore the mechanics of looking at the transgender body; but in this chapter on place, space, and regionality, I discuss the documentary film that greatly influenced *Boys Don't Cry*: *The Brandon Teena Story*, directed by Susan Muska and Greta Olafsdottir (1998). Like the feature film yet in different ways, *The Brandon Teena Story* tried to re-create the material conditions of Brandon's undoing, but like the feature film, it ultimately told a tall story about rural homophobia.

By designating the stories told about Brandon and his friends as "an archive" in this chapter, I am tracing the multiple meanings of this narrative for different communities. Ann Cvetkovich theorizes queer uses of the term "archives" in her book *An Archive of Feelings*: "Understanding gay and lesbian archives as archives of emotion and trauma helps to explain some of their idiosyncrasies, or, one might say, their 'queerness'" (Cvetkovich 2003, 242). The Brandon archive is exactly that: a transgender archive of "emotion and trauma" that allows a narrative of a queerly gendered life to emerge from the fragments of memory and evidence that remain. When Brandon was shot to death by John Lotter and Thomas Nissen, his failure to pass as a man in the harsh terrain of a small town in rural North America prompted a national response from transgender activists. This response has been amplified and extended by other queers for different and conflicting reasons. Some queers use Brandon's death to argue for hate-crime legislation; others have made Brandon into a poster child for an emergent transgender community dedicated to making visible the plight of cross-identified youth, and Brandon functions therefore as a reference point of what I called in chapter 1 transgressive exceptionalism; still others have pointed to Brandon's death as evidence of a continuing campaign of violence against queers despite the increasing respectability of some portions of the gay and lesbian community. But few of the responses have taken into consideration the specificity of Brandon's nonmetropolitan location, and few if any have used the murder and the production of activist and cultural activity that it has inspired as a way of reexamining the meaning of sexual identity in relation to a postmodern politics of place.

I use the Brandon material, then, to unpack the meaning of "local homosexualities" or transsexualities in the context of the United States. Like other narratives about nonmetropolitan sexuality, popular versions of this story posit a queer subject who sidesteps so-called modern models of gay identity by conflating gender and sexual variance. Indeed, in the popular versions of the Brandon narrative that currently circulate, like *Boys Don't Cry,* Brandon's promiscuity and liminal identity is depicted as immature and even premodern and as a form of false consciousness. When Brandon explores a mature and adult relationship with one woman who recognizes him as "really female," that film suggests, Brandon accedes to a modern form of homosexuality and is finally "free." Reconstituted now as a liberal subject, Brandon's death at the hands of local men can be read simultaneously as a true tragedy and an indictment of backward, rural communities. In this sense, Brandon occupies a place held by so-called primitives in colonial anthropology; he literally inhabits a different timescale from the modern queer, and using Johannes Fabian's formulation in *Time and the Other,* Brandon's difference gets cast as both spatially and temporally distant (Fabian 2002, 16). By reading Brandon's story in and through postcolonial queer theory and queer geography, we can untangle the complex links that this narrative created for the urban consumers who were its most avid audience between modern queerness and the rejection of rural or small-town locations.

I believe that an extensive analysis of the Brandon murders can serve to frame the many questions about identification, responsibility, class, regionality, and race that trouble queer communities today. Not only does Brandon represent a martyr lost in the struggle for transgender rights to the brutal perpetrators of rural hetero-masculine violences., Brandon also serves as a marker for a particular set of late-twentieth-century cultural anxieties about place, space, locality, and metropolitanism. Fittingly, Brandon has become the name for gender variance, for fear of transphobic and homophobic punishment; Brandon also embodies the desire directed at nonnormative masculinities. Brandon represents other rural lives undone by fear and loathing, and his story also symbolizes an urban fantasy of homophobic violence as essentially midwestern. But violence wherever we may find it marks different conflictual relations in different sites; and homicide, on some level, always depicts the microrealities of other battles displaced from the abstract to the tragically material. While at least one use of any Brandon Teena project must be to connect Brandon's gender presentation to other counternarratives of gender realness, I also hope that Brandon's story can be a vehicle linked to the discussions of globalization, transnational sexualities, geography, and queer migration. On some level Brandon's story, while cleaving to its own specificity, needs to remain an open narrative—not a stable narrative of female-to-male transsexual identity nor a singular tale of queer bashing, not a cautionary fable about the violence of rural America nor an advertisement for urban organizations of queer community. Brandon's story permits a dream of transformation that must echo in the narratives of queer life in other nonmetropolitan locations.

Falls City, Nebraska: A Good Place to Die?

> In little towns, lives roll along so close to one another; loves and hates beat about, their wings almost touching.
> —Willa Cather, *Lucy Gayheart* (Cather 1935, 167)

In *The Brandon Teena Story,* Muska and Olafsdottir attempt to place the narrative of Brandon's life and death firmly in the countryside of Nebraska, so much so that Nebraska takes on the role and the presence of a character in this drama. We see prolonged shots of the rolling Nebraska countryside, road signs welcoming the traveler to Nebraska's "good life," and scenes of everyday life and culture in small-town America. The filmmakers make it clear early on that their relationship to Falls City and its communities is ironic and distanced. They never appear in front of the camera even though about 75 percent of the documentary involves talking-head interviews with interviewees responding to questions from invisible interlocutors. In the few "local" scenes, the camera peers voyeuristically at the demolition derby and the line-dancing and karaoke bar, and in the interview sequences, the camera pushes its way rudely into the lives of the people touched by the Brandon story. In one significant scene, the camera pans the backs of local men watching a demolition derby. As the gaze sweeps over them, the men are rendered in slow motion, and they turn and gaze back at the camera with hostile stares of nonrecognition. Interactions between the camera and its subjects register the filmmakers as outsiders to the material realities of the rural Midwest, mark the objects of the gaze as literally haunted by an invisible camera, and finally, place the viewer at a considerable distance from the actors on the screen. This distance both allows for the emergence of multiple versions of the Brandon story but also pins the narrative of violent homophobic and transphobic violence firmly to the landscape of white trash America, and forces modes of strenuous disidentification between the viewer and the landscape.

The landscape of Nebraska serves as a contested site on which multiple narratives unfold—narratives, indeed, that refuse to collapse into simply one story, "the Brandon Teena story." Some of these narratives are narratives of hate, or of desire; others tell of ignorance and brutality; still others of isolation and fear; some allow violence and ignorant prejudices to become the essence of poor, white, rural identity; and still others provoke questions about the deployment of whiteness and the regulation of violence. While the video itself encourages viewers to distance themselves from the horror of the heartlands and to even congratulate themselves for living in an urban rather than a rural environment, ultimately we can use Brandon's story as it emerges here to begin the articulation of the stories of white, working-class, rural queers, and to map the immensely complex relations that make rural America a site of horror and degradation in the urban imagination.

For queers who flee the confines of the rural Midwest and take comfort in urban anonymity, this video may serve as a justification of their worst fears about the violent effects of failing to flee; closer readings of Brandon's story, however, reveal the desire shared by many midwestern queers for a way of staying rather than leaving. While some journalists in the wake of Brandon's murder queried his decision to stay in Falls City, despite having been hounded by the police and raped by the men who went on to murder him, we must consider the condition of "staying put" as part of the production of complex queer subjectivities. Some queers need to leave home in order to become queer, and others need to stay close to home in order to preserve their difference. The danger of small towns as Willa Cather described it, also in reference to rural Nebraska, emerges out of a suffocating sense of proximity: "lives roll along so close to one another," she wrote in *Lucy Gayheart,* "loves and hates beat about, their wings almost touching." This beautiful, but scary image of rural life as a space all-too-easily violated depends absolutely on an opposite image—the image of rural life as wide open and free ranging, as "big sky" and open plains. Cather captures perfectly the contradiction of rural life as the contrast between wide-open spaces and sparse populations, on the one hand, and small-town claustrophobia and lack of privacy, on the other.

The life and death of Brandon provokes endless speculation about the specificities of the loves and hates that characterized his experiences in Falls City, and any straightforward rendering of his story remains impossible. Some viewers of *The Brandon Teena Story* have accused the filmmakers of an obvious class bias in their depictions of the people of Falls City; others have seen the film as an accurate portrayal of the cultures of hate and meanness produced in small, mostly white towns. Any attempt to come to terms with the resonances of Brandon's murder will ultimately have to grapple with both of these proposals. One way in which *The Brandon Teena Story* deploys and perpetuates a class bias in relation to the depiction of anti-queer violence is by depicting many of its interview subjects in uncritical ways as "white trash." In their introduction to an anthology titled *White Trash: Race and Class in America,* Annalee Newitz and Matt Wray define white trash as both a reference to "actually existing white people living in (often rural) poverty," and a term designating "a set of stereotypes and myths related to the social behaviors, intelligence, prejudices, and gender roles of poor whites" (Newitz 1996, 7). The editors offer a "local politics of place" to situate, combat, and explain such stereotypes.

One way in which *The Brandon Teena Story* is able to grapple with the lives beneath the stereotypes (of white trash, of gender impersonation) is by allowing some of the women whom Brandon dated to explain themselves and articulate their own extraordinary desires. In the media rush to uncover the motivations behind Brandon's depiction of himself as a man, most accounts of the case have overlooked the fact that Brandon was actively chosen over more conventionally male men by the women he dated despite the fact that there were few social rewards for doing so. One girlfriend after another in the video characterizes Brandon as a fantasy guy, a dream guy, a man who "knew how a woman wanted to be treated." Gina describes him as romantic, special, and attentive, while Lana Tisdale calls him "every woman's dream." We might conclude that Brandon lived up to and even played into the romantic ideals that his girlfriends cultivated about masculinity. Brandon's self-presentation must be read, I believe, as a damaging critique of the white working-class masculinities around him; at the same time, however, his performance of courtly masculinity is a shrewd deployment of the middle-class and so-called respectable masculinities that represent an American romantic ideal of manhood. In the accounts that the women give of their relations with Brandon, we understand that he not only deliberately offered them a treatment they could not expect from local boys but he also acknowledged the complexity of their self-understandings and desires.

In order to understand the kinds of masculinities with which Brandon may have been competing, we can turn to the representations of the murderers themselves. While some accounts of the Brandon case have attempted to empathize with the men who murdered Brandon—Lotter and Nissen—by revealing their traumatic family histories and detailing their encounters with abuse, the video tries to encourage the men to give their own reasons for their brutality. The conversations with Lotter and Nissen are fascinating for the way they allow the men to coolly describe rape and murder scenes, and also because Lotter in particular articulates an astute awareness of the violence of the culture into which he was raised. Nissen, however, shows little power of self-reflection; the video represents him as ultimately far more reprehensible than his partner in crime. For one second in the video, the camera focuses on a small tattoo on Nissen's arm, but does not allow the viewer to identify it. In Aphrodite Jones's book on the Brandon case, *All S/he Wanted*, she provides information that situates this tattoo as a symbol of white supremacy politics. Nissen, we learn, was involved off and on throughout his early life with the White American Group for White America (Jones 1996, 154). While Nissen's flirtation with brutally racist white supremacist groups need not surprise us, it does nonetheless flesh out the particular nexus of hate that came to focus on Brandon, Lisa, and Philip.

Nowhere in the documentary, however, nor in media coverage of the case, does anyone link Nissen's racial politics with either the brutalization of Brandon or the execution of the African American, Philip; indeed, the latter is always constructed as a case of "wrong place, wrong time," but Philip's situation needs to be explored in more detail. In *The Brandon Teena Story*, Philip's murder is given little airplay, and none of his relatives or family make an appearance in the video. While every other character in the drama, including Lisa, is carefully located in relation to Brandon and the web of relations among Brandon's friends, Philip alone is given only the most scant attention. No explanation is given for the nonappearance of his family and friends, and no real discussion is presented about his presence in the farmhouse the night of the murders.[1]

It is hard to detach the murder of Philip from the history of Nissen's involvement in white supremacist cults. Many accounts of white power movements in the United States connect them to small, all-white towns in the Midwest and to economically disadvantaged white populations. While one would not want to demonize poor, white, rural Americans as any more bigoted than urban or suburban white yuppie populations in the United States, it is nonetheless important to highlight the particular fears and paranoia that take shape in rural, all-white populations. Fear of the government, fear of the United Nations, and fear of Jews, blacks, and queers mark white rural masculinities in particular ways that can easily produce cultures of hate (Ridgeway 1995). In small towns where few people of color live, difference may be marked and remarked in relation to gender variance rather than racial diversity. As Newitz and Wray point out in their anatomy of white trash, some degree of specificity is necessary when we try to describe and identify different forms of homophobia and transphobia as they are distributed across different geographies.

In "Get Thee to a Big City: Sexual Imaginary and the Great Gay Migration," anthropologist Kath Weston begins a much-needed inquiry into the difference between urban and rural "sexual imaginaries" (Weston 1995). She comments on the rather stereotyped division of rural/urban relations that "locates gay subjects in the city while putting their presence in the countryside under erasure" (262). Weston also traces the inevitable disappointments that await rural queers who escape the country only to arrive in alienating queer urban spaces. As Weston proposes, "The gay imaginary is not just a dream of a freedom to be gay that requires an urban location, but a symbolic space that configures gayness itself by elaborating an opposition between urban and rural life" (274). She wants us to recognize that the distinction between the urban and the rural that props up the gay imaginary is a symbolic one, and as such, it constitutes a dream of an elsewhere that promises a freedom it can never provide. But it is also crucial to be specific about which queer subjects face what kinds of threats, from whom, and in what locations. While in the city, for example, one may find that the gay or transsexual person of color is most at risk for violence from racist cops; in rural locations, one may find that even the white queers who were born and raised there are outlawed when they disrupt the carefully protected homogeneity of white, family-oriented communities. One may also discover that while the brutalization of a transgender sex worker of color raises little outcry in the city from local queer activists, the murder of a white boy in rural North America can stir up an enormous activist response that is itself symbolic of these other imaginary divisions.

The material in the Brandon archive has led me to question my own interest in the case and it has forced me to "know my place" in terms of the rural/urban divisions in queer communities that reactions to the story make visible. When I began thinking and writing about the Brandon murders in 1996, I approached the material with the bewilderment of a typical urban queer who wanted to know why Brandon, but also his African American friend Philip, did not pick up and leave Falls City as soon as they could, and furthermore, why they were there in the first place. Falls City, in all the literature, sounded like the last place in the United States where one would want to try to pass as a man while dating local girls; it was also clearly not a good place to be one of the few people of color in town and a black man dating a white woman. Deindustrialization and the farming crises of the 1970s and 1980s had made this town, like so many other midwestern small towns, a place of poverty and neglect where jobs were hard to come by. For the young white men in town, minorities were to blame for this latest downward swing in their fortunes, and certainly the federal government offered no real hope of retribution.

Having read much of the material on Brandon's short life and brutal murder, and having viewed this documentary about the case, I quickly rationalized the whole episode as an inevitable case of a queer running afoul of the rednecks in a place one would not want to live in anyway. In fall 1996, I was invited up to Seattle to speak at a gay and lesbian film festival following the screening of *The Brandon Teena Story*. I would be joined as a discussant by Seattle-local transman and anthropologist Jason Cromwell and Los Angeles–based philosophy professor and transman Jacob Hale. We conferred briefly before the panel, and after sitting through the disturbing documentary, we went to the stage to discuss the film with the audience. The organizers of the conference seemed to assume that the debate likely to be motivated by the documentary would involve whether we should understand Brandon as a female-to-male transsexual without access to sex reassignment surgery or a transgender butch who had deliberately decided not to transition. My comments skimmed over this debate, which seemed beside the point, and went straight to the question of regionality, location, and rural existence. I remarked that Nebraska was not simply "anywhere" in this video, but that the documentary filmmakers had skillfully tried to situate the landscape as a character in this drama. The audience made noises of approval. Next, I went on to the topic of life in small, mostly white, midwestern towns, and suggested that many of these places were the breeding grounds for cultures of hate and meanness that had both homophobic and racist dimensions. The audience was quiet, too quiet.

The question-and-answer session began without controversy, and a few people testified to the difficulties they had encountered as female-to-male transsexuals or as partners of female-to-males. Others talked about the traumatic experience of watching the video and coming so close to the horrific details of Brandon's murder. Then something strange happened. A harmless question came my way: "What do you think of the documentary? Do you think it is good? Do you think the directors were at all condescending?"

While I did have some real problems with the video and its representations of the people of Falls City, I felt that I had been invited to lead an even-handed discussion of *The Brandon Teena Story,* and so I shrugged off the implied criticism and said that I thought Muska and Olafsdottir had done some amazing interviews. The next question went a bit deeper: "What did you think about the depiction in the video of rural life, and furthermore, what do you mean by small towns in the heartland being 'cultures of hate and meanness?'" I tried to explain that I was describing the bigotry that resides in mostly white, nonurban constituencies. Then it got ugly. A woman stood up and denounced my comments as insensitive to those people present who may have come from small towns, and who, moreover, very much wanted to return to a small-town life and did not believe that the small town was an essentially racist or bigoted place. The audience broke out into spontaneous and sustained applause, and then one person after another stood up to testify that they too were from a small town or a rural background and that they too felt offended. Apart from a bruised ego (it is no fun to have an audience give a standing ovation to someone who has just told you that you are full of it), I left Seattle unscathed, but this experience forced me to reconsider what was at stake in the mythmaking that now surrounds Brandon's murder.[2] Confronted with my own urban bias, I decided that one could make use of the Brandon material to study urban attitudes toward queer rural life, and to examine more closely the essential links that have been made between urban life and queerness per se.

The murder of Brandon Teena, like the murder of Matthew Shepard some six years later, did in fact draw public attention to the peculiar vulnerabilities of queer youth (whether transgender or gay/lesbian) living in North America's heartland. In both cases, the victims became martyrs for urban queer activists fighting for LGBT rights, and they were mythologized in a huge and diverse array of media as extraordinary individuals who fell prey to the violent impulses of homophobic and transphobic middle-America masculinities. But while it is tempting to use the materials produced in the aftermath of the killings of both Brandon Teena and Matthew Shepard to flesh out the details of the lives and deaths of the subjects, it makes more sense to my mind to collect the details, the stories, the facts, and the fictions of the cases, and then to create deep archives for future analysis about the many rural lives and desires that were implicated in the lives ands deaths of these individuals. Here I do not mean simply a collection of data; rather, I use the word archive in a Foucauldian way to suggest a discursive field and a structure of thinking. The archive is an immaterial repository for the multiple ideas about rural life that construct and undergird urban identity in the twentieth and twenty-first centuries. In the case of Brandon, the archive that has posthumously developed contains vital information about racial and class constructions of identity and desire in rural areas, and it also provides some important details about the elaborate and complex desires of young women coming to maturity in nonurban areas; the young women who were drawn to Brandon's unconventional manhood must have lots to tell us about adolescent feminine fantasy. As I will elaborate in later chapters, all too often such girlish desires for boyish men are dismissed within a Freudian model of female sexuality as a form of immaturity and unrealized sexual capacity; the assumption that underpins the dismissal of adolescent female desires is that the young women who fall for a Brandon, a teen idol, or some other icon of youthful manhood, will soon come to full adulthood, and when they do, they will desire better and more authentic manhood. By reckoning only with Brandon's story, as opposed to the stories of his girlfriends, his family, and those other two teenagers who died alongside him, we consent to a liberal narrative of individualized trauma. For Brandon's story to be meaningful, it must be about more than Brandon.

Space and Sexuality in Queer Studies

In her lyrical rendering of life in an "other" America, the coal camps and "hollers" of West Virginia, Kathleen Stewart explores at length the meaning of memory for those who live life in forgotten places of neglect and poverty, or in what she calls the "space on the side of the road." In her ethnography, Stewart collects the untidy narratives that disorganize the conventional forward motion of ethnographic telling and thus allows us insight into the particular pull exerted by small-town life for even those subjects who are brutalized by it. One such narrative, for example, emerges when West Virginian Sylvie Hess offers Stewart a rambling recollection of a childhood experience in response to a question about why she could not make a life in the city. In order to explain the attraction of her dilapidated rural hometown, Sylvie recalls her favorite animal from childhood, a cow called Susie, who followed her around throughout her day. One day, however, some stray dogs savaged the cow, and "ripped out her throat and tore her all to pieces." Lingering for a moment over the brutal memory of her beloved cow "layin' there all tore up," Sylvie abruptly switches gears and comments, "But that place was sa perty!" As Stewart observes, "Here, home is a vibrant space of intensity where things happened and left their mark. Home is sweet not despite the loss of her favorite cow but because of it" (Stewart 1996, 65). Stewart's insightful rendering of the seemingly contradictory impulses animating Sylvie's memory provides momentary access for the urban reader to the appeal of the small rural town for the working-class subjects who stay there, finding beauty and peace in between the brutal realities of poverty, isolation, illness, and violence. For Stewart, the rural poor represent a forgotten minority in the U.S. imagination and offer a fertile site for the ethnographic project of documenting difference.

In gay/lesbian and queer studies, there has been little attention paid to date to the specificities of rural queer lives. Indeed, most queer work on community, sexual identity, and gender roles has been based on and in urban populations, and exhibits an active disinterest in the productive potential of nonmetropolitan sexualities, genders, and identities.[3] Or else when nonurban sexualities have been studied, most often within anthropological studies, they are all too often characterized as "traditional" and "non-Western."[4] And yet, at the same time that most theories of modern sexuality have made definitive links between the city and homosexuality, urban queers have exhibited an endless fascination for stories of gays, lesbians, and transgender people living outside the city. For example, we might explain the appeal of the case of Brandon to urban queers in terms of its ability to locate the continuing homophobic and transphobic violence directed at sex- and gender-variant people in the United States in spaces removed from urban life.

The deaths of Brandon and Matthew have sparked new considerations of the relationship between mainstream gay and lesbian rights movements and the harsh realities of lives lived far beyond the reach of rights-based policies. The response to these murders, in fact, suggests that they were, in the words of James C. Scott, "but a variant of affronts suffered systematically by a whole race, class, or strata" (Scott 1990). As Scott writes, "An individual who is affronted may develop a personal fantasy of revenge and confrontation, but when the insult is but a variant of affronts suffered systematically by a whole race, class, or strata, then the fantasy can become a collective cultural product" (9). While Scott's book *Domination and the Arts of Resistance* pertains mostly to class relations in nondemocratic societies, in the age of global capitalism, democracy is now riddled with pockets of intense and naked oppression that both shore up the attraction of democratic rule and fortify the myth of its totality. For those subjects—nonmetropolitan queers, prisoners, homeless people, undocumented laborers—who find themselves quite literally placed beyond the reach of federal protection, legal rights, or state subsidy, democracy is simply the name of their exclusion. For these subjects, the arts of resistance that Scott ascribes to slaves, serfs, and peasants become elaborate and necessary parts of a plan for survival. The Brandon archive is, in some ways, the "collective cultural product" that has responded to the affront of this brutal and phobic murder. And the archive reveals how little we actually know about the forms taken by queer life outside of metropolitan areas. The Brandon archive also makes historical and thematic links between the kinds of violences perpetrated against queer bodies and the documented violences against black bodies in lynching campaigns in the early twentieth century. Lisa Duggan has documented the ways in which lynching narratives and lesbian murder narratives in the 1890s mapped out overlapping histories of violence, and Duggan's powerful study of race, sex, and violence in her *Sapphic Slashers* makes these two seemingly distinct narratives tell a more complete story of the emergence of what she calls "twentieth century U.S. modernity" (Duggan 2000). Brandon's story, coupled as it is with the death of African American Philip DeVine, reminds us of the interchangeability of the queer and the racially other in the white American racist imagination.[5]

Most theories of homosexuality within the twentieth century assume that gay culture is rooted in cities, that it has a special relationship to urban life, and that as Gayle Rubin comments in "Thinking Sex," erotic dissidents require urban space because in rural settings queers are easily identified and punished; this influential formulation of the difference between urban and rural environments was, in 1984 when Rubin's essay was first published, a compelling explanation for the great gay migrations of young queers from the country to the city in the 1970s (Rubin 1984). And since Rubin's essay was heavily committed to the project of providing a theoretical foundation for "sexual ethnographesis" or the ethnographic history of community, it made sense to contrast the sexual conformity of small towns to the sexual diversity of big cities; such a contrast made crystal clear the motivations of young white gay men who seemed to flock in droves in the 1970s from small towns in the Midwest, in particular, to urban gay centers like San Francisco and New York. So in theory, the distinction between rural repression and urban indulgence makes a lot of sense, but in actuality, as recent research has shown, we might find that rural and small-town environments nurture elaborate sexual cultures even while sustaining surface social and political conformity. As John Howard argues in his book, *Men like That,* on rural gay male practices, "The history of gay people has often mirrored the history of the city" (Howard 1999). But he goes on to show that this history of gay migrations to the city depends on a "linear, modernist trajectory" and "effects a number of exclusions" (12). Howard's book resists the universal application of the gay migration narrative, and instead looks at "the interactions between men who experienced and acted on queer desire within a small, localized realm, [and] men who never took on gay identity or became part of a gay community or culture" (14).

Rural and small-town queer life is generally mythologized by urban queers as sad and lonely, or else rural queers might be thought of as "stuck" in a place that they would leave if they only could.[6] Only of late has the rural/urban divide and binary begun to produce some interesting inquiries into life beyond the metropolitan center; in some recent work, the rural/urban binary reverberates in really productive ways with other defining binaries like traditional/modern, Western/non-Western, natural/cultural, and modern/postmodern. The editors of one anthology of queer writings on sexual geographies, for example, *De-centering Sexualities: Politics and Representations beyond the Metropolis,* suggest that rural or nonmetropolitan sites have been elided within studies of sexuality and space, which typically focus on either "sexualized metropolitan areas such as New York and Berlin or on differently sexualized, marginalized and colonized spaces including the Orient and Africa" (Phillips et al. 2000). By comparison, "much less has been said about other liminal or in-between spaces including the small towns and rural parts of Europe, Australia and North America" (1). The volume as a whole points to the dominance of models of what David Bell in his "Eroticizing the Rural" terms helpfully "metrosexuality" and the concomitant representation of the rural as essentially either "hostile" or "idyllic" (Bell 2000).

The notion of metrosexuality as a cultural dominant in U.S. theorizing about gay/lesbian lives also gives rise to the term metronormativity. This term reveals the conflation of "urban" and "visible" in many normalizing narratives of gay/lesbian subjectivities. Such narratives tell of closeted subjects who "come out" into an urban setting, which in turn, supposedly allows for the full expression of the sexual self in relation to a community of other gays/lesbians/queers. The metronormative narrative maps a story of migration onto the coming-out narrative. While the story of coming out tends to function as a temporal trajectory within which a period of disclosure follows a long period of repression, the metronormative story of migration from "country" to "town" is a spatial narrative within which the subject moves to a place of tolerance after enduring life in a place of suspicion, persecution, and secrecy. Since each narrative bears the same structure, it is easy to equate the physical journey from small town to big city with the psychological journey from closet case to out and proud. As Howard comments in *Men like That,* the rural is made to function as a closet for urban sexualities in most accounts of rural queer migration. But in actual fact, the ubiquity of queer sexual practices, for men at least, in rural settings suggests that some other epistemology than the closet governs sexual mores in small towns and wide-open rural areas. In reality, many queers from rural or small towns move to the city of necessity, and then yearn to leave the urban area and return to their small towns; and many recount complicated stories of love, sex, and community in their small-town lives that belie the closet model.

Metronormativity, while it reveals the rural to be the devalued term in the urban/rural binary governing the spatialization of modern U.S. sexual identities, can also shed light on the strangely similar constructions of nonmetropolitan queer sexualities in the United States and nonmetropolitan sexualities in other parts of the world.[7] The recent work on "global gays," to use Dennis Altman's term, has assumed a model of global consciousness-raising within which "unenlightened" sexual minorities around the world, and particularly in Asia, come into contact with Euro-American models of gay identity and begin to form rights-oriented activist communities. In his book *Global Sex,* Altman repeatedly describes the flows of cultural influence between the United States and the "developing" world in terms of the sway of "modern" sexualities on traditional understandings of gender and desire. Sometimes Altman articulates his awareness of the fact that "sexuality becomes an important arena for the production of modernity, with 'gay' and 'lesbian' identities acting as the markers for modernity" (Altman 2001, 91). But he quickly falls back onto thoroughly unexamined assumptions about contemporary forms of embodiment and liberation; for example, he implies repeatedly that gender variance is an anachronistic marker of same-sex desire. Altman writes, "I remain unsure just why 'drag,' and its female equivalents, remains a strong part of the contemporary homosexual world, even where there is increasing space for open homosexuality and a range of acceptable ways of 'being' male or female" (91). Altman's model of "contagious liberation," which is passed on from Westerners to those "closeted" folks in third world countries who remain committed to an anachronistic model of gender inversion and "drag," is deeply flawed. From his conception of a "universal gay identity" to his equation of Western identity with modernity

37

and Asian and Latin American homosexualities with tradition, Altman persistently conjures up a complex model of globalization only to reduce it at the level of sexuality to a false opposition between sexual liberation and sexual oppression.[8] What is more, his projections of sex/gender anachronism onto so-called developing nations unnecessarily simplifies and streamlines sex/gender systems in dominant nations.[9]

In an illuminating essay that acknowledges the difference between the kind of inevitable model of global gay life that Altman proposes and the active imposition of U.S. sexual hegemonies, Alan Sinfield notes that "the metropolitan gay model will be found in Johannesburg, Rio de Janeiro and Delhi, as well as New York and London, in interaction with traditional local, nonmetropolitan, models" (Sinfield 2000, 21). In other words, Sinfield recognizes that a global gay model is always interacting with other, often nonmetropolitan sexual economies. At the same time, then, that we find evidence of the (uneven) spread of U.S. sexual hegemony within these metropolitan areas named by Altman and Sinfield as centers for gay cross-cultural contact, could it be possible that nonmetropolitan models also share certain characteristics cross-culturally? These shared characteristics might be attributed less to capitalist modalities like gay tourism on which the metropolitan model depends and more to the separation of localized sexual economies from the so-called gay global model. In other words, could there be some level of correspondence between a nonmetropolitan sexual system in rural Indonesia and one in rural Nebraska? And could both regions be considered other in relation to the dominant metropolitan model of gay male sexual exchange? In an essay on "gay" men in Indonesia, for example, Tom Boellstorff posits this potential for "someone thousands of miles away (to be) closer than someone next door," and helpfully labels this confluence of distance and similarity "translocal" (Boellstorff 1999, 480). Calling for a "more serious engagement with postcoloniality as a category of analysis" within queer studies, Boellstorff argues that such an engagement "might improve our understanding of sexualities outside the 'West'" (478). But the full deployment of translocal analysis—by which Boellstorff means a way of moving beyond the local/global and sameness/difference binaries that have characterized much of the work on transnational sexualities—would presumably also potentially improve and indeed complicate our understanding of sexualities *within* the "West."

The kinds of sexual communities, identities, and practices that Howard describes in *Men like That,* and that have been depicted and "discovered" in relation to narrative events like the murder of Brandon Teena, may indeed have less in common with the white gay and lesbian worlds associated with the Castro in San Francisco, West Hollywood in Los Angeles, and Chelsea in New York, and they may share some significant traits with the sexual and gender practices associated with *tombois* in Indonesia and Thailand, *travesti* in Brazil, and *bakla* in the Philippines (Morris 1994; Manalansan 1997; Donham 1998). Like other nonmetropolitan sex/gender systems, U.S. small-town and rural alternative sexual communities may often be characterized by distinct gender roles, active/passive sexual positioning, and passing practices; and like other nonmetropolitan models, they may exist in proximity to, rather than in distinction from, heterosexualities.

In the United States, rural populations are studied more often in relation to class or the formation known as white trash, and only rarely is the plight of the rural poor linked to other subaltern populations around the world. There are of course good reasons for not simply lumping all rural populations into one large subaltern formation: as George Lipsitz has documented, even working-class whites in the United States have a "possessive investment in whiteness" that situates them in often contradictory relations to power and dominant discourses (Lipsitz 1998). In the Midwest, moreover, the history of whiteness is linked to the early-twentieth-century Alien Land Laws, which restricted landownership only to those eligible for citizenship, thereby excluding, for example, Asian immigrants (Lowe 1996). As the federal government waged war on native populations in states like Nebraska, "white" immigrants from Scandinavia and other northern European destinations were encouraged to settle in the Midwest by specific government policies aimed at recruiting "white" settlers (Lieberman 1998; Hietala 2003). White rural populations in the United States, particularly in the Midwest, must in fact be thought about through the racial project of whiteness and the historical construction of working-class "whiteness" as a place of both privilege and oppression. Because of this complex construction, we must avoid either romanticizing rural lives or demonizing them: rural queers in particular may participate in certain orders of bigotry (like racism or political conservatism) while being victimized and punished by others (like homophobia and sexism). If we turn to the case of Brandon's murder, we discover a developing archive for the further consideration of queer rural lives. In the narratives and accounts that have poured out of the tragic murder of a young transgender man and his two friends in rural Nebraska, we find an intricate knot of questions about how Brandon passed; the desire he elicited from local girls; his relationship to gay, lesbian, and transgender identities; the hate and violence his performance drew from two young white male friends; and the enduring legacy of the whiteness of the heartland.

One account of gay life in the Midwest that records the combination of privilege and oppression that characterizes the lives of the white gay men who live there, can be found in an oral history project called *Farm Boys* (Fellows 2001). In this volume, historian Will Fellows collected the memories and testimonies of a group of midwestern gay men, all of whom grew up on farms in Scandinavian American or German American families. The narratives presented by Fellows in *Farm Boys* were all submitted in response to a questionnaire that he circulated, and so the stories have an unfortunate generic quality that emphasizes the similarities rather than the differences between the life experiences of the men. In this stock format, each man speaks of his relationship with his father and brothers, describes some childhood sexual experiences (many with livestock, for example), and discusses his move from his rural hometown to the city and (sometimes) back again. But despite the repetitive and formulaic nature of these stories, some important features do emerge. Many of the men stress, for instance, the isolation and lack of queer community in rural settings. Their isolation has sometimes led to a lengthy delay in the man's coming-out process, and many take detours through unwanted marriages. Yet the isolation can, on occasion, also allow for an array of gay or queer identities since the men are not modeling themselves on one stereotypical narrative. The emergence of idiosyncratic formulations of sexual identity implies that if certain sex/gender categories are not presented as inevitable, other options may emerge. Howard claims as much in *Men like That*: "What is apparent is that gay identity in Mississippi (surely as elsewhere) existed alongside multiple queer desires that were not identity based or identity forging" (29).

Farm Boys also shows that rural settings and small towns may offer a reduced amount of contact between the queer person and the kinds of medical discourses that have been so influential on the lives of gays, lesbians, and transsexuals in the twentieth century (Terry 1999). Also, in climates where homosexual identity is not forbidden but simply unthinkable, the preadult sexual subject who pursues same-sex eroticism may do so without necessarily assuming that this sexual activity speaks the truth of one's identity. Furthermore, according to the male narrators of *Farm Boys*, same-sex sexual activity for them was not necessarily accompanied by noticeable degrees of effeminacy, and in fact, male effeminacy was actively discouraged within their communities less as a sign of homosexual tendencies and more because it did not fit with the heavy labor expected of boys in farm families. By the same logic, however, rural women were more likely to be characterized by gender inversion because masculinity in women seems not to have been actively discouraged. A masculine woman, in the context of a farm, is not automatically read as a lesbian; she is simply a hardworking woman who can take care of herself and her farm. Farm masculinities for men and women, then, result in an asymmetrical development of gay and lesbian identities in terms of their relations to gender-inversion models of sexual identity.

Many of the men in *Farm Boys* disassociated themselves from the metropolitan gay worlds that they discovered once they left their rural and small-town homes. Some were puzzled and disturbed by gay effeminacy in the cities, and others were annoyed by the equation of gay with "activist." This desire to have a sexual practice separate from an overt ideological critique of the state or heteronormativity can be taken as one legacy of the history of whiteness that marks the communities the gay rural men left behind. Fellows makes no comment on the often reactionary political sentiments of these white gay men and his remarks focus instead on the importance of pluralistic accounts of gay life. As an oral historian, furthermore, who has actively solicited and shaped the responses of his informants, Fellows has left himself little room for critical commentary. His project points to the difficulties involved in taking account of rural gay lives, but it also charts the contradictory nature of rural queers who have been omitted from dominant accounts of queer life and yet must not be represented as a subaltern population.

As Fellows's volume argues, it is not always easy to fathom the contours of queer life in rural settings because, particularly in the case of gay men, queers from rural settings are not well represented in the literature that has been so much a hallmark of twentieth-century gay identity. Gay men and lesbians from rural settings tend not to be artists and writers in such great numbers, and so most of the coming-out stories that we read are written by people from cities or suburbs. As Eve Kosofsky Sedgwick's work has shown in compelling detail, the history of twentieth-century literature in an Anglo-American context has been indelibly marked and influenced by the contributions of white gay men; consequently, literature has been a powerful vehicle for the production and consolidation of gay identity (Sedgwick 1986, 1990). But again, little of this literature has anything at all to say about rural life, and most of it ties homosexual encounters to the rhythms of the city. Just a quick glance at some of the most influential high-culture texts of queer urban life would reveal gay guidebooks to Oscar Wilde's London, Jean Genet's Paris, Christopher Isherwood's Berlin, E. M Forster's Florence, Thomas Mann's Venice, Edmund White's New York, John Rechy's Los Angeles, Allen Ginsberg's San Francisco, and so on. Canonized literary production by Euro-American lesbian writers like Radclyffe Hall, Djuna Barnes, Jeanette Winterson, and Gertrude Stein similarly focuses, although less obsessively, on urban locations like Paris, London, and New York. But in queer writing by women, we do find some of the themes that we might also expect to see in accounts of rural queer life like stories of isolation and numerous passing narratives.

While fictional narratives of queer rural life are quite hard to find, some ethnographic work and oral histories did emerge in the 1990s. Howard's *Men like That* is an exemplary and unique history and ethnographic survey of the sexual practices and social mores of men who have sex with men in southern Mississippi. His book examines "sexual and gender nonconformity, specifically male homosexualities and male-to-female transgender sexualities in Mississippi from 1945–1985" (Howard 1999, xiv). Arguing that men "like that" in the rural South in the 1950s were "largely homebound, living in familial households," Howard shows that these men did travel nonetheless, but most did not migrate to big cities; instead, "queer movement consisted of circulation rather than congregation" (xiv). Most queers, he claims, found partners within their immediate vicinity, and in the 1950s, these men were able to escape state surveillance of their illicit activities and their queer sexual practices went undetected. By the supposedly liberal 1960s, however, a new discourse of perversion allowed for the large-scale harassment and arrest of large numbers of queer men. What Howard's book perhaps does not emphasize enough is the impunity from legal and moral scrutiny in Mississippi that was extended specifically to white men while the sexual activities of black men (gay or straight) were constantly watched by fretful white citizens. In fact, it is not *so* surprising that white patriarchs during the same period were able to have sex with boys, black men, and each other without incurring any kind of comment. Howard's book also has little to say about female sexual practices in rural areas, and we are left to wonder whether the histories of men like that can tell us anything at all about the women who were also homebound and yet had no opportunities for congregation or circulation.

While Brandon fits only nominally into the category of "woman" and while his complex story cannot at all be called "lesbian," Brandon's choices do give us some insight into what kinds of options may exist for cross-identified, female-born transgender people in rural settings. Many urban gays, lesbians, and transgender people responded to the murder of Brandon with a "what do you expect" attitude, as if brutality was an inevitable consequence of trying to pull off such a risky endeavor as passing for male in some godforsaken place. But what such a response ignores is the fact that Brandon had been passing for male with only mixed success in the city of Lincoln, Nebraska, since his early teenage years; indeed, it was only when he left the city and made a reverse migration to the small town of Falls City that he really pulled off a credible presentation as male. Obviously, the small town can accommodate some performances even as it is a dangerous place for others— for example, an exhibition of normative masculinity in a transgender man may go unnoticed while an overt and public demonstration of nonnormative gendering may be severely and frequently punished. Urban responses to Brandon's decisions also misunderstand completely the appeal of the small town to certain subjects. Like Sylvie Hess, the West Virginian in Stewart's ethnography who remembers the loss of a favorite animal and the beauty of the place of its death side by side, the rural queer may be attracted to the small town for precisely those reasons that make it seem uninhabitable to the urban queer.

Brandon clearly knew what was possible in Falls City, Nebraska, and he seemed to know what limits might be imposed on his passing performance. He moved to Falls City not in order to be a stranger with no history but because he had friends there. As Angelia R. Wilson observes in an essay about "Gay and Lesbian Life in Rural America": "Unknown outsiders are never welcomed in small towns." And she continues: "The key to survival in a rural community is interdependence" (Wilson 2000, 208). Brandon quite quickly developed a friendship network in Falls City, which included both his girlfriends and his killers, but he seemed to take a certain comfort in being known and in knowing everyone in town. By moving to a small town and setting up life as a young man, moreover, Brandon was operating within the long tradition of passing women in rural areas of North America that has been documented by historian Lisa Duggan among others.[10] Wilson mentions at least one such narrative in her essay involving an "African American woman who lived as a man for 15 years" in Mississippi in the 1940s and 1950s. Jim McHarris/Annie Lee Grant lived in a small town called Kosciusko, working and dating women, and was only discovered when he was arrested by the local police for a traffic violation. After that, Jim left town and began his life as a man elsewhere. The story was reported in *Ebony* in 1954.[11] And there are many more. While gender codes may be somewhat more flexible in urban settings, this also means that people become more astute in urban contexts at reading gender. In the context of a small town where there are strict codes of normativity, there is also a greater potential for subverting the codes surreptitiously.

The Brandon story brings to light at least three historiographical problems related to the topic of studying queer rural life. First, this narrative reveals how difficult transgender history has been to write in general, but also how there may be specific dimensions of transgender identity that are particular to a rural setting. Given that many gay, lesbian, and transgender people who grow up and live in small rural areas may not identify at all with these labels, the rural context allows for a different array of acts, practices, performances, and identifications. Second, the Brandon story suggests that too often minority history hinges on representative examples provided by the lives of a few extraordinary individuals. And so in relation to the complicated matrix of rural queer lives, we tend to rely on the story of a Brandon Teena or a Matthew Shepard rather than finding out about the queer people who live quietly, if not comfortably, in isolated areas or small towns all across North America. The "representative individual" model of minority history, furthermore, grows out of the particular tendency in Western culture to think about sexuality in terms of, as Foucault describes it, "the implantation of perversions," which in turn surface as identities (Foucault 1980). The history of sexuality in a Euro-American context has therefore traced the medical and legal histories of the formation of identities like "homosexual," "lesbian," "transsexual," and "heterosexual." While Foucauldian histories have been careful to depict the sexological production of identities over space and time, still much critical attention focuses on the individual, the formation and transformations of self, the psychology of desire, the drama of pathology and pathologization, the emergence of types, and even the biographies of famous representative individuals (like Radclyffe Hall, Oscar Wilde, and so on). Less time, as George Chauncey has pointed out, has been spent on considering the developments of queer communities, and the negotiations of desire and identity within communities that may be unified or disunified by other modes of identification (Chauncey 1989). Even less time has been spent in consideration of those subjects who remain outside the ambit of the medical and psychological productions of identity, and the reverse discourses that greet and shape their use. Precisely because queer history has been so preoccupied with individuals, it has been harder to talk about class and race, and it has seemed much more relevant to discuss gender variance and sexual practices. All too often, community models are offered only as a generalized model of many individuals rather than as a complex interactive model of space, embodiment, locality, and desire. The Brandon archive, then, needs to be read less in terms of the history of one extraordinary person, and more in terms of the constructions of community and self that it brings to light.

The third and final historiographical problem in relation to this case has to do with the stakes of authenticity. What is real? What is narrative? As I argue in chapter 6 in relation to Austin Powers and drag king subcultures, queer genders profoundly disturb the order of relations between the authentic and the inauthentic, the original and the mimic, the real and the constructed. And as we will see in the next chapter in relation to transgender biographies, there are no true accounts of "passing lives" but only fictions, and the whole story turns on the production of counterfeit realities that are so convincing that they replace and subsume the real. This case itself hinges on the production of a "counterfeit" masculinity that even though it depends on deceit and illegality, turns out to be more compelling, seductive, and convincing than the so-called real masculinities with which it competes.

Future Histories

Ultimately, the Brandon archive is not simply the true story of a young queer misfit in rural North America. It is also a necessarily incomplete and ever expanding record of how we select our heroes as well as how we commemorate our dead. James Baldwin, in his account of the 1979 Atlanta murders of black children, calls our attention to the function of streamlining in the awful vicinity of violent erasure. In *The Evidence of Things Not Seen,* Baldwin writes: "The cowardice of this time and place—this era—is nowhere more clearly revealed than in the perpetual attempt to make the public and social disaster the result, or the issue of a single demented creature, or, perhaps, half a dozen such creatures, who have, quite incomprehensibly, gone off their rockers and must be murdered and locked up" (Baldwin 1995, 72). The desire, in other words, the desperate desire, to attribute hate crimes to crazy individuals and to point to the U.S. justice system as the remedy for unusual disturbances to the social order of things must be resisted in favor of political accounts of crime and punishment. In the end, we are not simply celebrating a Brandon Teena and denouncing a John Lotter or Thomas Nissen, nor should we be seeing love as the redemptive outcome to a tale of hate; the real work of collecting the stories of a Brandon Teena, a Billy Tipton, or a Matthew Shepard must be to create an archive capable of providing a record of the complex interactions of race, class, gender, and sexuality that result in murder, but whose origins lie in state-authorized formations of racism, homophobia, and poverty. Justice in the end lies in the unraveling of the crime not simply in its solution, and when we cease to unravel we become collaborators. "The author of a crime," notes Baldwin, "is what he is . . . but he who collaborates is doomed forever in that unimaginable and yet very common condition which we weakly call hell" (125). The stories we collect in the Brandon archive should stretch far beyond the usual tales of love and hate and the various narratives of accommodation; this archive lends us precisely the kind of evidence for things not seen that Baldwin sought, and in the end, if we read it right, it may tell us a different story about late-twentieth-century desire, race, and geography. With careful organization now, this archive may also become an important resource later for future queer historians who want to interpret the lives we have lived from the few records we have left behind.

3

Unlosing Brandon

Brandon Teena, Billy Tipton, and Transgender Biography

> What is remembering? Remembering brings the absent into the present, connects what is lost to what is here. Remembering draws attention to lostness and is made possible by emotions of space that open backward into a void. Memory depends upon void, as void depends upon memory, to think it. Once void is thought, it can be canceled. Once memory is thought, it can be commodified.
>
> —Anne Carson, *Economy of the Unlost*

The act of remembering, says poet and essayist Anne Carson, "connects what is lost to what is here." And to be unlost is to exist in that space between retrieval and obliteration where erasure waits on one side and something well short of salvation waits on the other side. In many ways, Brandon exists among the unlost; he is actively remembered by people who never knew him, and he is endlessly memorialized as a symbol for the lives that have passed unnoticed and the deaths that have gone unrecorded. When we "remember" Brandon, what do we remember, who do we remember, and why do we invest so much hope in the remembering of an individual who would have appeared unremarkable and possibly unsympathetic had most of his mourners met him today? By calling the legacy of Brandon an "archive," as I did in my last chapter, I draw attention to the material and phantasmatic investments in this figure who stands enigmatically for a generation or community of the lost, and I show how the act of remembering Brandon constitutes an act of mourning for a life unlived, a potential unrealized, and an identity unformed. In *Economy of the Unlost*, Carson comments: "Once void is thought, it can be canceled. Once memory is thought, it can be commodified." In this chapter, I will trace the commodification of memory by biographers of transgender subjects. If some memories are motivated by an idealizing and sentimental desire to elevate these characters to iconic states, others, as we will see in the examples that follow, are motivated by the anxious need to protect a fragile status quo. In the idealized narrative, the transgender subject occupies the status of "unlost"; he is retrieved and preserved in the amber of those memories that would hold him up as an example, an icon, a symbol. In the excoriating narratives, the transgender man is lost to history, and in his place we find only a magician disappearing in a puff of smoke and leaving in his wake a perfectly arranged tableau of heterosexual order.

Transgender Histories

> Following the ghosts is about making a contact that changes you and re-fashions the social relations in which you are located. It is about putting life back in where only a vague memory or a bare trace was visible to those who bothered to look.
>
> —Avery Gordon, *Ghostly Matters* (1997, 22)

The names Brandon Teena and Billy Tipton have become synonymous with a cluster of questions and concerns about passing, gender identities, memory, history, space, and transgender biography. Brandon was a young woman who passed successfully as a man in a small town in Nebraska and who was brutally murdered when some local men decided to take their bloody revenge for what they considered to be a grand deception. Billy Tipton was a jazz musician who was only discovered to have a female body after his death. Since Tipton had married several times and was survived by a wife and adopted children, the revelation of his biological sex created a minor sensation. In the case of each of these transgender subjects, their lives were dismantled and reassembled through a series of biographical inquiries. This chapter situates transgender biography as a sometimes violent, often imprecise project that brutally seeks, retroactively and with the benefit of hindsight, to erase the carefully managed details of the life of a passing person, and that recasts the act of passing as deception, dishonesty, and fraud. I will be asking here what kind of truths about gender we demand from the lives of people who pass, cross-dress, or simply refuse normative gender categories. None of the transgender subjects whom I examine here can be definitively identified as transsexual, and none can be read as lesbian; all must be read and remembered according to the narratives they meticulously circulated about themselves when they were alive. In this chapter, I address thorny questions about the ethics of biography, biographical temporality, and who has the right to tell tales about whose life; and I explore and flesh out the postmodern category "transgender." This chapter also makes contact with the ghosts who animate contemporary queer consciousness about transgender life.

While transgender has served as a kind of umbrella term in recent years for cross-identifying subjects, I think the inclusivity of its appeal has made it quite unclear as to what the term might mean and for whom. Some theorists like Bernice Hausman have dismissed transgenderism as a form of false consciousness that circulates through the belief that genders can be voluntary and chosen, and she concludes in *Changing Sex* that "the new gender outlaws are just newer versions of the old gender conformists" (Hausman 1995, 197). Others, like transsexual theorist Henry Rubin for one, read transgender politics as a postmodern critique of the commitment to the "real" that is implied by transsexualism (Rubin 1996). Still others, like Biddy Martin, identify transgenderism as a faddish celebration of gender crossing that assigns non-cross-identified queers to the ignominy of gender conformity (Martin 1994). But as I will show in this chapter, we have hardly begun to recognize the forms of embodiment that fill out the category of transgenderism, and before we dismiss it as faddish, we should know what kind of work it does, whom it describes, and whom it validates. Transgender proves to be an important term not to people who want to reside outside of categories altogether but to people who want to place themselves in the way of particular forms of recognition. Transgender may indeed be considered a term of relationality; it describes not simply an identity but a relation between people, within a community, or within intimate bonds.

I will engage here with the somewhat paradoxical, but necessary project of transgender history: paradoxical because it represents the desire to narrate lives that may willfully defy narrative, but necessary because without such histories, we are left with only a bare trace of a life lived in defiance of gender norms. At least one of the reasons that the term transgender quickly became popular and widespread in the early 1990s was the emergence of communities of cross-identifying women who did not comply with medical models of transsexuality. And as female-to-male transsexuals became more numerous and visible in urban queer communities, there was inevitably a reshuffling of categories and etiologies. Young people coming out in the 1990s, as my introduction showed, may be forgiven for not quite knowing what their experiences of cross-identification might mean. If "lesbian" in this context becomes the term for women who experience themselves as female and desire other women, and if "FTM transsexual" becomes the term for female-born people who experience prolonged male-identification and think of themselves as male, then what happens to those female-born people who think of themselves as masculine but not necessarily male and certainly not female? We do use the term "butch" for this last category, but it cannot adequately bridge the categorical gap between lesbian and transsexual.

Jay Prosser's book *Second Skins: The Body Narratives of Transsexuality,* in particular, has been enormously useful in thinking through the relations between the terms transgender and queer, and elucidating the continuities and difference between butch and FTM (Prosser 1998). Prosser's work helps us map the theoretical terrain of transgender studies. His formulation of the role of narrative in transsexual transition has established itself in opposition to what he understands to be a queer and indeed postmodern preference for performativity over narrativity. In *Second Skins,* Prosser asks what the effect of a theory of gender performativity has been on our understanding of transsexuality; he also argues that for all our talk about "materiality" and "embodiment," it is precisely the body that vanishes within ever more abstract theories of gender, sexuality, and desire. Prosser points out that in *Gender Trouble,* Judith Butler implied that it was the transgender subject in particular who symbolized the "gender trouble" to which every subject is heir; in other words, the split between sex and gender, which is so readable within the transgender or transsexual body, reveals the constructedness of all sex and gender. Gender normativity, within this schema, is a place of self-deception inasmuch as the "straight" subject imagines his or her gender to be consistent with his or her sex and the relation between the two to be "natural" (Butler 1990). As Prosser comments: "While within this framework, this allocation is a sign of the devaluation of straight gender and conversely queer's alignment of itself with transgender performativity represents queer's sense of its own 'higher purpose,'" in fact there are transgendered trajectories, in particular transsexual trajectories, that aspire to what this scheme devalues. Namely, there are transsexuals who seek very pointedly to be nonperformative, to be constative, quite simply to be" (32). This is a complicated passage, but I think it can be rendered as: many transsexuals do not want to represent gender artifice; they actually aspire to the real, the natural, indeed the very condition that has been rejected by the queer theory of gender performance.

While I am totally sympathetic to Prosser's argument that the transsexual has been used in queer theory as a symbol for the formulation of a subjectivity that actually threatens transsexual claims to legitimacy, I do think there are problems with his formulation of a transsexual desire for realness and his sense that gender realness is achievable. After all, what actually constitutes the real for Prosser in relation to the transsexual body? The penis or the vagina? Facial hair or shaved legs? Everyday life as a man or a woman? The main example of a transsexual desire for realness that Prosser examines involves Venus Extravaganza from the film *Paris Is Burning*, a figure whom Butler discusses at length in *Bodies That Matter*. Prosser critiques Butler for making a distinction between transgender transgression and transsexual capitulation to "hegemonic constraint," and he notes that as long as Venus remains gender ambiguous, then she can represent the transgression of the "denaturalization of sex"; but because she expresses a desire to become a white woman and live in the suburbs, Butler talks of the "reworking of the normative framework of heterosexuality" (Butler 1993, 133). Prosser, on the other hand, not only wants to release the transsexual from the burden of representing subversive sexuality and gender; he also wants to draw attention to the fact that Venus Extravaganza is killed by a transphobic john not because she is a woman but because she is mid-transition, not quite a woman. Prosser notes ominously that "Butler's essay locates transgressive value in that which makes the subject's life most unsafe" (49).

In the critique of Butler waged by Prosser, I believe a distinction needs to be made between realness and the real—a distinction that would have been meaningful to Venus, who lived in the world of balls, voguing, and realness. Realness in *Paris Is Burning* is, in the words of drag queen ball elder Dorian Corey, "as close as we will ever come to the real." It is not exactly performance, not exactly an imitation; it is the way that people, minorities, excluded from the domain of the real, appropriate the real and its effects. Another category in the world of drag balls exemplifies the inflections of realness: "butch realness." Masculine women compete within this category for the trophy that recognizes the most compelling, exciting, or convincing performance of passing by a butch. Here, as in other drag categories, the term realness offsets any implications of inauthenticity within the category, and it invites masculine women, passing women, to put their masculinity on display and inhabit it with style and emphasis for the entertainment and scrutiny of the judges of the competition. While it may seem to imply manipulable agency, butch realness actually describes less of an act of will and more of a desire to flaunt the unpredictability of social gendering.

Realness—the appropriation of the attributes of the real, one could say—is precisely the transsexual condition. The real, on the other hand, is that which always exists elsewhere, and as a fantasy of belonging and being. Venus Extravaganza, in the clips from *Paris Is Burning* discussed by Prosser and Butler, accordingly expresses her desire for the real in the form of things she will obviously never attain, such as white suburban respectability; meanwhile, in another performance of realness, the transgender man expresses his desire for a manhood that will on some level always elude him. The ever receding horizon of the real, however, need not be the downfall of transsexual aspiration; indeed, it may be its strength. Needless to say, the fantasy that many queers may entertain of gender realness is extremely important as we challenge the limits of theories of performance. Prosser suggests that transsexuals become real literally through authorship, by writing themselves into transition. "Narrative," Prosser notes, "is not only the bridge to embodiment but a way of making sense of transition, the link between locations: the transition itself" (9). Gender discomfort can be alleviated by narratives that locate the oddly gendered subject in the world and in relation to others. While I cast the relationship between the transgender subject and narrative in slightly different terms, I find Prosser's understanding of the role of narrative in transsexual self-authorization to be crucial. What happens when the transgender subject has died and is unable to provide a narrative of his complex life? What is the difference between transsexual autobiography and transgender biography?

One way in which queers and transgenders have put themselves in the way of gender realness is to inhabit categories of their own making. While some people suggest that categories (gay, lesbian, transsexual) are themselves the site of regulation, trouble, and repression, I would argue that categories represent sites of "necessary trouble," to use one of Butler's terms (Butler 1991, 4). Queer theory has long been preoccupied with the relationship between identity and regulation; post-Foucault, we recognize that to embrace identities can simply form part of a "reverse discourse" within which medically constructed categories are lent the weight of realness by people's willingness to occupy those categories (Foucault 1980). Nevertheless, it may be that we have allowed this Foucauldian insight to redirect discussions of identification away from the subject of categories themselves. The term "reverse discourse" in Foucault's *The History of Sexuality: An Introduction, Vol. 1*, identifies and rejects the traditional formulations of gay and lesbian political struggle as essentially oppositional. Since certain sexual liberation discourses recapitulate the terms of the homo/hetero binary that oppress minority sexual subjects in the first place, then these discourses become part of the installation of the very sexual hierarchy that they seek to oppose. Foucault, however, also understands emancipation struggles as strategically and historically necessary. Furthermore, a reverse discourse is in no way the "same" as the discourse it reverses; indeed, its desire for reversal is a desire for transformation.

We may not want to reject all reverse discourses per se, but may instead want to limit the ways in which we invest in them (coming out, for example) as end points: Foucault, and Butler for that matter, clearly believe that resistance has to go beyond the taking of a name ("I am a lesbian"), and must produce creative new forms of being by assuming and empowering a marginal positionality. The production of categories is also different in different spaces: expert-produced categories ("the homosexual," "the invert," "the transsexual") are ultimately far less interesting or useful than sexual vernaculars or the categories produced and sustained within sexual subcultures. The naming of sexual vernaculars and the production of community histories can be traced back to the work of Gayle Rubin in particular, and she has spoken eloquently about the limits of expert discourses on sexuality (like psychoanalysis) and the importance of questions of "sexual ethnogenesis" (the formation of sexual communities).[1] Scientific discourses have tended to narrow our ability to imagine sexuality and gender otherwise, and in general the discussions that take place in medical communities about embodiment and desire may be way behind those on e-mail lists, in support groups, and in sex clubs. Accordingly, we should take over the prerogative of naming our experience and identifications.

Nowhere has the effect of naming our identifications been clearer in recent years than in relation to the experience we call "transgendered." Transgender is for the most part a vernacular term developed within gender communities to account for the cross-identification experiences of people who may not accept all of the protocols and strictures of transsexuality. Such people understand cross-identification as a crucial part of their gendered self, but they may pick and choose among the options of body modification, social presentation, and legal recognition available to them. So you may find that a transgender male is a female-born subject who has had no sex-reassignment surgery, takes testosterone (with or without medical supervision), and lives as a man mostly, but is recognized by his community as a transgendered man in particular. The term transgender in this context refuses the stability that the term transsexual may offer to some folks, and it embraces more hybrid possibilities for embodiment and identification. At the same time, the term transsexual is itself undergoing reconstruction by publicly identifiable transsexuals; Kate Bornstein, for one, has made a career from reshaping the public discourse around gender and transsexuality (Bornstein 1998). In other words, transsexual is not simply the conservative medical term to transgender's transgressive vernacular; instead, both transsexuality and transgenderism shift and change in meaning as well as application *in relation to each other* rather than in relation to a hegemonic medical discourse.

In relation to the female-born person who passes as male (with or without hormones) for most of his life, the term transgender registers the distinction between *his* cultivated masculinity and a male's biological masculinity, and it addresses the question of the transgender man's past history as female. For these subjects, of course, we need a transgender history, a method for recording the presence of gender-ambiguous subjects sensitive enough not to reduce them to either "women all along" or "failed men." Transgender bodies seem to be both illogical and illegible to any number of "experts" who may try to read them. At the same time, transgender lives often seem to attract enormous attention from biographers, filmmakers, talk show hosts, doctors, and journalists, all of whom are dedicated to forcing the transgender subject to make sense. While one would not wish to assign the transgender life to the inauspicious category of nonsense, we should be wary of overly rational narratives about lives filled with contradiction and tension. Ultimately, we must ask questions about history, documentation, and the sometimes dangerous project of scrutinizing lives that were organized around gender passing.

The lives and deaths of Brandon Teena and Billy Tipton have suffered the untimely and rude effects of overexposure. While obviously my efforts to examine the flurry of representation surrounding Brandon, Billy, and other transgender figures actually adds to this effect, the production of counternarratives seems all-important in a media age when suppression of information is virtually impossible (nor would I necessarily argue for the suppression of information under any circumstances). In the cases of Brandon and Billy, however, it serves some purpose to examine the motives behind various representations of transgender lives. In general, we can identify three different and often competing sets of motivations for the representation of a transgender life by nontransgender people. First, there is *the project of stabilization*. In this narrative project, the destabilizing effects of the transgender narrative are defused by establishing the transgender narrative as strange, uncharacteristic, and even pathological. Stabilization, for example, is the underlying principle of cable television shows like *Weird Lives* on the Biography channel, a show that has featured the life stories of both Billy Tipton and male-to-female transsexual Christine Jorgenson.

Then there is *the project of rationalization.* Within a rationalizing project, the biographer, filmmaker, or writer finds reasonable explanations for behavior that may seem dangerous and outrageous at first glance. A good example of a rationalizing narrative about gender passing would be Maggie Greenwald's film *The Ballad of Little Jo.* In this account of a passing woman in postbellum America, the heroine is assigned an economic motive for her masquerade and she ultimately gives up her disguise when she falls in love with a man. This narrative placates mainstream viewers by returning the temporarily transgender subject to the comforting and seemingly inevitable matrix of hetero-domesticity.

Finally, there is *the project of trivialization.* A third narrative told about transgender subjects in order to contain the threat they represent to gender stability is a trivializing one in which the transgender life is dismissed as nonrepresentative and inconsequential. Such a containment strategy can be found in numerous tales of female-to-male cross-dressing soldiers in the nineteenth and twentieth centuries. Usually in such narrative accounts, the cross-dressing "military maid" is cast as an adventure seeker or a brave nationalist, but only rarely is she characterized as cross-gendered.

The term transgender can be used as a marker for all kinds of people who challenge, deliberately or accidentally, gender normativity. Jazz singer Little Jimmy Scott, just to give one example, is a male vocalist whose high countertenor voice causes him to be heard as female. His voice has been described as "angelic," and he has influenced many famous female jazz vocalists like Nancy Wilson. The term transgender can be applied here not to remove Scott from the category "male" but to prevent him from being heard as "female." In interviews, he strenuously objects to criticisms of his voice that liken it to a woman's and he insists, in a way, that his voice, his transgender voice, extends the category of maleness rather than capitulates to the strict dictates of gender normativity. In this context, the term transgender appears as an adjective to describe a voice rather than as an identification category that describes Scott's gender identity or sexual orientation. In what follows, I will use transgender as a descriptive term for several different forms of nonnormative gender presentation. While Scott has recently given interviews about the medical condition (Kallman's syndrome—a hormonal dysfunction) that gave him his high voice and androgynous appearance, other people who present their gender ambiguously may not be given the opportunity to explain what motivates their gender variance.[2] Transgender history should allow the gender ambiguous to speak; too often, I will claim, the histories of women who pass as men or the narratives of transgender men attempt to rationalize rather than represent transgender lives in the glory of all their contradictions. In the rest of this chapter, I examine the biographical accounts that have been produced about transgender men in the last decade and argue that with only a few notable exceptions, these biographies cast transgender men in the somewhat salubrious roles of cad, deceiver, seducer of young women, or simply the delusional charmer.

Ghost Writing: The Case of Billy Tipton

> Many ghost writers believe they are the real authority on their subject and not the ghost themselves.
>
> —Jackie Kay, *Trumpet* (1998, 262)

Early on in *Trumpet,* a haunting novel by British author Jackie Kay, Millicent Moody, the widow of the celebrated jazz musician Joss Moody, comments: "The only thing that feels authentic to me is my past" (37). Shortly after her husband dies, the secret that she and Joss have kept meticulously over the years of their marriage leaks out to the press: Joss was born a woman. As Millicent mourns the death of her beloved husband, she also has to fend off journalists, try to repair the damaged relationship with her son, and protect the memories of her life with Joss from the vicious rewritings to which they are now subject. "I am the only one," she says, "who can remember him the way he wanted to be remembered" (40).

Trumpet, as even a short summary of the novel makes clear, models the character of Joss Moody on the life and death of the U.S. jazz musician Billy Tipton.

When Tipton died in 1992, paramedics called by his son were shocked to find breasts beneath the man's clothing. Tipton's son and his last wife claimed to have no knowledge of Tipton's secret. Unlike Tipton's wife, Millicent in Kay's novel *Trumpet* is depicted as having full knowledge of the "facts" of her husband's embodiment. For Millicent, her husband's breasts and female genitalia were "our secret"—a secret not all that different from the many secrets kept between spouses: "Lots of people have secrets, don't they? The world runs on secrets. What kind of place would the world be without them?" (10). The revelation of the secret of the passing man or woman, however, seems to occasion a particular kind of curiosity, and has produced sometimes cruel and disrespectful revisions of life narratives. The revelation of Tipton's "secret," for example, prompted speculation and investigation of the so-called true identity of Tipton.

In her highly publicized biography of Tipton, *Suits Me: The Double Life of Billy Tipton,* academic biographer Diane W. Middlebrook comes dangerously close to claiming that Tipton's life as a man was simply the result of his overwhelming ambition to perform as a musician (Middlebrook 1998). Despite recent research providing evidence to the contrary (Dahl 2001; Tucker 2001), Middlebrook argues that jazz gigs were hard to come by for women in the 1930s and 1940s. And by emphasizing the impenetrable nature of this music scene for women, she is able to make Tipton's desire to perform and tour seem like motivation enough for his momentous decision to live his life as man with a woman's body. This rationalizing rubric then forces Middlebrook to view his relationships with women as elaborate deceptions within which Tipton finds younger women to date and then exploits their sexual naïveté, using them as a "beard." Middlebrook depicts Tipton accordingly and variously as a "magician" and as someone who preyed on innocent and naive women. Of one wife, Betty, who was very young when she married Tipton, Middlebrook writes, "Billy made a shrewd choice in choosing Betty as a partner, and it is the shrewdness that diminishes Billy's moral stature" (177). In such moments, the supposedly objective and scholarly biographer turns abruptly into judge and juror, and the life hanging in the balance is measured by impossibly high standards.

While obviously transgender and transsexual critics may also be guilty of manipulating the subject matter of transgender lives, more often than not transgender or transsexual researchers will reveal their own investment in the subject matter at hand (Stryker 1994; Hale 1998). Other analysts, biographers, and historians, like Middlebrook, remain hidden from view, content to allow the spotlight to shine on the strangeness and duplicity of the transgender subject. For this reason, Middlebrook's academic biography is subtitled *The Double Life of Billy Tipton,* and Kate Summerscale's biography of butch lesbian Joe Carstairs marks Carstairs life story as "eccentric" in its subtitle (Summerscale 1997). Eccentric, double, duplicitous, deceptive, odd, self-hating: all of these judgments swirl around the passing woman, the cross-dresser, the nonoperative transsexual, the self-defined transgender person, as if other lives—gender-normative lives—were not odd, not duplicitous, not doubled and contradictory at every turn. When Middlebrook tries to reveal herself to the reader's gaze, she oddly places herself in the position of a duped wife: "What if I had met Billy at age eighteen, Betty's age when they became lovers? In 1957 I was as ignorant about the specifics of sexual intercourse as most of my girlfriends, and I did not know much about male anatomy. Would I have discovered Billy's secret?" (175). In fact, this isolated moment of self-revelation in a text completely trained on the eccentricity of Tipton, does tell us much about the biographer, Middlebrook. It tells us that she identifies and is in sympathy with Billy's wives rather than Billy; it tells us that her particular perspective may allow her unique insight into the lives of those women who chose to ignore and accept Billy's anatomy while loving and honoring his chosen gender. Indeed, Billy's last wife commissioned this biography, and it is written for her (or at least on her behalf), to her, and in concert with her desires. In many ways, in fact, *Suits Me* well suits the wife who wants to distance herself from her late husband's legacy of queerness, and it suits too the needs of a mainstream reading public who want to be fascinated but not challenged, provoked but not transformed. What would the biography look like if the biographer identified with Billy? Should such an identification be a precondition for writing such a biography? Why is the life of Tipton the life on show when the lives of his wives share in the eccentricity that so fascinates Middlebrook? Those wives also lived double lives, also made choices—shrewd choices. How does the scandal of the transgender body drain attention away from the extraordinary qualities of other conflicted lives?

Returning again to Kay's novel, we find a character closely mirroring Middlebrook. In *Trumpet*, a biographer is hot on the trail of Joss's secrets, and tries to bribe both his son and his wife to give her information about Joss. In the last half of the novel, Kay details the struggle between journalist Sophie Stones and Joss's son, Colman, over the documenting of Joss's life; it is in this section of the novel that Kay forcefully brings to a crisis questions about naming, identity, and narrative. In the characterization of Stones, moreover, it is impossible not to read parallels between her and Middlebrook. While Middlebrook's biography of Tipton was commissioned by his last wife, Kitty, in *Trumpet*, Joss's wife steadfastly refuses to have anything to do with a biography of Joss, and Millicent comments in outrage, "The idea that I could cooperate with a book about my life, that I could graft myself into this life that they think I had. . . . My life is up for grabs. No doubt they will call me a lesbian. They will find words to fit onto me. Words that don't fit me. Words that don't fit Joss" (Kay 1998, 153–54). Kay depicts the biographer as a stranger who seeks intimacy with the dead for the purposes of telling a good story: "The public might hate perverts, she [Stones] tells herself, but they love reading about them" (264). In order to tell the story of the cross-dresser or the transgender subject, the biographer must convince herself that her own life is normal, beyond reproach, honest. But Kay shows that biography as a project is inevitably bound to deception and manipulation in its own way. How else does the biographer get loved ones to inform on their former father/husband/son? How else to create a position from which to judge? At one point, however, Stones questions her own motivations, asking herself, "I wonder what I would have felt if I had been Mill Moody. Would I have fallen for Joss Moody too?" (126). This question is an uncanny echo of Middlebrook's own questions about her motivation for rewriting Tipton's carefully constructed life. And in both cases, the biographer is shown as one with no identification with the subject of their biographical project; in both cases, the biographer can only wonder about the desire directed at the transgender subject.

In a flurry of investigative zeal, Kay's novel shows us that a life carefully written by its author, owned and shielded by loved ones, may suddenly stand exposed as a lie. The beauty of Kay's narrative is that she does not try to undo the life narrative of a passing man; rather, she sets out to honor it by weaving together a patchwork of memories from Joss's survivors, but mainly his wife, and making that patchwork into the authentic narrative. When Millicent asserts, "I am the only one who can remember him the way he wanted to be remembered," she rejects the attempts made by the press to revise, reform, and rescript her husband. Although the blurb on the back cover of *Trumpet* refers to the love between Millicent and Joss as something built "out of a complex, dazzling lie," the novel itself quietly sidesteps the equation between passing and lying, and instead investigates the particularity of desire: "I didn't feel like I was living a lie," Millicent thinks. "I felt like I was living a life" (95).

While Tipton was born a white midwesterner, Kay's character, Moody, is a black Briton: "His father was African, his mother Scottish" (17). Joss and Millicent adopt a black son together, Colman, who later in life wonders how his parents pulled off their masquerade. In the wake of the revelation of his father's sex, he struggles with the complex legacy of ambiguity that Joss leaves him: "I didn't feel Scottish. Didn't feel British either. Didn't feel anything. My heart is a fucking stone" (51). He remembers how Joss could not tell him stories about his grandparents, but told him instead to make up his own bloodline, imaginatively create his own family tree. He remembers the accidental resemblance between his father and himself: "I am the same kind of colour as my father. We even look alike. Pure fluke" (50). And Colman takes pride in the ways in which his father and he are related despite the lack of a biological link. Finally, Colman struggles to make sense of his masculinity, modeled so clearly on his father's and destabilized now by the revelation of female body parts. Is his own masculinity a lie? he wonders. Does his own identity dissolve in the wake of his father's death?

The voices that tell the life and death of Joss are various, like the lives he lived, like the lives we all live. His wife's memories approximate most closely the life he made and narrated for himself. His son's struggle with his father's legacy creates a complex and contradictory story of fatherhood and forgiveness. But there are other voices as well: a doctor, a registrar, a funeral director. The doctor and registrar both play their part in the construction and destruction of identities: the doctor crosses out "male" on the death certificate and quietly inserts "female"; the registrar agrees to record Joss as "Joss Moody" on the death papers and not "Josephine." So too the funeral director states, "There are as many different deaths as there are different people" (103), and he carefully guards the genre of death that Joss has chosen. But the biographer is a different story, has a different story, and it is the battle between competing narratives about Joss that speaks to the ethics of biography.

By taking aim at the project of narrating a life built around passing, Kay's novel also produces important questions about the project of transgender history and biography. The danger of biography, Kay's novel suggests, lies in the way "many ghost writers believe they are the real authority on their subject and not the ghost themselves" (Gordon 1997, 262). Kay warns us here to listen to the ghost. In her beautiful sociological study of haunting, *Ghostly Matters,* Avery Gordon also advises us to listen to the ghost, to hear the unspoken, and to see the invisible. She remarks that "the ghost is not simply a dead or a missing person, but a social figure, and investigating it can lead to that dense site where history and subjectivity make social life" (8). Obviously, the ghost for Gordon is not quite the same as the ghost for Kay, yet both texts share a sense of the mechanism of haunting as an articulate discourse. Both texts also suggest that haunting is a mode within which the ghost demands something like accountability: to tell a ghost story means being willing to be haunted. "Following the ghosts," Gordon says "is about making a contact that changes you and refashions the social relations in which you are located" (22). The error of the willful biographer lies in her refusal to be changed by her encounter with the ghost she chases; the method of the transgender historian must be encounter, confrontation, transformation.

Kay's novel raises thorny questions about biography, about precisely the kind of biography that Middlebrook has written. Should identification be a prerequisite for writing up someone's life? Is a biography that tells tales and reveals secrets an act of violence? Should there be an ethics of biography? Kay herself points to the danger of biography and warns us to listen to the ghost. And unlike the ghostwriter who cares nothing about the ghost, Kay grants her ghost the last word. In the novel's final section, Joss returns from the dead in a letter he leaves for his son to finally tell his own story. This simple but effective gesture of giving Joss the last word summarizes Kay's particular interest in the Tipton legend and its retelling. She comes to praise, memorialize, and elegize Tipton/Moody and countless transgender men, and not to bury them.

Male Fraud: The Case of Brandon

While Tipton died a so-called natural death in 1992 only to have his life rearranged by the discovery of his "secret," Brandon, one year later, was exposed and then killed precisely for his secret. While the death of Tipton and the subsequent discovery of his "true" sex created a ripple in the media, the Brandon murders created a veritable landslide of both queer and mainstream narratives. As I suggested in the previous chapter, this mountain of documentation can now be recognized as an archive of marginalized queer lives. But we can also find a fair share of "ambulance chasers" among the multitudes of writers and artists who have felt drawn to the case. What does this narrative symbolize about late-twentieth-century gender norms, and what is its appeal, not simply to queer communities who mourn Brandon's passing, but to straight writers over whom the narrative exerts a mesmerizing effect? Just a quick rundown of the fictional material inspired by the "true" story of Brandon would include the following: the case has been fictionalized in a novel by Dinitia Smith called *The Illusionist*; it has been written up as a true-crime mystery called *All S/he Wanted* by Aphrodite Jones; and John Gregory Dunne wrote about the murders for the *New Yorker* (Smith 1997; Jones 1996; Dunne 1997). In terms of cinematic representations, Diane Keaton tried unsuccessfully to produce a feature film about the case, starring Drew Barrymore, but fortunately she was beaten to the punch by *Boys Don't Cry,* which in turn drew heavily from *The Brandon Teena Story*. At the same time, queer media artist Shu Lea Cheang has created a Web site for the Guggenheim Museum simply called *Brandon* that she describes as a "multi-artist, multi-author, multi-institutional collaboration."[3] In my next chapter, I will look at the feature film made about Brandon more closely, but here I want to consider what the implications might be of such a rush to represent, fictionalize, and document this case in print media.

The story of Brandon has been carefully disguised and written up in Smith's *The Illusionist*, a tale of a young man called Dean Lily who seduces young women without revealing to them that he is really a woman. *The Illusionist* recasts the Brandon story in Sparta, New York, and makes the Brandon character into an amateur magician who picks up women in the Wooden Nickel bar; the novel insists, in other words, that since Dean Lily is only a counterfeit man, "a wooden nickel," he must seduce his unknowing heterosexual partners by using a deadly combination of charm and magic. Smith's narrative characterizes the appeal of Brandon's charms as a deliberate mode of pandering to feminine adolescent fantasies of nonthreatening and nonadult masculine sexuality. Smith never actually acknowledges that her novel is based on the Nebraska murders, and the novel carries the usual disclaimer stating that "names, characters, places, and incidents either are products of the author's imagination or are used fictitiously. Any resemblance to actual events or locales or persons, living or dead, is entirely coincidental." Blurbs from reviews printed inside the book confirm that the power of this narrative lies in Smith's particular skill as an author, and so reviewer Hilma Wolitzer exclaims, "Dinitia Smith is the true illusionist." And another reviewer, Rosellen Brown, pinpoints Smith's skill as her ability to "make the bizarre plausible." Gay author Larry Kramer notes simply that the novel is "an overwhelming accomplishment of the imagination." The insistence on the originality of this narrative, of course, is highly ironic here. The basis for the narrative in this book springs not from the mind or the imagination of Smith but is inspired by the "true-crime" mystery of the Brandon murders; and the lack of originality within the novel is not of negligible interest since her depiction of the Brandon character has everything to do with the difference between the real and the fake.

While Brandon used many names during his brief life, Smith gives her hero only one: Dean Lily. This name plays all too obviously on some combination of "James Dean" and a virginal "lily of the valley."[4] Whereas Brandon's life was full of complicated relations to his female lovers and male buddies, Smith reduces all desire directed at Dean Lily to the vulnerabilities of adolescent females, and she simplifies Dean Lily's relations to other men by depicting his masculinity as inadequate, lacking, and endangered. The novel's title, *The Illusionist,* refers to the performance of magic tricks by the protagonist. As Smith writes, "He curls a dime around his fingers and it changes into a penny. . . . The partyers watch him, mocking smiles on their faces, skeptical. They only half believe what he is doing is magic. They've seen his tricks before. They know he's an imposter and a con man. . . . And they love him anyway" (Smith 1997, 97). This simple and even simplistic literary device, which marks Brandon as a magician and then uses magic to explain his gender performance, certainly accesses some of the power of Brandon's "act," but it dangerously confirms a conservative view of his gender performance as trickery, illusion, subterfuge, and sleight of hand. By casting him and his gender as magical, the narrative actually reiterates the logic that sentences Brandon to death: his gender is unreal, it is indeed ethereal like magic, it is dangerous and it must be punished. The magician may be a special character, protected and charmed, but he is also, after all, an impostor and a con man. He is the illusion that disappears into thin air when his magic wand is challenged by the real wand of manhood. This notion of Brandon as a magician, furthermore, echoes Middlebrook's characterization of Tipton as a "magician" (147) weaving a "tangled web of deceit" (176). The metaphoric use of magic in both instances implies that the transgender man creates a gender act that takes advantage of a trusting audience, forcing them to invest hope and desire in an illusory identity. Both Middlebrook and Smith place their antiheroes in the realm of magic in order to assert that true manhood exists in the space of the real and does not rely on a set of tricks that conjure up masculinity. For both writers, the real man is solid and present while the transgender man has an identity that can appear or disappear like a rabbit in a hat.

While this novel misses many of the nuances of Brandon's life, a review of the book in the *New York Times* is simply homophobic and transphobic. In her strange summation, reviewer Patricia Volk tells us that this novel is about "two dumb homophobic hoodlums, needy girls, a depressed town and a transgender stranger with a Casanova complex" (Volk 1997). And she continues, it is not about "homosexual love. It is about being so emotionally deprived that anything that fills the void looks viable." Volk concludes that "Miss Smith has no trouble convincing the reader that Dean was the answer to these maidens' prayers. You just wish they had prayed for something better. 'I mean if he does everything that a man does,' one of his girlfriends says, 'what does it matter?' He doesn't and it does" (B7). This paranoid insistence that "he doesn't" do everything that a man does and that "it does" make a difference that Brandon is not biologically male, yet again repeats in a different mode the eradicating violence aimed at Brandon throughout his life. Also, the use of the term "maidens" characterizes the girls as virginal and even presexual—in other words, as lacking the basic adult knowledge that would allow them to tell the difference between authentic and unauthentic maleness. Volk also insists that the plight of both Dean Lily and the girls he seduced has to do with an emotional deprivation arising out of class circumstances. Within Volk's flip reading of the already simplified version of Brandon's story, emotional complexity emerges as a symbol of bourgeois identity and working-class identity must be reduced to the impoverishment of all aspects of life.

Early on in his career as a man, Brandon passed as "Billy." As Billy, he dated a young woman called Heather Kufahl while still living in Lincoln, sometimes at home with his mother; in addition to Heather, he regularly dated girls who thought he was male. Certainly at this stage in his life, the ambiguities of adolescent gender aided him in his ability to pass, but he was also helped by the fact that so many of the girls he dated, like fourteen-year-old Heather, found that there were huge contradictions between the romances they saw depicted on television and in magazines and the realities of teenage sexual etiquette. Heather said of Billy: "He was everyone's dream guy. . . . He was romantic. He took you out to dinner, bought flowers, roses, just everything" (Jones 1996, 61). Billy, unlike other guys, lived up to her romantic notion of masculinity. When Billy told Heather that he was a "hermaphrodite," she was satisfied with this explanation of his bodily difference, not because she was stupid, but precisely because she was satisfied with Billy's performance of masculinity. Later, Billy would leave Lincoln and deploy different explanations for his male identification ranging from transsexuality to intersexuality; even then his girlfriends accepted these explanations without question.

As a counternarrative, then, to bourgeois and heteronormative renderings of heroic individualism, Brandon's self-presentation was itself—and must be read as—a damaging, indeed threatening critique of middle-class as well as working-class male masculinity. Not only did he deliberately offer the women with whom he went out those things that he knew they could never get from local boys, he also acknowledged the complexity of their own self-understandings. By showing his girlfriends respect, generosity, sweetness, and politeness, Brandon excelled in the performance of masculinity that we most often associate with middle-class values of self-restraint and courtliness. His masculinity destabilizes the essential nature of not only male masculinity but also middle-class masculinity. One of his lovers, Lana Tisdale, commented that she was attracted to him "because he was well-dressed and really polite. The guys I knew in Falls City weren't like that. They weren't like that at all" (Jones 1996, 128). Another called him "the perfect woman's man," and still another dubbed him "a perfect gentleman" (Minkowitz 1994). Many of the women in their accounts of Brandon describe him as a fantasy, an ideal, an improved and even aristocratic version of the usual forms of masculinity that they came across. But mainstream writers like Smith and Volk insist that these women deserved something better than Brandon despite the fact that the women insisted that he was their dream come true. Something better in this context constructs authentic maleness as the combination of middle-class status and male embodiment.

If Brandon was convincing to his girlfriends, it was certainly in part because these young women wanted to be convinced by his romantic persona, but it was also in part because they clearly felt some dissatisfactions with other versions of maleness that they had encountered. Brandon knew all too well what these other versions of masculinity looked like. Indeed, in relation to his male friends, Brandon constantly walked a dangerous line between identification, friendship, and rivalry. While many of his male friends knew on some level that he was not a man, for short periods of time they did accept him as such. Since so much of what we recognize as masculinity and masculine relations revolve around intense sites of competition and aggression, Brandon's performance might be expected to raise the stakes considerably within the everyday contestations of manhood. In one cocky picture of Brandon reproduced in Jones's informative true-crime mystery, we see Brandon grabbing his crotch while his "buddy" John Lotter makes a bicep. Brandon compares his manhood to his friend's by offering his crotch as a gender marker equal to John's bicep. This photo has an eerie oracular quality when we realize that the comparison would come down to a deadly standoff only days later when Lotter would demand to see the crotch, no longer satisfied with the symbolic evocation of it. Lotter and Nissen knew on some level that the only thing that disqualified Brandon from manhood was the contradiction of his body, and while this contradiction signified no obstacle at all as far as Brandon's girlfriends were concerned, for the men, the body must be the final arbiter of manhood because, in a sense, this is the only competition within which they can beat the version of masculinity that Brandon champions. When Brandon literally did not measure up to the physical test of manhood, his two male "friends" took him out to a remote spot, where they then raped and sodomized him. The punishment, as far as they were concerned, fit the crime inasmuch as Brandon must be properly returned to the body he denied. If Jones's research on the Nebraska murders is correct, this was a punishment with which Brandon had been threatened many times. Jones comments on an earlier friendship between Brandon and a roommate named Drew: "Some of Drew's buddies didn't like Brandon's charade. They felt they were being made fools. 'If she wants to be a man, she better well fight like one,' one of them threatened. 'If all she wants is dick, she could ask me,' another teased, 'I'll give her some'" (Jones 1996, 71). While Brandon's relations with his girlfriends demonstrates that a penis is neither necessary to nor inevitable within heterosexual encounter, the men whom he antagonizes insist that "all she wants" (where "she" means both Brandon and the girlfriends) is penis, and the penis becomes the sum total of what they are willing to give. Brandon, as I will elaborate on later, gives in very different ways.

According to the documentary account, when he went to the police after the rape, Brandon was further abused by a police officer, who chastised him for "running around with girls instead of guys." The response of Police Chief Laux, of course, confirms that Brandon deserved what he got and that he had it coming; Laux's unethical questioning of Brandon uses the traditional charge against a woman in a rape case—namely, that she was to blame all along—but annexes it to the idea that gender nonconformity must be corrected through the enforcement of heterosexuality. What is made all too clear in this case is that heterosexuality is violently enforced in multiple sites. Accordingly, Brandon's gender "disorder" wreaks havoc within the unstable arena of adolescent and early-adult gender relations, and must be brutally eliminated within that same space. But Brandon also represents an abiding threat to the law itself, and within the confines of the police station, he must be coerced back into the role of female victim. Naturally, then, the police did not act immediately on the rape charge against Lotter and Nissen, and one week later, as a consequence of some combination of police inactivity and vigilante enthusiasm, Brandon was shot to death at the age of twenty-one in a deserted farmhouse by the two men. In her woefully unimaginative rendition of the violent dispatch of Brandon, the counterfeit male, Smith can only collude with the representational system that makes Brandon a target for brutalization. By casting his masculinity as inadequate, slight, deceptive, and made up of tricks and sorcery, Smith fails to see that for the girls of Falls City, Brandon's masculinity occupied the space of the real comfortably and without contradiction. When she discounts Brandon's masculinity, Smith inadvertently discounts his female suitor's ability to desire particularity, and the ensuing narrative marries a transphobic narrative to a sexist one.

Smith also misunderstands the nature of Dean Lily's gender role. Depicted as a mysterious stranger who enters the lives of young and impressionable women, Smith compares Dean to Shakespeare's Viola from *Twelfth Night*, and a quotation from that play frames the novel as a whole. By making the connection between Viola and Dean, Smith implies that Dean's cross-dressing transformation, like Viola's, is only a temporary disruption to the heterosexual romantic narrative. Furthermore, through the comparison to Viola, Smith promises to restore gender order by the story's end. Ominously, then, the last section of the book is named for the last part of the quote from *Twelfth Night*: "I am not that I play." This section, which records the aftermath of Dean's brutal murder, implies that a kind of unmasking has occurred, and that the real Dean and the mystery of Dean Lily has finally been solved. By relegating Dean's life to a play and his gender to a role that Dean has assumed unsuccessfully, the novel ultimately insists that the real Dean, the Dean beneath the costume, was always and only a woman. This impression is further emphasized by the form of the narrative within which Dean's lovers take turns describing their experiences with him while Dean speaks only once. Dean's sole first-person narrative presents the rape scene, and so his authority in speaking is undercut by the self-eradicating experience that he describes. By the novel's end, Dean has been dismantled completely; no longer an illusionist, he seems finally to be simply an illusion.

Another writer, Dunne, similarly tried to disentangle the desires of the girls from the identity of Brandon, and while Smith simply dismisses the whole teenage gang in Falls City as simplistic, Dunne actually manages to champion the masculinity of Brandon's murders even as he casually dismisses Brandon's own. In a long account of the case titled "The Humboldt Murders," Dunne casts Brandon in the role of a confused and pathetic androgyne. He describes "her" as "small and vaguely androgynous," and claims that "her" appearance is more "unisex" then "masculine" (Dunne 1997, 49). Given what he sees as Brandon's unconvincing masculine appearance,

Dunne can only explain Brandon's successful performances as male as evidence of the ignorance of working-class youth. He calls the women Brandon went out with "child women" trapped in cycles of sexual abuse and domestic violence, and suggests that Brandon's appeal boiled down to the fact that he was "an unthreatening romantic, a lean and unmuscular quasi-man who offered sex without pregnancy or fisticuffs" (50). Dunne repeats here Smith's insistence that Brandon's masculinity was unthreatening, and that it looks tame compared to the real armed and dangerous masculinity of working-class male youth. He also repeats Volk's assertion that Brandon passes because he mingles with ignorant working-class adolescents. Of course, this construction of Brandon masks a much more complicated reading of his masculinity in which his successful and romantically viable approximation of heterosexual masculinity attracts women precisely because it *is* denaturalized; furthermore, the insistence that Brandon's masculinity is unthreatening sounds anxious here given how clearly threatened all the men (including Dunne) involved in this case obviously were. Dunne bluntly refuses to take Brandon's masculinity seriously and depicts him as a poor deluded woman who lacked even "the imaginative range to consider the idea that she was truly at risk." The boys who kill Brandon, on the other hand, are shown to be victims of unstable families who are trapped by their class backgrounds and lack of opportunities.

In relation to Nissen in particular, Dunne's sympathies run riot and, in the course of writing his story, he begins a long correspondence with Nissen. He goes on to present pieces of this correspondence to show that despite Nissen's low IQ and grammatical errors, this young man is perceptive and insightful. In short, Dunne attributes to Nissen the complex subjectivity and sense of self that he consistently denies to Brandon. While Nissen is a heroic consciousness struggling with a hopeless situation, Brandon is "self-indulgent" and "uses her gender confusion as an excuse to abdicate personal responsibility." There are, of course, many ways in which Dunne could have expressed a degree of empathy for the Nissens of this world—working-class, uneducated white men—without doing so at the expense of Nissen's victim and without erasing the disastrous choices that this man made throughout his life. Indeed, Nissen's life was a record of abuse, suicide attempts, and foster homes; it was also a record of flirtations with white supremacist military cults and episodes of violence. What bears examination, in other words, in relation to Dunne's representation of the Brandon case is the way Dunne can casually justify male expressions of violence, but cannot account for transgender expressions of rage; Nissen's flirtation with white racism is simply described as a wrong turn, while Brandon's criminal record for forging checks becomes evidence of a deep pathology.

At one point, Dunne turns to Willa Cather in order to evoke the hard landscape of rural Nebraska. He comments on Cather's preferred name—William Cather—and her habit of wearing short hair and mannish clothes. He classifies Cather as a discreet lesbian and notes approvingly: "Her relationships with women had the virtue of constancy." Ultimately, Dunne concludes, Cather used the backdrop of Red Cloud, Nebraska, as "raw material" and then converted it into novels—*My Antonia, Lucy Gayheart*. By contrast, Brandon, he notes, "was the raw stuff distilled to its very essence, . . . a young woman from that constituency living at or below society's safety net. The tyranny from which she could not escape was less that of gender than of class; a prison more tyrannical than Willa Cather's prairie town, especially in white America, where class distinctions are not supposed to exist" (49). Dunne uses a troubling metaphor here in order to subsume the drama of gender instability within what he sees as the more general theater of U.S. class politics. Brandon has become the raw material that cannot be rescued from the turmoil of poverty. While earlier for Dunne, Brandon in relation to the women he seduced was anything but raw, an all-too-cooked version of gender trouble and self-indulgent masquerade, now he becomes the savage of the heartland who can never escape the primitive landscapes of social injustice and thuggery.

To add insult to injury, Dunne even tries to imagine what Cather's response to Brandon might have been. He uses Cather's depiction of the servant girl Antonia Shimerda in *My Antonia* as paradigmatic of Cather's attitudes toward working-class women and then notes, "I suspect that Brandon Teena would have made Cather impatient: Teena was socially and economically no more disadvantaged than Antonia and one can assume that Cather would have regarded her obsession with gender and its discontents as self-indulgent, and her gender confusion as an excuse to abdicate personal responsibility" (50). Perhaps it is pointless to be shocked by such pronouncements, and perhaps Dunne's do not matter so much in the general scheme of things, but this particular move, the projection of harsh judgment onto Cather, reveals precisely how a figure like Brandon becomes snared in the space between recognizable categories and doomed therefore to a bloody dissection. Dunne first evokes Cather in order to provide an aesthetic landscape for the drama he describes, but then she becomes the acceptable and indeed middle-class version of gender and sexual deviance against which Brandon's particular experiences and actions must be measured.

Cather and Brandon, of course, do not represent the cooked and the raw, the refined and the primitive, the civilized and the savage elements of rural America. Rather, they exist in more of a continuum of gender impropriety. It is not hard to imagine that gender nonconformity and what Dunne calls self-indulgent gender confusion provided Cather with precisely those startling insights into small-town bitterness to which Dunne is so drawn. Cather and Brandon are less close and less distant than Dunne would think. The violence directed at Brandon may in some way explain why sixty years earlier Cather had to leave Red Cloud; but at the same time, both Cather and Brandon found Nebraska to be a place where they could pass, where they could assume male identities, and where they could move around in men's clothing. When Cather left rural Nebraska for urban life, she also abandoned her cross-dressing practices. Since his maleness was so important to him, we might assume, Brandon chose not to stay in urban Lincoln and seek help at the gay and lesbian center (and we know that people suggested just this to him). His plans were better served by the daily routine of life in a small town where most people lived far apart, asked few questions, and kept their opinions to themselves. Brandon lived within the freedoms offered by a small town and he died because for two boys the version of masculinity that Brandon paraded, exposed the lack at the heart of their own enactments of manhood. But the brutality that visited Brandon late one night in a deserted farmhouse was not simply the violence of rural working-class maleness, as Dunne would love to believe, it was also a violence linked to a bourgeois investment in the economy of authenticity.

What I have tried to show here is that the murder of Brandon has been followed by other violences that do not merely repeat the original trauma but rather extend and stretch the punishment of Brandon to other potential sites for gender transgression. Furthermore, Brandon's masculinity clearly presents a threat not only to male masculinity in general but particularly to notions of the authenticity of bourgeois manhood. Dunne, Volk, Smith, and Police Chief Laux as well as Lotter and Nissen all seem to agree on one thing: Brandon is a fake man. In Smith's book, as mentioned earlier, Brandon is named "counterfeit" by making a bar called the Wooden Nickel into the backdrop for his magic tricks. The naming of his masculinity as counterfeit, ensures that Brandon's impersonation will be read within a class narrative as both a quest for social mobility and an ill-fated assault on masculine privilege. While Smith, Dunne, and others are fascinated by the sexual drama surrounding Brandon and the women he dated, they also insist that this story is merely a subplot to the narrative of working-class degradation. Gender for Smith and Dunne is merely a personal crisis, an opportunity for self-indulgence, but class is a prison. Along these lines, then, Brandon's gender presentation threatens some people and seduces others, but the dark and brutal events that lead to his death are reduced to the volatile combination of poverty, lack of education, and childhood abuse. The subordination of gender to class here allows for both Smith and Dunne to assure themselves that the Brandon story happens in another world far from the one in which they live with their families.

At the heart of the narrative of Brandon stands an economy of representation. It is no coincidence that Smith's novels takes place at a bar called the Wooden Nickel, and most accounts of this story suggest that Brandon's habit of forging checks and fraudulently using his girlfriend's credit cards represents in economic terms the contours of his gender masquerade. Both Smith and Dunne fetishize Brandon by making him the figure for both excessive power and extreme degradation. It is a little easier to understand the anxious attempts to cast Brandon as counterfeit if we read the metaphor of the Wooden Nickel as a fetishizing device, but also as an economic metaphor that attempts to grapple with the value of Brandon's iconic status rather than simply with its content. The fetish, within psychoanalysis, is the thing that masquerades as a phallus and creates an illusion of wholeness. To say that Brandon is a fetish figure for the straight white writers who dissect his life, not to mention the killers who shot him, is to understand that for his supporters and detractors alike, Brandon represents both what is missing and what is present for the observer. For Smith, Brandon serves as a fetish object that covers over the lack at the heart of heterosexual romance. Smith can deny that romance itself offers young girls a promise it cannot make good on and instead she can project that failed promise onto the seemingly inadequate body of Brandon. The fetish of Brandon also allows Dunne to shore up white middle-class manhood by projecting the blurred and weak boundary between the passing woman and the biological man onto working-class forms of masculinity. And for numerous other contemporary viewers and readers, Brandon's body becomes the marker of a gender disorder that always resides elsewhere.

The postmortem productions of narratives about Brandon that continue to defuse the obviously potent and effective masculinity that he carefully

crafted for himself despite overwhelming odds, are themselves violent attempts to reassert the primacy of even a damaged and mutilating male masculinity over and above the simulated, but pleasurable transgender masculinity that Brandon created. This pleasurable masculinity was characterized by most of the women who went out with him as tender, romantic,
caring, and above all generous. Everyone depicted him as a man who loved
to give and asked for nothing in return. This spirit of generosity, even where
the generosity was funded by someone else's credit card, should be read as
the economy of a radical form of manhood that Brandon pioneered. While
Brandon's crimes of forgery and embezzlement have been held up as evidence of the pathological and indeed illegal nature of all of Brandon's so-
called impersonations, such prognostications refuse to acknowledge the
power of the forgery, the endless generosity of the Robin Hood figure who
transfers wealth and currency from one place of abundance to another place
of need.

The word counterfeit has been used against passing women long before
anyone had heard of Brandon. For example, in a book called *Counterfeit
Ladies*, Janet Todd and Elizabeth Spearing edit the life histories of two women
who took liberties with their womanhood in the seventeenth century (Todd
1994). These two women, Mary Frith (Moll Cutpurse) and Mary Carleton (a
German princess) both trespassed beyond the boundaries of accepted feminine behavior, but they did so in different ways. While Carleton's crime was
one of impersonating nobility in order to seduce a rich husband, Frith's
crime was that she wore male clothing, engaged in masculine activities, and
pursued a career in embezzlement of one kind or another. Obviously, the
term counterfeit in relation to each of these historical figures conjures up the
combination of impersonation and theft. Carleton uses class impersonation
to find her way to a wealthy marriage, but Frith uses male impersonation to
make her own money. The idea of counterfeiting, then, both reduces male
impersonation to an economic opportunity and collapses it into the phenomenon of social climbing. In other words, if male impersonation can be
safely explained in terms of economic advantage, then the gender crisis it
also names can be avoided.

Rather than reduce male impersonation to a form of counterfeiting, I
think we can read an economics of impersonation into both historical and
contemporary acts of gender passing. There are ultimately few material gains
to be garnered from the kind of passing performances perpetrated by Brandon and his historical antecedents; but the act of passing does damage the

investments made in conventional gender, sexuality, and domesticity. As a wooden nickel passing as silver, a Brandon Teena throws into doubt the value of conventional currency and also shows how easy it is to circumvent the monetary system altogether. In a controversial commentary on the meaning of Brandon's gender act that appeared in the *Village Voice* soon after the murders became public, lesbian journalist Donna Minkowitz attempted to read Brandon's complex economy of gender and desire. Minkowitz harshly judged Brandon as a selfish con artist who had to leave Lincoln, Nebraska, because his debts were in danger of catching up with him. Minkowitz ends her problematic account of the case with the following judgment: "Brandon had to go to Humboldt because everyone who loved her [*sic*] in Lincoln was finally too infuriated with her, whether she'd stolen their love or taken the money they needed to live" (Minkowitz 1994, 30). Brandon traded in love and desire; he gave love and attention to the girls he dated, and sometimes took money in return or sometimes asked for nothing. But his bad checks, financial tricks, and forgeries do not add up to cheap love in impoverished circumstances. Unlike the men he exposes, Brandon gave something of worth in exchange for the money he took, and because his attentions to the girls were worth more to them than credit cards and money in the bank, he earned the undying hate of the men he supplanted.

The Unlost

The stories of Brandon Teena and Billy Tipton, their own stories, the stories that are told about them, and the stories that the people around them produce, help to conclude several outmoded narratives about gender and embodiment in the United States at the end of the twentieth century. Neither Brandon nor Billy comfortably fit into the sexological categories of inversion from the early twentieth century, but neither do they represent new transsexual discourses involving bodily transformations. Brandon and Billy have little to do with modern gay and lesbian identities, nor are they indicative of future renderings of gender, class, and embodiment. Perhaps they are the unresolved tales of gender variance that will follow us from the twentieth to the twenty-first century, not resolved, not neat, not understood. Perhaps the only way to honor the memories of Teena and Tipton is to remember them as they wish to be remembered: not as heroes or demons but as examples of what Gordon calls in *Ghostly Matter* "complex personhood." At the very least, Gordon tells us, "complex personhood is about conferring the respect on others that comes from presuming that life and people's lives are simultaneously straightforward and full of enormously subtle meaning" (5). When we read transgender lives, complex and contradictory as they may seem, it is necessary to read for the life and not for the lie. Dishonesty, after all, is just another word for narrative.

Returning to Carson's extraordinary study of memory and preservation, *Economy of the Unlost*, I suggest that we try not to "unlose" the complex figures of Brandon and Billy to the fates of biography and sentimental remembrance. Carson's study of the historically distinct poets Simonides and Paul Celan situates poetry as a mode of expression caught between different economic structures. While the Greek poet Simonides literally found himself trapped between two systems of money, the gift and the commodity, Celan wrote poetry in the shadow of the Holocaust and found language, particularly German, to be an inadequate tool for mourning, memory, and rage. "Remembering," writes Carson, "draws attention to lostness and is made possible by emotions of space that open backward into a void." As we have seen, poetic moments in Kay's lyrical novel *Trumpet* captured the lasting imprint of a transgender character in a mood of remembrance rather than in a description or rationalization. While the biographer remembers through fact, Kay's narrative suggests, the poet remembers through "emotions of space," and it is poetic memory that best approaches the legacy of a life that has become symbolic through death. Again, in the case of Brandon, his murder reorganized the meaning of his life as well as the significance of the choices he made about passing as a man and engaging the desires of others. Until the murder, Brandon was a slightly foolish, fairly brave, oddly confident youth who had the luxury to live an inconsistent life made up of equal parts of courage and myopia. After his murder, Brandon's life—the jumbled desires and deeds—becomes frozen into either a heroic narrative of derring-do or a reprehensible story of deception and denial. In most accounts of Brandon's life, the wild strands of narrative incoherence are reined in by an all-encompassing fantasy of moral order. All future attempts to recapture this life will now have to chip away at the laminate that fixes this narrative to its place and time. In many ways, the moralizing narratives that I examine here commit Brandon to the status of "lost" soul, and the task that remains to queer archivists is to render Brandon "unlost."

Like the poets about whom Carson writes so movingly, Brandon is a figure standing between different economic orders. While for Simonides, the economic orders that trapped him were materially identifiable as gift and commodity cultures, Carson is less concerned with the transition between economic systems and more focused on the impact of this transition on the role of the poet. If formerly the poet was a figure who penned verses for a host in return for hospitality, in a new economic system, the poet must reconcile himself to being someone who sells grace. Simonides, Carson says, never could make the clean transition to currency and so redefined the role of the poet: "Simonides spent his literary as well as his historical life exerting a counterpressure to the claims of the merely visible world" (60). Celan's work, according to Carson, continues in this poetic tradition of "*not* seeing what *is* there" (62). Like the poet in Carson's essay who refuses to sell poems to the highest bidder, a Brandon figure refuses to recognize the current values and meanings of masculinity, and circulates as and within an alternative system of value. The task that faces us now as we write epitaphs, elegies, and encomiums for Brandon, Billy, and others like them is to craft a poetic rather than a moral framework of remembrance—a framework, moreover, that tackles the economic charge that propels Brandon out of the realm of flesh and into the order of fetish, icon, commodity.

4

The Transgender Look

> Certain social groups may be seen as having rigid or unresponsive selves
> and bodies, making them relatively unfit for the kind of society we now
> seem to desire.
>
> —Emily Martin, *Flexible Bodies*

In the last two chapters, we have seen how an archive of print and visual materials have accumulated around the figure of Brandon Teena, a young transgender man who defied the social mandate to be and to have a singular gender identity. Here, I continue to build on that archive with a consideration of the feature film *Boys Don't Cry*, but I also try to expand the archive of visual representations of gender ambiguity, placing this expanded archive within what Nick Mirzoeff calls "the postmodern globalization of the visual as everyday life" (Mirzoeff 1999, 3). I begin with a study of the transgender gaze or look as it has developed in recent queer cinema (film and video), and then in the next chapter, turn to photography and painting to examine the clash between embodiment and the visual that queer art making has documented in vivid detail. Gender ambiguity, in some sense, results from and contests the dominance of the visual within postmodernism.

The potentiality of the body to morph, shift, change, and become fluid is a powerful fantasy in transmodern cinema. Whether it is the image of surgically removable faces in John Woo's *Face/Off*, the liquid-mercury type of slinkiness of the Terminator in *Terminator 2: Judgment Day*, the virtual bodies of *The Matrix*, or the living-dead body in *The Sixth Sense*, the body in transition indelibly marks late-twentieth- and early-twenty-first-century visual fantasy. The fantasy of the shape-shifting and identity -morphing body has been nowhere more powerfully realized recently than in transgender film. In films like Neil Jordan's *The Crying Game* (1992) and *Boys Don't Cry*, the transgender character surprises audiences with his/her ability to remain attractive, appealing, and gendered while simultaneously presenting a gender at odds with sex, a sense of self not derived from the body, and an identity that operates within the heterosexual matrix without confirming the inevitability of that system of difference. But even as the transgender body becomes a symbol par excellence for flexibility, transgenderism also represents a form of rigidity, an insistence on particular forms of recognition, that reminds us of the limits of what Martin has called "flexible bodies." Those bodies, indeed, that fail to conform to the postmodern fantasy of flexibility that has been projected onto the transgender body may well be punished in popular representations even as they seem to be lauded. And so, Brandon in *Boys Don't Cry* and Dil in *The Crying Game* are represented as both heroic and fatally flawed.

Both *The Crying Game* and *Boys Don't Cry* rely on the successful solicitation of affect—whether it be revulsion, sympathy, or empathy—in order to give mainstream viewers access to a transgender gaze. And in both films, a relatively unknown actor pulls off the feat of credibly performing a gender at odds with the sexed body even after the body has been brutally exposed. Gender metamorphosis in these films is also used as a metaphor for other kinds of mobility or immobility. In *The Crying Game,* Dil's womanhood stands in opposition to a revolutionary subjectivity associated with the Irish Republican Army (IRA), and in *Boys Don't Cry,* Brandon's manhood represents a class-based desire to transcend small-town conflicts and a predictable life narrative of marriage, babies, domestic abuse, and alcoholism. While Brandon continues to romanticize small-town life, his girlfriend, Lana, sees him as a symbol of a much-desired elsewhere. In both films, the transgender character also seems to stand for a different form of temporality. Dil seems deliberately removed in *The Crying Game* from the time of the nation and other nationalisms, and her performance of womanhood opens up a ludic temporality. Brandon in *Boys Don't Cry* represents an alternative future for Lana by trying to be a man with no past. The dilemma for the transgender character, as we have seen in earlier chapters, is to create an alternate future while rewriting history. In *Boys Don't Cry,* director Peirce seems aware of the imperative of queer time and constructs (but fails to sustain) a transgender gaze capable of seeing through the present to a future elsewhere. In experimental moments in this otherwise brutally realistic film, Peirce creates slow-motion or double-speed time warps that hint at an elsewhere for the star-crossed lovers that is located in both time and space.

The transgender film confronts powerfully the way that transgenderism is constituted as a paradox made up in equal parts of visibility and temporality: whenever the transgender character is seen to be transgendered, then he/she is both failing to pass and threatening to expose a rupture between the distinct temporal registers of past, present, and future. The exposure of a trans character whom the audience has already accepted as male or female, causes the audience to reorient themselves in relation to the film's past in order to read the film's present and prepare themselves for the film's future. When we "see" the transgender character, then, we are actually seeing cinematic time's sleight of hand. Visibility, under these circumstances, may be equated with jeopardy, danger, and exposure, and it often becomes necessary for the transgender character to disappear in order to remain viable. The transgender gaze becomes difficult to track because it depends on complex relations in time and space between seeing and not seeing, appearing and disappearing, knowing and not knowing. I will be identifying here different treatments of the transgenderism that resolve these complex problems of temporality and visibility.

In one mode that we might call the "rewind," the transgender character is presented at first as "properly" gendered, as passing in other words, and as properly located within a linear narrative; her exposure as transgender constitutes the film's narrative climax, and spells out both her own decline and the unraveling of cinematic time. The viewer literally has to rewind the film after the character's exposure in order to reorganize the narrative logic in terms of the pass. In a second mode that involves embedding several ways of looking into one, the film deploys certain formal techniques to give the viewer access to the transgender gaze in order to allow us to look *with* the transgender character instead of *at* him. Other techniques include ghosting the transgender character or allowing him to haunt the narrative after death; and doubling the transgender character or playing him/her off another trans character in order to remove the nodal point of normativity. *The Brandon Teena Story,* discussed in chapter 2, provides an example of the ghosting technique, and in this film, Brandon occupies the space of the ghost; he literally haunts the film and returns to life only as an eerie voice recorded during a brutal police interrogation. Two other transgender films, Kate Davis's documentary *Southern Comfort* (2001) along with Harry Dodge and Silas Howard's feature film *By Hook or by Crook* (2001), work through the strategy of doubling. In *Southern Comfort,* the transgender man, Robert Eads, is in the process of disappearing as the film charts his decline and death from uterine and ovarian cancers. Robert is doubled by other male transgender friends, but also by his transgender girlfriend, Lola. By showing Robert to be part of a transgender community rather than a freakish individual, the film refuses the medical gaze that classifies Robert as abnormal and the heteronormative gaze that renders Robert invisible. Instead, *Southern Comfort* portrays Robert as a transgender man among other transgender people.

In *By Hook or by Crook,* transgenderism is a complex dynamic between the two butch heroes, Shy and Valentine. The two collude and collaborate in their gendering, and create a closed world of queerness that is locked in place by the circuit of a gaze that never references the male or the female gaze as such. The plot of *By Hook or by Crook* involves the random meeting of two trans butches and the development of a fast friendship. Shy tries to help Valentine, who has been adopted, find his mother, while Valentine introduces the lonely Shy, whose father has just died, to an alternative form of community. The dead or missing parents imply an absence of conventional family, and afford our heroes with the opportunity to remake home, family, community, and most important, friendship. As the story evolves into a shaggy-dog tale of hide-and-seek, we leave family time far behind, entering into the shadow world of queers, loners, street people, and crazies. Transgenderism takes its place in this world as a quiet location outside the storm of law and order, mental health, and financial stability. Unlike other transgender films that remain committed to seducing the straight gaze, this one remains thoroughly committed to the transgender look, and it opens up, formally and thematically, a new mode of envisioning gender mobility. In this chapter, I pay close attention to three versions of the "transgender film"— *The Crying Game, Boy's Don't Cry,* and *By Hook or by Crook*—to track the evolution of a set of strategies (each with different consequences) for representing transgender bodies, capturing transgender looks, and theorizing transgender legibility.

Crying Games

> *crying—verb*: announce in public, utter in a loud distinct voice so as to be heard over a long distance; *noun*: the process of shedding tears (usually accompanied by sobs or other inarticulate sounds); *adj*.: conspicuously bad, offensive or reprehensible.
>
> —*Oxford English Dictionary*

When *The Crying Game* was released, the media was instructed not to give away the "secret" at the heart of the film—but what exactly was the film's secret? Homosexuality? Transsexuality? Gender construction? Nationalist brutalities? Colonial encounters? By making the unmasking of a transvestite character into the preeminent signifier of difference and disclosure in the film, director Jordan participates, as many critics have noted, in a long tradition of transforming political conflict into erotic tension in order to offer a romantic resolution.[1] I want to discuss *The Crying Game* briefly here to illustrate the misuse or simply the avoidance of the transgender gaze in mainstream films that purport to be about gender ambiguity. By asking media and audiences to keep the film's secret, then, *The Crying Game*'s producers created and deepened the illusion that the film would and could offer something new and unexpected. In fact, the secrecy constructs a mainstream viewer for the film and ignores more knowing audiences.

The Crying Game concerns a number of different erotic triangles situated within the tense political landscape of the English occupation of Northern Ireland. The film opens by animating one triangle that links two IRA operatives, Fergus and Jude, to the black British soldier, Jody, whom they must kidnap. Jude lures Jody away from a fairground with a promise of sexual interaction, and then Fergus ambushes Jody and whisks him away to an IRA hideout. The whole of the opening scene plays out to the accompaniment of "When a Man Loves a Woman." The song equates femininity with trickery, falsehood, and deceit, and it sets up the misogynist strands of a narrative that envision the white male as unknowing victim of feminine wiles. The first third of the film concerns the relationship between captors and captive, and particularly between the warmhearted Fergus and the winning Jody. Fergus and Jody bond and connect over the picture of Jody's absent lover, Dil. After Jody dies in a foiled escape effort, Fergus leaves Ireland to escape the IRA and heads to England, where he becomes a construction worker. Fergus goes looking for Dil, and when he finds her, he romances her while seemingly unaware of her transgender identity. The last third of the film charts the course of Fergus's discovery of Dil's secret and his reentanglement with the IRA.

There are three major narrative strands in *The Crying Game,* all of which seem bound to alternative political identities, but none of which actually live up to their own potential. In the first strand, which involves the IRA, we expect to hear a critique of English colonialism, English racism, and the occupation of Northern Ireland by England. Instead, the film uses Jody to critique Irish racism and Fergus to delegitimize the IRA. The second narrative strand, which concerns the romance between Fergus and Dil, seems committed to a narrative about the "naturalness" of all types of gender expression, and here we expect to see the structures of heteronormativity exposed and the male gaze de-authorized. Instead, *The Crying Game* uses Dil's transvestism only to re-center the white male gaze, and to make the white male into the highly flexible, supremely human subject who must counter and cover for the gender rigidity of the transvestite Dil (rigidity meaning that she cannot flow back and forth between male and female; she insists on being recognized as female) and the political rigidity of the IRA "fanatic" Jude. The triangulations that prop up each half of the film create the illusion of alternatives, but return time and again to the stable political format of white patriarchy. The third narrative strand has to do with cinematic time, and it projects an alternative ordering of time by positioning Dil as a character who seems to be able to cross back and forth between past, present, and future. When we first see Dil, she appears in a photograph representing Jody's past. When Fergus finally meets Dil, she represents his new present-tense life away from the IRA, and as the film winds down, Dil represents for Fergus a conventional future of marriage and family that awaits him when he obtains his release from jail, where he is "doing time." The seeming temporal fluidity of Dil is undercut, however, by the normative logic of the narrative's temporal drive, which seeks, through Fergus, to pin Dil down within the logic of heteronormative time.

Ultimately, the transgender character Dil never controls the gaze, and serves as a racialized fetish figure who diverts the viewer's attention from the highly charged political conflict between England and Ireland. The film characterizes Irish nationalism as a heartless and futile endeavor while depicting England ironically as a multicultural refuge, a place where formerly colonized peoples find a home. To dramatize the difference between Irish and English nationalism, the kidnapped black soldier, Jody, describes Ireland as "the only place in the world where they'll call you a nigger to your face." England, on the other hand, is marked for him by class conflicts (played out in his cricket tales), but not so much by racial disharmony. By the time Dil enters the film, about a third of the way in, England has become for Fergus a refuge and a place where he can disappear.

Disappearing is, in many ways, the name of the crying game, and the film plays with and through the fetishistic structure of cinema itself, with, in other words, the spectator's willingness to see what is not there and desire what is. In a series of scenes set in the gay bar, the Metro, where Dil performs, the viewer's gaze is sutured to Fergus's. In the first few scenes, the bar seems to be populated by so-called normal people, men and women, dancing together. But in the scene at the Metro that follows Fergus's discovery of Dil's penis, the camera again scans the bar and finds the garish and striking faces of the drag queens who populate it. Like Fergus, we formerly saw bio men and women, and like Fergus, we suddenly see the bar for what it is: a queer site. And our vision, no matter how much we recognized Dil as transgender earlier, makes this abrupt detour around the transgender gaze along with Fergus. Indeed, *The Crying Game* cannot imagine the transgender gaze any more than it can cede the gaze to an IRA perspective. Here the revelation of a queer bar community sets up new triangulations within which the relationship between Fergus/Jimmy and Dil is now coded as homosexual. The homo context erases Dil's transsexual subjectivity, and throws the male protagonist into a panic that is only resolved by the symbolic castration of Dil when Fergus cuts Dil's hair. He does this supposedly to disguise Dil and protect her from the IRA, but actually the haircut unmasks her and serves to protect Fergus from his own desires.

If we recall the three definitions of "crying" with which I began this section, we will see that Jordan's film makes use of all of them in order to confirm the alignment of humanity with Fergus and otherness with Dil, Jody, and Jude. The first definition—"to announce in public, utter in a loud distinct voice so as to be heard over a long distance"—references the open secret of Dil's gender, and equates the "crying game" with the subtle interplay between being "out" and being "in." While Dil's secret is equated with dishonesty and sickening deceit (literally since Fergus/Jimmy vomits when he sees Dil's penis), the film makes no particular moral judgments about the secret that Fergus keeps from Dil—namely, his involvement in the death of her lover. Only Dil is shown to be playing the crying game and so it is her treacherous deceptions rather than his that must be punished. His punishment (jail time) is earned for his traitorous behavior of the nation rather than his betrayal of Dil. The second definition—"the process of shedding tears (usually accompanied by sobs or other inarticulate sounds)"—speaks to the potential for tragedy in and around the transgender figure. The tragic transgender, indeed, weeps because happiness and satisfaction, according to transphobic narratives, is always just out of reach. In this film, Dil cries when she thinks that Fergus is leaving her for Jude. Fergus uses Dil's tears to wipe her makeup off her face and begin the transformation from female to male that he says will be her cover from the violence of the IRA. By using her tears to erase her mask, the film once again creates a model of true humanity that is equated with gender and temporal stability. Dil's transformation from girl to boy matches up both sex and gender, past and present. The final definition of crying is "conspicuously bad, offensive or reprehensible," and ultimately this is the judgment that the film hands down on the transgender character and the fanatic IRA members.

Boys Don't Cry: Beyond Tears

Given the predominance of films that use transgender characters, but avoid the transgender gaze, Peirce's transformation of the Brandon story into the Oscar-winning *Boys Don't Cry* signaled something much more than the successful interpretation of a transgender narrative for a mainstream audience. The success of Peirce's depiction depended not simply on the impressive acting skills of Hilary Swank and her surrounding cast, nor did it rest solely on the topicality of the Brandon narrative in gay, lesbian, and transgender communities; rather, the seduction of mainstream viewers by this decidedly queer and unconventional narrative must be ascribed to the film's ability to construct and sustain a transgender gaze. Debates about the gendered gaze in Hollywood film have subsided in recent years, and have been replaced by much more flexible conceptions of looking and imaging that account for multiple viewers and perspectives. The range of subject positions for looking has been expanded to include "queer looks," "oppositional gazes," "black looks," and other modes of seeing not captured by the abbreviated structures of the male and female gaze (hooks 1992; Gever 1993). But while different styles of looking have been accounted for in this expanded range, the basic formula for generating visual pleasure may not have shifted significantly. In other words, while different visual styles and pallets have helped to construct an alternative cinema, the structures of mainstream cinema have remained largely untouched. The success of *Boys Don't Cry* in cultivating an audience beyond the queer cinema circuit depends absolutely on its ability to hijack the male and female gazes, and replace them surreptitiously with transgender modes of looking and queer forms of visual pleasure.

In a gesture that has left feminist film theorists fuming for years, Laura Mulvey's classic essay "Visual Pleasure and Narrative Cinema" argued, somewhat sensibly, that the pleasure in looking was always gendered within classic cinema. Mulvey went on to claim that within those classic cinematic narrative trajectories that begin with a mystery, a murder, a checkered past, or class disadvantage, or that advance through a series of obstacles toward the desired resolution in heterosexual marriage, there exist a series of male and female points of identification (Mulvey 1990). In other words, to the extent that the cinema depends on the power to activate and attract desiring relations (between characters, between on-screen and offscreen subjects, between images and subjects, between spectators), it also depends on a sexual and gendered economy of looking, watching and identifying. The desiring

Hillary Swank as Brandon Teena in *Boys Don't Cry*. Press packet for *Boys Don't Cry*.

positions within conventional cinematic universes tend to be called "masculine" and "feminine." While the masculine character in the film (whether or not that character is male or female) negotiates an obstacle course in order to advance toward a romantic reward, the feminine character waits at the course's end for the hero to advance, succeed, and arrive.[2] These gendered characters play their parts within a field of extremely limited and finite variation, and yet, because gendered spectators have already consented to limited and finite gender roles before entering the cinema, they will consent to the narrow range of narrative options within narrative cinema. Entertainment, in many ways, is the name we give to the fantasies of difference that erupt on the screen only to give way to the reproduction of sameness. In other words, as much as viewers want to believe in alternatives, the mainstream film assumes that they also want to believe that the choices they have made and the realities within which they function offer the best possible options. So for example, while gay or lesbian characters may appear within heterosexual romances as putative alternatives to the seemingly inevitable progression within adulthood from adolescence to romance to marriage to reproduction to death, the queer characters (say, Greg Kinnear in *As Good as It Gets,* or any and all lesbian characters in films about homo triangulations like *Basic Instinct, French Twist,* and so on) will function only to confirm the rightness of heterosexual object choice.

How does conventional narrative cinema allow for variation while maintaining a high degree of conformity? Sometimes the masculine character will be a woman (Barbara Stanwyck in *Walk on the Wild Side;* Michelle Rodriguez in *Girlfight;* Mercedes McCambridge in anything) and the narrative twist will involve her downfall or domestication. Sometimes the feminine character will be a man (Jeremy Irons in *Dead Ringers;* Jet Li in *Romeo Must Die*) and the narrative will compel him to either become a male hero or self-destruct. And sometimes, as we saw in *The Crying Game,* the transgender character will be evoked as a metaphor for flexible subjecthood, but will not be given a narrative in his/her own right. But every now and then, and these are the instances that I want to examine here, the gendered binary on which the stability, the pleasure, and the purchase of mainstream cinema depend will be thoroughly rescripted, allowing for another kind of gaze or look. Here, I track the potentiality of the transgender gaze or the "transverse look," as Nick Mirzoeff describes it. Mirzoeff suggests that in an age of "multiple viewpoints," we have to think beyond the gaze. He writes about a "transient, transnational, transgendered way of seeing that visual culture seeks to define, describe and deconstruct with the transverse look or glance—not a gaze, there have been enough gazes already" (Mirzoeff 2002, 18).

While Mulvey's essay created much vigorous debate in cinema studies on account of its seemingly fatalistic perspective on gender roles and relations, the messenger in many ways was being confused with the message. Mulvey was not *creating* the gendered dynamics of looking, she was simply describing the remarkably restricted ways in which spectators can access pleasure. And so, for example, conventional narratives cannot conceive of the pleasure of being the image, the fetish, or the object of the gaze. Nor can they allow for the ways in which thoroughly scrambled gender relations might impact the dynamics of looking, at least not for long. Within conventional cinema, Mulvey proposed that the only way for a female viewer to access voyeuristic pleasure was to cross-identify with the male gaze; through this complicated procedure, the female spectator of a conventional visual narrative could find a position on the screen that offered a little more than the pleasure of being fetishized. Mulvey suggests that the female viewer has to suture her look to the male look. Others have talked about this as a form of transvestism—a cross-dressed look that allows the female spectator to imagine momentarily that she has the same access to power as the male viewer. The problem with the cinematic theory of masquerade, of course, is that it requires no real understanding of transvestism and of the meaning of male transvestism in particular. Mary Ann Doane, for example, in "Film and the Masquerade," simply theorizes all female subject positions as masquerade, and makes no particular distinction between a cross-dressing masquerade and a hyperfeminine one (Doane 1990). In doing so, she misses the queer dimension of the masquerade. In a trenchant critique of Doane, Chris Straayer in *Deviant Eyes, Deviant Bodies* has described the appeal of the "temporary transvestite film" for mainstream viewers, and she claims that the popularity of these films has to do with "the appeasement of basic contradictions through a common fantasy of over-throwing gender constructions without challenging sexual difference."[3] But what happens when the transvestite narrative is not temporary, and when gender constructions are overthrown and sexual difference is shaken to its very foundations?

In the classic Hollywood film text, the camera looks from one position/character and then returns the gaze from another position/character, thereby suturing the viewer to a usually male gaze and simultaneously covering over what the viewer cannot see. This dynamic of looking is called shot/reverse shot and it occupies a central position within cinematic grammar. The shot/reverse shot mode allows for the stability of narrative progression, ensures a developmental logic, and allows the viewers to insert themselves into the filmic world by imagining that their access to the characters is unmediated. The dismantling of the shot/reverse shot can be identified as the central cinematic tactic in *Boys Don't Cry*. In her stylish adaptation of the true-to-life story of Brandon, director Peirce self-consciously constructs what can only be called a transgender look. *Boys Don't Cry* establishes the legitimacy and the durability of Brandon's gender not simply by telling the tragic tale of his death by murder but by forcing spectators to adopt, if only provisionally, Brandon's gaze, a transgender look.[4] The transgender look in this film reveals the ideological content of the male and female gazes, and it disarms, temporarily, the compulsory heterosexuality of the romance genre. Brandon's gaze, obviously, dies with him in the film's brutal conclusion, but Peirce, perhaps prematurely, abandons the transgender look in the final intimate encounter between Lana and Brandon. Peirce's inability to sustain a transgender look opens up a set of questions about the inevitability and dominance of both the male/female and hetero/homo binary in narrative cinema.

One remarkable scene, about halfway through the film, clearly fore-grounds the power of the transgender look, making it most visible precisely where and when it is most threatened. In a scary and nerve-racking sequence of events, Brandon finds himself cornered at Lana's house. John and Tom have forced Candace to tell them that Brandon has been charged by the po-lice with writing bad checks and that he has been imprisoned as a woman. John and Tom now hunt Brandon, like hounds after a fox, and then they begin a long and excruciating interrogation of Brandon's gender identity. Lana protects Brandon at first by saying that she will examine him and de-termine whether he is a man or a woman. Lana and Brandon enter Lana's bedroom, where Lana refuses to look as Brandon unbuckles his pants, telling him, "Don't. . . . I know you're a guy." As they sit on the bed together, the camera now follows Lana's gaze out into the night sky, a utopian vision of an elsewhere into which she and Brandon long to escape. This is one of several fantasy shots in an otherwise wholly realistic film; Peirce threads these shots in which time speeds up or slows down through the film, creating an imag-istic counternarrative to the story of Brandon's decline.

As Brandon and Lana sit in Lana's bedroom imagining an elsewhere that would save them from the impoverished reality they inhabit, the camera cuts back abruptly to "reality" and a still two-shot of Brandon in profile and Lana behind him. As they discuss their next move, the camera draws back slowly and makes a seamless transition to place them in the living room in front of the posse of bullies. This quiet interlude in Lana's bedroom establishes the fe-male gaze, Lana's gaze, as a willingness to see what is not there (a condition of all fantasy), but also as a refusal to privilege the literal over the figurative (Brandon's genitalia over Brandon's gender presentation). The female gaze, in this scene, makes possible an alternative vision of time, space, and em-bodiment. Time slows down while the couple linger in the sanctuary of Lana's private world, her bedroom; the bedroom itself becomes an other-worldly space framed by the big night sky, and containing the perverse vi-sion of a girl and her queer boy lover; and the body of Brandon is preserved as male, for now, by Lana's refusal to dismantle its fragile power with the scrutinizing gaze of science and "truth." That Lana's room morphs seam-lessly into the living room at the end of this scene, alerts the viewer to the possibility that an alternative vision will subtend and undermine the chill-ing enforcement of normativity that follows.

Back in the living room—the primary domestic space of the family— events take an abrupt turn toward the tragic. Brandon is shoved now into the bathroom, a hyperreal space of sexual difference, and is violently de-pantsed by John and Tom, and then restrained by John while Tom roughly examines Brandon's crotch. The brutality of John and Tom's action here is clearly identified as a violent mode of looking, and the film identifies the male gaze with the factual, the visible, and the literal. The brutality of the male gaze, however, is more complicated than simply a castrating force; John and Tom not only want to see the site of Brandon's castration but more important, they need Lana to see it. Lana kneels in front of Brandon, confirming the scene's resemblance to a crucifixion tableau, and refuses to raise her eyes, declining, again, to look at Brandon's unveiling.

At the point when Lana's "family" and "friends" assert their heteronormative will most forcefully on Brandon's resistant body, however, Brandon rescues himself for a moment by regaining the alternative vision of time and space that he and Lana shared moments earlier in her bedroom. A slow-motion sequence interrupts the fast and furious quasi-medical scrutiny of Brandon's body, and shots from Brandon's point of view reveal him to be in the grips of an "out-of-body" and out-of-time experience. Light shines on Brandon from above, and his anguished face peers out into the crowd of onlookers who have gathered at the bathroom door. The crowd now includes a fully clothed Brandon, a double, who returns the gaze of the tortured Brandon impassively. In this shot/reverse shot sequence between the castrated Brandon and the transgender one, the transgender gaze is constituted as a look divided within itself, a point of view that comes from two places (at least) at the same time, one clothed and one naked. The clothed Brandon is the one who was rescued by Lana's refusal to look; he is the Brandon who survives his own rape and murder; he is the Brandon to whom the audience is now sutured, a figure who combines momentarily the activity of looking with the passivity of the spectacle. And the naked Brandon is the one who will suffer, endure, and finally expire.

Kaja Silverman has called attention to cinematic suture in an essay of the same name, as "the process whereby the inadequacy of the subject's position is exposed in order to facilitate new insertions into a cultural discourse which promises to make good that lack" (Silverman 1983, 236). Here, in *Boys Don't Cry*, the inadequacy of the subject's position has been presented as a precondition of the narrative, and so this scene of the split transgender subject, which would ordinarily expose "the inadequacy of the subject's position," actually works to highlight the *sufficiency* of the transgender subject. So if usually the shot/reverse shot both secures and destabilizes the spectator's sense of self, now the shot/reverse shot involving the two Brandons serves both to destabilize the spectator's sense of gender stability and confirm Brandon's manhood at the very moment that he has been exposed as female/castrated.

Not only does *Boys Don't Cry* create a position for the transgender subject that is fortified from the traditional operations of the gaze and conventional modes of gendering but it also makes the transgender subject dependent on the recognition of a woman. In other words, Brandon can be Brandon because Lana is willing to see him as he sees himself (clothed, male, vulnerable, lacking, strong, and passionate), and she is willing to avert her gaze when his manhood is in question. With Brandon occupying the place of the male hero and the male gaze in the romance, the dynamics of looking and gendered being are permanently altered. If usually it is the female body that registers lack, insufficiency, and powerlessness, in *Boys Don't Cry*, it is Brandon who represents the general condition of incompleteness, crisis, and lack, and it is Lana who represents the fantasy of wholeness, knowledge, and pleasure. Lana can be naked without trauma while Brandon cannot; she can access physical pleasure in a way that he cannot, but he is depicted as mobile and self-confident in a way that she is not. Exclusion and privilege cannot be assigned neatly to the couple on the basis of gender or class hierarchies; power, rather, is shared between the two subjects, and she agrees to misrecognize him as male while he sees through her social alienation and unhappiness, recognizing her as beautiful, desirable, and special.

By deploying the transgender gaze and binding it to an empowered female gaze in *Boys Don't Cry*, director Peirce, for most of the film, keeps the viewer trained on the seriousness of Brandon's masculinity and the authenticity of his presentation as opposed to its elements of masquerade. But toward the end of the film, Peirce suddenly and catastrophically divests her character of his transgender look and converts it to a lesbian and therefore female gaze. In a strange scene following the brutal rape of Brandon by John and Tom, Lana comes to Brandon as he lies sleeping in a shed outside of Candace's house. In many ways, the encounter between the two that follows seems to extend the violence enacted on Brandon's body by John and Tom since Brandon now interacts with Lana *as if he were a woman*. Lana, contrary to her previous commitment to his masculinity, seems to see him as female, and she calls him "pretty" and asks him what he was like as a girl. Brandon confesses to Lana that he has been untruthful about many things in his past, and his confession sets up the expectation that he will now appear before

Lana as his "true" self. Truth here becomes sutured to nakedness as Lana disrobes Brandon, tentatively saying that she may not know "how to do this." "This" seems to refer to having sex with Brandon as a woman. They both agree that his whole journey to manhood has been pretty weird and then they move to make love. While earlier Peirce created quite graphic depictions of sex between Brandon and Lana, now the action is hidden by a Hollywood dissolve as if to suggest that the couple are now making love as opposed to having sex. The scene is disjunctive and completely breaks the flow of the cinematic text by having Lana, the one person who could see Brandon's gender separate from his sex, now see him as woman. Moreover, the scene implies that the rape has made Brandon a woman in a way that his brutal exposure earlier in the bathroom and his intimate sex scenes with Lana could not. And if the scene seems totally out of place to the viewer, it apparently felt wrong as well to Hilary Swank. There are rumors that Swank and Peirce fought over this scene, and that Peirce shot the scene without Swank by using a body double. A close reading of the end of the scene indeed shows that the Brandon figure takes off his T-shirt while the camera watches from behind. The musculature and look of Brandon's back is quite different here from the toned look of Swank's body in earlier exposure scenes.

The "love" scene raises a number of logical and practical questions about the representation of the relationship between Brandon and Lana. First, why would Brandon want to have sex within hours of a rape? Second, how does the film pull back from its previous commitment to his masculinity here by allowing his femaleness to become legible and significant to Lana's desire? Third, in what ways does this scene play against the earlier, more "plastic" sex scenes in which Brandon used a dildo and would not allow Lana to touch him? And fourth, how does this scene unravel the complexities of the transgender gaze as they have been assembled in earlier scenes between Brandon and Lana? When asked in an interview about this scene, Peirce reverts to a tired humanist narrative to explain it and says that after the rape, Brandon could not be either Brandon Teena or Teena Brandon and so he becomes truly "himself," and in that interaction with Lana, Brandon "receives love" for the first time as a human being.[5] Peirce claims that Lana herself told her about this encounter and therefore it was true to life. In the context of the film, however, which has made no such commitment to authenticity, the scene ties Brandon's humanity to a particular form of naked embodiment that in the end requires him to be a woman.

Ultimately in *Boys Don't Cry*, the double vision of the transgender subject gives way to the universal vision of humanism; the transgender man and his lover become lesbians, and the murder seems to be simply the outcome of a vicious homophobic rage. Given the failure of nerve that leads Peirce to conclude her film with a humanist scene of love conquers all, it is no surprise that she also sacrificed the racial complexity of the narrative by erasing the story of the other victim who died alongside Brandon and Lisa Lambert. As discussed earlier, Philip DeVine, a disabled African American man, has in general received only scant treatment in media accounts of the case, despite the connections of at least one of the murderers to a white supremacist group (Jones 1996, 154). Now in the feature film, Philip's death has been rendered completely irrelevant to the narrative that has been privileged. Peirce claimed that this subplot would have complicated her film and made the plot too cumbersome, but race is a narrative trajectory that is absolutely central to the meaning of the Brandon murder. Philip was dating Lana's sister, Leslie, and had a fight with her the night he showed up at Lisa's house in Humboldt County. His death was neither accidental nor an afterthought; his connection to Leslie could be read as a similarly outrageous threat to the supremacy and privilege of white manhood that the murderers Lotter and Nissen rose to defend. By taking Philip out of the narrative and by not even mentioning him in the original dedication of the film ("To Brandon Teena and Lisa Lambert"), the filmmaker sacrifices the hard facts of racial hatred and transphobia to a streamlined romance.[6] Peirce, in other words, reduces the complexity of the murderous act even as she sacrifices the complexity of Brandon's identity.

In the end, the murders are shown to be the result of a kind of homosexual panic, and Brandon is offered up as an "everyman" hero who makes a claim on the audience's sympathies first by pulling off a credible masculinity, but then by seeming to step out of his carefully maintained manhood to appear before judge and jury in the naked flesh as female. By reneging on her earlier commitment to the transgender gaze and ignoring altogether the possibility of exposing the whiteness of the male gaze, *Boys Don't Cry* falls far short of the alternative vision that was articulated so powerfully and shared so beautifully by Brandon and Lana in Lana's bedroom. But even so, by articulating momentarily the specific formal dimensions of the transgender gaze, *Boys Don't Cry* takes a quantum leap away from the crying games, which continued in the past to locate transgenderism in between the male and female gazes and alongside unrelenting tragedy. Peirce's film, in fact, opens the door to a nonfetishistic mode of seeing the transgender body—a mode that looks with, rather than at, the transgender body and cultivates the multidimensionality of an indisputably transgender gaze.

What would a transgender film look like that did not punish the transgender subject for his or her inflexibilities and for failing to deliver the fantasy of fluidity that cinematic audiences so desire? *By Hook or by Crook* offers the spectator not one but two transgender characters, and the two together represent transgender identity as less of a function of bodily flexibility and more a result of intimate bonds and queer, interactive modes of recognition.

Lovely and Confusing:
By Hook or by Crook and the Transgender Look

> We feel like we were thrown almost every curve in the game. And we managed to make this thing by hook or by crook.
>
> —Harry Dodge and Silas Howard, *By Hook or by Crook* directors

By Hook or by Crook marks a real turning point for queer and transgender cinema. This no-budget, low-tech, high-concept feature, shot entirely in mini digital video, tells the story of two gender bandits, Shy and Valentine. Described by its creators as "utterly post-post-modern, a little bit of country and a little bit of rock and roll," the film conjures up the twilight world of two loners living on the edge without trying to explain or rationalize their reality.[7] The refusal to explain either the gender peculiarities of the heroes or the many other contradictions they embody allows directors Howard and Dodge instead to focus on developing eccentric and compelling characters. While most of the action turns on the bond between Shy and Valentine, their world is populated with a stunning array of memorable characters like Valentine's girlfriend, Billie (Stanya Kahn), and Shy's love interest, Isabelle (Carina Gia). The film also features fabulous guest appearances by queer celebrities like Joan Jett as a news interviewee, the late Kris Kovick typecast as a crazy nut in the park, and Machiko Saito as the gun store clerk. These cameos establish the world of *By Hook or by Crook* as a specifically queer universe and clearly mark a studied indifference to mainstream acceptance by making subcultural renown rather than Hollywood glamour into the most desirable form of celebrity.

Both *The Crying Game* and *Boys Don't Cry* relied heavily on the successful solicitation of affect—whether revulsion, sympathy, or empathy—in order

Silas Howard and Harriet Dodge in *By Hook or by Crook*. Reproduced by permission of the filmmakers.

to give mainstream viewers access to a transgender gaze. And in both films, a relatively unknown actor (Jay Davidson and Hilary Swank, respectively) performs alongside a more well-known actor (Stephen Rea and Chloe Sevigny, respectively); the relative obscurity of the transgender actors allow them to pull off the feat of credibly performing a gender at odds with the sexed body even after the body has been brutally exposed. *By Hook or by Crook* resists the seduction of crying games and the lure of sentiment, and works instead to associate butchness and gender innovation with wit, humor, and style. The melancholia that tinges *The Crying Game* and saturates *Boys Don't Cry* is transformed in *By Hook or by Crook* into the wise delirium of Dodge's character, Valentine. Dodge and Howard (Shy) knowingly avoid engaging their viewers at the level of sympathy, pity, or even empathy, and instead they "hook" them with the basic tools of the cinematic apparatus: desire and identification.

Dodge and Howard pioneer some brilliant techniques of queer plotting in order to map the world of the willfully perverse. As they say in interviews, neither director was interested in telling a story about "being gay." Nor did Dodge and Howard want to spend valuable screen time explaining the characters' sexualities and genders to unknowing audiences. In the press kit, Dodge and Howard discuss their strategy in terms of representing sexuality and gender as follows: "This is a movie about a budding friendship between two people. The fact that they happen to be queer is purposefully off the point. If you call them something, other than sad, rambling, spirited, gentle, sharp or funny . . . you might call them *'butches.'*" Instead of a humanist story about gay heroes struggling to be accepted, Dodge and Howard tell a beautifully fragmented tale of queer encounter set almost entirely in a queer universe. In other words, the heroes are utterly unremarkable for their queerness in the cinematic world that the directors have created. In this way, Dodge and Howard offer a tribute to the San Francisco subcultural worlds that they inhabit. As Howard remarks, "We've always hoped this project would reflect the creativity and actual valor of the community of people we came from. And I think it does. From the get-go, this movie had its roots in our extended family of weirdos in San Francisco."

In the film, Shy and Valentine visit cafes, clubs, shops, and hotels where no one reacts specifically to their butchness. This narrative strategy effectively *universalizes queerness* within this specific cinematic space. Many gay and lesbian films represent their characters and their struggles as "universal" as a way of suggesting that their film speaks to audiences beyond specific gay and lesbian audiences. But few do more than submit to the regulation of narrative that transforms the specific into the universal: they tell stories of love, redemption, family, and struggle that look exactly like every other Hollywood feature angling for a big audience. *By Hook or by Crook* actually manages to tell a queer story that is more than a queer story by refusing to acknowledge the existence of a straight world. Where the straight world is represented only through its institutions such as the law, the mental institution, or commerce, the queer cinematic world comes to represent a truly localized place of opposition—an opposition, moreover, that is to be found in committed performances of perversity, madness, and friendship. While some of Dodge's comments in the press notes imply a humanist aim for the project ("We wanted to make a film about people with big ideas and big dreams who end up dealing with the shadowy subtleties of human life"; "I want to make work that touches people's hearts. . . . I am interested in the human spirit"), the film resists the trap of liberal humanism (making a film about gays who are, in the end, just like everybody else). So *By Hook or by Crook* universalizes queerness without allowing its characters to be absorbed back into the baggy and ultimately heterosexist concept of the "human."

Different key scenes from the film build, capture, and sustain this method of universalizing queerness. In one scene soon after they meet, Shy and Valentine go to a club together. The club scene, filmed in San Francisco's notorious Lexington Bar, is a riotous montage of queer excess. The camera lovingly pans a scene of punky, pierced, tattooed, perverted young queers. The montage lasts much longer than necessary, signaling that the beauty and intrinsic worth of this world transcends its diegetic purpose. In *The Crying Game*, the bar scenes were used first to establish the credibility of Dil's womanhood and then, after she has "come out" to Fergus as male bodied, the bar scenes are used to cast her womanhood as incredible. So while *The Crying Game* casts the bar as a place of perversion and a primal scene of deception, Dodge and Howard situate the queer bar as central to an alternative vision of community, space, time, and identity. In the bar, Valentine dances wildly and ecstatically while Shy sits apart from the crowd watching. The camera playfully scans the bar and then lines up its patrons for quick cameos. Here, Dodge and Howard are concerned to represent the bar as both a space of queer community and a place of singularity. The singularity of the patrons, however, does not create the kind of transgressive exceptionalism that I discussed in chapter 1; it instead reveals a difference to be a shared and a collaborative relation to normativity rather than an individualist mode of refusal.

After watching Valentine dance, Shy gets up and steals Valentine's wallet before leaving. The theft of Valentine's wallet should create a gulf of distrust and suspicion between the two strangers, but in this looking-glass world, it actually bonds them more securely within their underground existence. Shy uses Valentine's wallet to find out where she lives, and when Shy returns Valentine's wallet the next day, she is greeted like a long-lost brother—this has the effect of inverting the morality of the world represented in this film by the police. Other scenes deepen this refusal of conventional law and order. The two butches as wannabe thieves try to hold up a drugstore only to be chased off by an aggressive salesclerk; they try to scam a hardware store and, in a citation of Robert De Niro's famous scene from *Taxi Driver*, they pose with guns in front of the mirror in Shy's run-down motel room. All of these scenes show Shy and Valentine as eccentric, but gentle outlaws who function as part of an alternative universe with its own ethics, sex/gender system, and public space.

De Niro's taxi driver, muttering "you looking at me" as he pointed a loaded gun at his own mirror image, is a vigilante loner, a man turned inward and lost to the city he skims across in his yellow cab. But while De Niro's character accidentally hits a vein of humor with his mohawked "fuck you," Shy and Valentine deliberately ride butch humor rather than macho vengeance into the sunset. If the vigilante wants to remake the world in his image, the queer outlaws of *By Hook or by Crook* are content to imagine a world of their own making. When asked about the title of the film, Silas Howard responded: "The title refers to what is involved in inventing your own world—when you don't see anything that represents you out there, how can you seize upon that absence as an opportunity to make something out of nothing, by hook or by crook. We take gender ambiguity, for example, and we don't explain it, dilute it or apologize for it—we represent it for what it is—something confusing and lovely!"

The recent explosion of transgender films forces us to consider what the spectacle of the transgender body represents to multiple audiences. For some audiences, the transgender body confirms a fantasy of fluidity so common to notions of transformation within the postmodern. To others, the transgender body confirms the enduring power of the binary gender system. But to still other viewers, the transgender body represents a utopian vision of a world of subcultural possibilities. Representations of transgenderism in recent queer cinema have moved from a tricky narrative device designed to catch an unsuspecting audience off guard to truly independent productions within which gender ambiguity is not a trap or a device but part of the production of new forms of heroism, vulnerability, visibility, and embodiment. The centrality of the figure of Brandon in this drama of postmodern embodiment suggests, as I argued in chapter 2, that we have a hard time thinking of seismic shifts in the history of representations separate from individual stories of transformation. The hopes and fears that have been projected onto the slim and violated body of one transgender loner in small-town Nebraska make clear the flaws of "representative history," and call for the kind of shared vision that we see in *By Hook or by Crook*—a vision of community, possibility, and redemption through collaboration.

5

Technotopias

Representing Transgender Bodies in Contemporary Art

> For visual culture, visibility is not so simple. Its object of study is precisely
> the entities that come into being at the points of intersection of visibility
> with social power, that is to say, visuality.
> —Nick Mirzoeff, "The Subject of Visual Culture"

Contemporary images of gender-ambiguous bodies by artists like Del La-
Grace Volcano, Linda Besemer, and Jenny Saville, when considered in con-
junction with the surprising success of the transgender film *Boys Don't Cry*
and the subcultural popularity of *By Hook or by Crook*, imply that the transgender body represents something particular about the historical moment
within which it suddenly and spectacularly becomes visible. While the transgender body has been theorized as an in-between body, and as the place of
the medical and scientific construction of gender, when it comes time to picture the transgender body in the flesh, it nearly always emerges as a transsexual body. In the images I consider here, the transgender body is not re-
ducible to the transsexual body, and it retains the marks of its own ambiguity and ambivalence. If the *transsexual* body has been deliberately
reorganized in order to invite certain gazes and shut down others, the transgender body performs self as gesture not as will, as possibility not as proba-
bility, as a relation—a wink, a handshake and as an effect of deliberate mis-
recognition.

In one particularly stunning example of the representation of transgender
hybridity by way of faux collage, JA Nicholls's paintings imagine transgenderism in the form of conglomerate creatures who emerge from the paint itself. In a painting titled *in another place,* for example, the body *is* postmodern
surface, the very gesture of representation, and it struggles to emerge from
the canvas enclosing its form. *in another place* splits the body into two non-
complementary forms, each one in motion on the road to "another place."
Each figure stands on his or her own path, in his or her own place, and the
two exchange a look that can never arrive. The roads that frame each hybrid

body lead in different directions and the two separate(d) selves can never meet. The body itself in Nicholls's painting is a collage form, but the collage is made up of not only different body parts but different perspectives (a side view, full frontal) and different modes of representation. Resisting the traditional form of collage that draws other materials into the sphere of painting, Nicholls creates the effect of collage with paint and canvas alone. She refuses the clear separation of the real and the represented that collage implies, and makes representation into a primary realm of signification. Nicholls's work lies somewhere between abstraction and figural representation, marking out beautifully the other place of queer embodiment in contemporary aesthetics.

Postmodernism and Transgenderism

Postmodernism, as I proposed in chapter 1, cannot simply be reduced to the cultural formations that accompany a new mode of capitalism; as Anna Tsing points out, this kind of reductive reading of culture misunderstands the potential for cultural production to exceed and resist economic imperatives (Tsing 2002). Indeed, the assumption that cultural production will always only represent the dominant economic order, erases the multiple disruptions to hegemony that have emerged from subcultural and avant-garde art practices in the past, and it leaves us with a sense of inevitability about our relation to the dominant. Debates about the relationship between the economy and art production, base and superstructure, have a long history in art criticism, and I attempt to revisit some of these debates here in order to refute the return of a Frankfurt school paradigm of cultural capitulations, on the one hand, and to define the political and aesthetic contributions made by "ludic" body artists to oppositional politics in postmodernism, on the other. In this chapter, I define postmodernism as the generative clash between new modes of cultural production and late capitalism. Within postmodernism, subcultural activities are as likely to generate new forms of protest as they are to produce new commodities to be absorbed back into a logic of accumulation; and new sites of opposition or "geographies of resistance" become available even as new modes of domination are formed (Pile 1997).

The link between transgenderism and postmodernism has emerged in a number of late-twentieth-century philosophies of embodiment, from Judith Butler's *Gender Trouble*, to Jean Baudrillard's essay "Transsexuality," to Rita Felski's "Transsexuality, Postmodernism, and the Death of History" (Butler

1990; Baudrillard 1990; Felski 1996). Butler takes the transgender subject seriously and uses transgenderism to represent the contradictions of being—specifically gendered being—in postmodernism. Baudrillard, on the other hand, uses transsexuality and, by implication, transgenderism as simply a metaphor for the unlocatability of the body. For Baudrillard, no one actually inhabits transgender subjectivity; rather, transgenderism represents the subject floating free of the body in cyberspace. And for Felski, the fate of the transsexual body in postmodern theory spells out the "death of history" in that transsexuality as an experience, as a specific history of gender and sexuality, has been cast as a disembodied, metaphoric signifier of pure difference. Felski argues for an ethical account of difference that respects the specific historical locations of embodied forms in space and time. My account of the representations of transgendered bodies in this chapter takes heed of Felski's challenge to "remain attentive to disjuncture and nonsynchrony in the experience of temporality while simultaneously acknowledging systematic connections and relations among discrete cultural practices" (Felski 1996, 348), and provides an account of the emergence of the transgender body within art in relation to the various histories of art making that have involved the visibly gendered body.

The connection between postmodernism and transgenderism also makes an oblique and somewhat surprising appearance in Fredric Jameson's classic essay "The Cultural Logic of Postmodernism" (Jameson 1997). In this essay, Jameson sounded the warning bell on a new form of cultural production, which, he believes, participates in a global cultural industry. Jameson noted that "aesthetic production today has become integrated into commodity production generally" (4). He was concerned to point out that the seemingly resistant and oppositional strains of postmodern cultural production (the blending of high and low culture, for example, or the inclusion and even foregrounding of sexually explicit material) were actually the marks of institutionalization rather than revolution, and he identified a postmodern aesthetic of pastiche with "a consequent weakening of historicity" (6). Jameson identified high modernism with the singular master works of artists like Vincent van Gogh and Edvard Munch, and postmodernism, for him, could be grasped through the easily reproduced silk screens of glamour icons by Andy Warhol. Jameson identifies political postmodern only in relation to the historical novels of E. L. Doctorow and, ultimately, expresses a pessimistic vision of the political utility of postmodern cultural production—a pessimism, moreover, that has been echoed in the work of other Marxist theorists like

David Harvey, and that has been subtly blamed on the preponderance within postmodernism of a ludic and parochial body politics.

As Mandy Merck has pointed out, Jameson's rigid identification of postmodernism with queer consumption and of modernism with heterosexual production is startling and troubling (Merck 1996). And indeed, his essay depends utterly on a homophobic repudiation of the superficial, the depthless, and the spectacular. In his essay, Jameson sets up a binary division between postmodernism and modernism that in its comparison of a van Gogh painting called *Peasant Shoes* and a Warhol silk screen titled *Diamond Dust Shoes*, associates modernist work with politically urgent representations of working-class and male labor, and postmodernist art with politically anemic representations of bourgeois and female leisure. Jameson deepens this contrast by noting the three-dimensionality of the painting versus the one-dimensionality of the silk-screened image. Van Gogh's shoes, he observes, are caked with mud and materiality; they are of history, nature, and the world. Meanwhile, Warhol's shoes are clean, new, manufactured; they speak only of consumption and luxury. Van Gogh's painting tells us about class struggle, exploitation, and historical process while Warhol's image transmits only the triumph of global capitalism. In her reading of Jameson's art history lesson, Merck restores a queer history of sex work and gay community to Warhol's pile of unmatched footwear, and she situates van Gogh's matched pair firmly in relation to the centrality of heterosexual domestic arrangements within the stability of capitalism. Jameson's narrative of aesthetic (and specifically queer) capitulation to the forces of consumption falters in the face of this buried "other" history and his evolutionary cycle of cultural collusion with economic imperatives grinds to a halt.

Surprisingly, then, Jameson unwittingly offers a queer proposal as the only antidote to global capitalism. Jameson claims repeatedly that postmodern architecture is the best example of the sinister underside of postmodern cultural production. "Of all the arts," he writes, "architecture is the closest constitutively to the economic, with which, in the form of commissions and land values, it has a virtually unmediated relationship" (5). And architecture, he proposes, serves as the clearest example of the momentous changes within late capitalism that have unsettled relations between subjects and objects. Postmodern architecture, Jameson alleges, constitutes a "mutation in built space itself" with which we humans have not kept pace: "there has been a mutation in the object unaccompanied as yet by any equivalent mutation in the subject." Here, Jameson dips into the very body politics that he elsewhere seems to hold in such contempt. This spatial mutation, he argues, constitutes a form of postmodern evolution, and indeed "stands as something like an imperative to grow new organs, to expand our sensorium and our body to some new, yet unimaginable, perhaps ultimately impossible, dimensions" (39). This utopian, technotopian, or spatially imaginative formulation of a body with new organs and expanded sensorium corresponds precisely to the new forms of embodiment that have come to be called transgender in certain queer communities.

Apart from the patently homophobic rejection of postmodern cultural logics as queer and ludic, Jameson's casting of postmodern cultural production as a logic of late capitalism resonates with, and in many ways simply replicates, many of the earlier twentieth-century debates about art and politics. Jameson's essay, in some respects, is an update of Clement Greenberg's famous essay from 1939, "Avant-Garde and Kitsch." Greenberg's piece is often located in art history as something of an anomaly in Greenberg's own output given its avowedly Marxist emphasis and its critique of bourgeois culture. Later on, of course, Greenberg became the foremost defender of abstract art, and his work led the way to an association of modernist aesthetics with political autonomy and disinterestedness. And the early essay, in some sense, paves the way for later proposals by Greenberg about the subordination of ideology to form. Yet in "Avant-Garde and Kitsch," Greenberg still has one eye on a utopian socialist future and the other on the growing global threat of fascism, and in this historical context, he defines the role of the avant-garde as "not to 'experiment,' but to find a path along which it would be possible to keep culture *moving* in the midst of ideological confusion and violence" (Greenberg 2000, 49).[1] Greenberg then contrasts and opposes the avant-garde to "kitsch," which he associates with "folk or rudimentary culture" (55). Despite positing a seemingly clear-cut opposition between kitsch and the avant-garde, Greenberg does argue that kitsch and the avant-garde are "simultaneous cultural phenomena," and that they can coexist organically in a stable society; but where fascism or demagoguery take hold, kitsch can provide the dictator with access to the masses. Greenberg writes: "The main trouble with avant-garde art and literature, from the point of view of the Fascists and the Stalinists, is not that they are too critical, but that they are too 'innocent,' that it is too difficult to inject effective propaganda into them, that kitsch is more pliable to this end. Kitsch keeps a dictator in closer contact with the 'soul' of the people" (57).

101

Many critics have detailed what is wrong with Greenberg's delineation of the relations between avant-garde culture and kitsch, and as Thomas Crow summarizes it in his "Modernism and Mass Culture in the Visual Arts," "The critique of Greenbergian modernism is now well advanced and its defenders are scarce" (Crow 1996, 9). But Crow goes on to reexamine contradictions in Greenberg's opus in order to recast the relationship between high and low cultures in modernism as well as to demonstrate, in fact, the indebtedness of avant-garde cultural production to what Crow calls oppositional publics. T. J. Clark also returns to Greenberg in an essay titled "Clement Greenberg's Theory of Art" to propose other histories of the relationship between artistic production and political resistance. By tracing other, somewhat buried histories of modernism itself, Clark is able to claim that far from being totally disarmed by the rise of mass politics and publics, "the avant-garde . . . has regularly and rightly seen an *advantage* for art in the particular conditions of 'ideological confusion and violence' under capitalism" (Clark 2000, 75). Both Crow and Clark stop short of endorsing or even describing the "cultural possibilities," as Clark puts it, of postmodernism, but both do reject completely the formalist solution to the problem of the commodification of art. I will return later to the provocative way that Crow rehistoricizes the relationship between subcultures and avant-garde cultural production as one way out of the retreat of art into formalism; but Clark's rejection of Greenbergian modernism also has appeal to my project in that he resists both the retreat into abstraction and grim, fatalistic conclusions about the function of art in late capitalism. As Clark reminds us forcefully, "Art wants to address someone, it wants something precise and extended to do; it wants *resistance*, it needs criteria; it will take risks in order to find them, including the risk of its own dissolution" (83).

Given the vehement rejections in art history of gloom-and-doom scenarios within which art either withdraws into a private world of abstraction or becomes completely complicit with capitalism, it is surprising to see the notion of an oppositional modernism overwhelmed by mass culture reassert itself so insistently in Jameson's essay without the accompaniment of an historical accounting by him of the relationship between art and capitalism, bourgeois avant-garde traditions and aristocratic patronage, mass culture and subcultural resistance. It is surprising too that a one-to-one relationship between capitalism and culture would emerge so strongly among Marxist critics of postmodernism when even Friedrich Engels himself warned against seeing "the economic situation" as "cause, solely active while everything else is just passive effect." Engels continues: "No. Men make their history themselves, only they do so in a given environment" (Engels 1894).[2] Just as Greenberg could only see kitsch as the debased alternative to a rigorously committed avant-garde tradition, so Jameson can only cast postmodern pastiche as a dehistoricized and depoliticized capitulation to an economic imperative.

Our present, of course, is no longer the present that Jameson wrote about just a decade ago; and the new aesthetics he explored in the late 1980s have been upstaged by another aesthetic that does develop along the lines of pastiche but also exceeds it. And while for Jameson, a grand narrative of historicity allowed him to trace the passage from the modern to the postmodern, this new moment is characterized by the tumbling and uneven advent of an era of simultaneity and instantaneous communication. One aesthetic no longer follows neatly on from another (if it ever did), replacing it and critiquing it at the same time; rather, one aesthetic collides with the next, and hyperrealism will compete and collude with high abstraction, which will supplement and contrast with the return of narrative and a new experimentalism. This overlap of styles signifies not cultural confusion but an immense array of strategies deployed to make sense of and resist capitalism at a historical moment within which several generations can neither remember nor imagine the world otherwise. What constitutes the alternative now is, as Jameson predicted, a technotopic vision of space and flesh in a process of mutual mutation. But while for Jameson, hyperspace was always corporate space, for some postmodern artists, the creation of new bodies in an aesthetic realm offers a way to begin adapting to life after the death of the subject.

In what follows, I want to trace the collision of postmodern space and postmodern embodiment in a technotopic aesthetic, or one that tests technological potentialities against the limits of a human body anchored in time and space, and that powerfully reimagines the relations between the organic and the machinic, the toxic and the domestic, the surgical and the cosmetic. In doing so, I will try to account for new relations between what was earlier called the avant-garde and contemporary subcultural production. While Marxists see the disappearance of the avant-garde accompanied by the rise of mass culture, in actuality, postmodernism elevates the subculture to the status of the avant-garde. Since the avant-garde no longer solely represents class interests and class contradictions, and since subcultures, as I will show in my next chapter, cannot be understood as simply the localized containment of class struggle, we need to rethink the definitions of advanced, subcultural, and mass cultural production in an age of diversified struggle and multiple hegemonies. Representations of the transgender body by both advanced and subcultural artists provide one arena for the examination of new dynamics of resistance.

Since gender assignations rely so heavily on the visual, the postmodern dismantling of gender certainty in the realm of the visual has wide-ranging effects. Even though postmodernism tends to be represented by Jameson and others as a definitive break between different modes of capitalism, the lines of rupture are not so easy to trace in different genres of cultural production. And while literary history or even architecture may well show signs of a rupture between the formal complexities of high modernism and the emphasis on pastiche, repetition, and nonoriginality in postmodern works, visual culture contains different histories of transition between old and new modes of representation. Or at least, the changes in visual culture have adhered to different schedules and have played out somewhat differently from changes in literary culture. The break between abstract expressionism and pop art perhaps comes closest to replicating the rupture that cultural critics identify in literary histories, but even here the debates about the avant-garde, ideology and art, and genius look different.[3] And abstract expressionism, unlike experimental writing, neither faded away nor remained the location of an avant-garde impulse. While experimental writing still represents some kind of resistance to the easily digested narratives and ideas of what used to be called a "culture industry" (Adorno 1993), and while experimental film is still closely associated with independent, alternative, and often queer cinemas, abstract expressionist work is quite likely to find a place on the walls of a bank or a corporate office. And so the cultural logic of late capitalism that Jameson wants to attribute so completely to postmodernism does not pan out as neatly as he proposes. Some postmodern work certainly collaborates with corporate interests just as some strands of modernism line up with the political mandates of fascism. But the wholesale reduction of postmodernism to a cultural logic of late capitalism looks particularly suspect when we turn to visual culture, where some of the art objects, like certain forms of sculpture for example, change and age over time, giving rise to a sense of the impermanence of the art object as well as a different sense of both history and futurity.

The artistic rendering of ambiguous embodiment as representative of an unstable and chaotic self emerged in late modernism/early postmodernism. Mostly queer and female artists in the late 1960s used representations of the body to resist the move to total abstraction and, by implication, to return a representational mode of political urgency to the practice of making art. While Warhol's work represents one obvious rejection of abstract expressionism, Eva Hesse's work, which I discuss in detail later in this chapter, is representative of a wide range of art that rejected the U.S. turn to abstraction. Hesse, for instance, began her career making abstract paintings, but she quickly expressed dissatisfaction with a total emphasis on abstraction and began to produce organic, sculptural "part-objects." As Hesse explains, "I don't believe art can be based on an idea of composition or form" (Nemser 1970, 6). This chapter gathers together a scattered and selective history of the representation of gender ambiguity in art in order to chart the new understandings of time, space, and cultural production that emerge from a "transgender aesthetic." Indeed, the sliding of the postmodern into the transgender, which has been noted with concern by some transgender theorists (most notably Jay Prosser), is not simply an appropriation of the material body of the transsexual by queer theorists or postmodernists (Prosser 1998). The appearance of the transgender body in visual culture is instead part of a long history of the representation of unstable embodiment. We might even say that this form of postmodernism can be read as the cultural logic of anticapitalist, subcultural queer politics.

Building on the insights about a transgender look that emerged out of my detailed consideration of transgender cinema in the last chapter, I now turn to representations of the transgender body in contemporary art and photography. While there are some fascinating areas of overlap and dialogue between cinematic modes of representation and other methods of visualization, "still" images actually offer different logics of gender flexibility and dynamism; in highly abstract representations of embodiment in painting, sculpture, Web art, and photography, we find new formulations of the transgender look and different applications of this look to an understanding of the meaning of gendered embodiment in late postmodernism. The museum, as opposed to the cinema, offers a different set of opportunities for the representation of gender ambiguity and the reception of those images by a viewer. In the cinema, the viewer is positioned in a seemingly passive mode of reception, but in a studio, installation, or museum space, the viewer walks, sits, observes, and passes through space, and thus creates meaning in a different way.

In my reading of *Boys Don't Cry*, I suggested that the shot/reverse shot building block of contemporary cinema comes apart under the pressure of representing a subject essentially divided within himself and explicitly unreadable through the logics of visual gender. This dismantling of the shot/reverse shot forms the basis of two quite different art installations that can be called transgender for very different reasons. The first provides an eccentric example of transgender forms of looking that are not anchored solely to transgender identity and that create a "turbulent" field of vision. In Iranian-born artist Shirin Neshat's installation art, viewers are trapped between two mutually inclusive video spaces in which competing narratives unfold about the relations between men and women in Iran since the 1979 Islamic revolution. In *Rapture,* for instance, one wall tells a story of female flight and the resistance of veiled female bodies to the religious male gaze; and simultaneously, the other wall shows males massing to pray and to participate in the rituals of a militaristic faith. In *Turbulent,* the two walls depict singers, one male and one female. The male singer faces the camera as he stands in front of a full auditorium of men, and he sings a haunting and moving piece to wild applause. The female singer stands opposite in real time with her back turned to the camera and occupies a space utterly apart from the homosocial auditorium, and she waits until the male singer completes his song. Once he has concluded, the male singer turns to face the female singer, who now sings her response to an empty hall; she is greeted by silence. The video installation as a whole addresses the exclusion of women from public space, and the difficulty and heroism of female art production in the absence of audience, publicness, liveness, and voice. Neshat has said that *Turbulent* was inspired by the experience of seeing a young, blind, female singer on the streets of Istanbul. The woman was singing for money, but could not see her audience. The piece as a whole, Neshat has said, is "based on the idea of opposites, visually and conceptually" (Danto 2000, 64). Like the young blind woman, the singers in *Turbulent* cannot see their audiences, and the female singer literally has no audience except the museum patron, who situated in the dark space of the installation, becomes a silent witness to the staging of gender. The space where the viewer sits is a space most significantly of turbulence, a place where lines of sight between the two singers cross, where their voices compete, where they perform for each other and for the audience that remains invisible to them. And it is the space of the museum itself, the location where value is ascribed to culture and where bodies navigate the cultural codes of relevance. But the turbulence that Neshat's video creates is specifically a gender turbulence, and the space between the male singer and the female singer could provisionally be called a transgender space in the sense that it conjures up a site between two distinct genders where social conduct, religious doctrine, performance rituals, and cultural histories clash.

I want to claim for the images that I examine here an aesthetic of turbulence that inscribes abrupt shifts in time and space directly onto the genderambiguous body, and then offers that body to the gaze as a site of critical reinvention. Within this turbulence we can locate a transgender look, a mode of seeing and being seen that is not simply at odds with binary gender but that is part of a reorientation of the body in space and time. In her remarkable installations, for example, Neshat conjures up something like the transgender look that I identified as central to *Boys Don't Cry*. Neshat also rearticulates the shot/reverse shot sequence of Hollywood cinema so as to force spectators to acknowledge and confront their role in the process of suturing. By taking the shot/reverse shot sequence apart, as Neshat does in *Turbulent,* the male gaze and the female spectacle are fragmented, and viewers themselves become the camera pivoting their own gaze back and forth, looking at the singer singing, looking at the witness witnessing, and all the time making space for their own turbulent relations to seeing and being seen. The camera hardly moves in either video; rather, the spectators' bodies are forced to turn and look, look again, look back, modulate, mediate, hesitate, and finally see.

For a different example of manipulations of the shot/reverse shot sequence and the anchoring of transgenderism to tragedy, we can turn to an experimental video, which also constructs and explores the possibilities of the transgender gaze, and also plays in and is made for gallery rather than cinematic viewing. In his video *I probably want perfection in everything and a little more. Maybe that'll be my downfall,* Brian Dawn Chalkley uses a combination of bodily and vocal immobility to reorganize space and subjectivity in relation to gender ambiguity. Relying not at all on the trickery of visual gender attribution, Chalkley deliberately makes his gender work "voice activated." Chalkley effectively splits his selves between Brian and Dawn, and allows them to dialogue. The dialogue becomes an auditory equivalent to the sequence in *Boys Don't Cry,* which split Brandon in two, and allowed one self to remain whole while the other is brutally and violently disassembled. In Chalkley's video, Chalkley supplements the image track of a bulky woman/transvestite lying lifeless in a floodlit forest while night creatures fly back and forth in front of the camera light with a sound track of a conversation between a transvestite and a john in a transvestite pickup bar. The spooky combination of the inert body and the lively insects makes it hard to concentrate on the banter between "Brian" and "Dawn," or the john and the tranny, all of which is rendered in one male voice.

As so many transsexuals will attest, the voice can be a powerful gender marker for the person trying to pass, and the "wrong" voice can confuse or even anger an unsuspecting listener who may have already made a confident gender attribution that must now be reversed. Chalkley does not attempt to make his voice higher when speaking as Dawn or lower when speaking as Brian. Instead, he just patters on at an even and banal clip as the transvestite and her john exchange irrelevant information before deciding to leave the bar together. The ominous figure laid out on its bed of leaves in the background of the shot, however, suggests that the subsequent encounter slipped violently from desire to rage. As in *Boys Don't Cry*, violence is almost an inevitable outcome when the gender-ambiguous subject inspires not disgust but desire; the desire directed at the transgender body is a turbulent desire— one that must be paid for in blood. Because *Boys Don't Cry* is very much a narrative film with only a few experimental moments, it is not, in the end, entirely successful in sustaining a transgender gaze; but Chalkley's piece offers a more critical perspective in its depiction of the parameters of a transgender gaze. This work violates genres as well as genders by using video to create a *still life* as opposed to a moving picture and by calling attention to the violence, which literally stills the shot/reverse shot sequence of transgender reality. Nothing moves in *I probably want perfection*. The camera remains fixed on the immobile body, and the voices that crisscross the surface of the text cannot call the body back to life.

As Chalkley's video makes clear, subcultural or avant-garde as opposed to mainstream configurations of the transgender look refuse to subordinate narratives of alternative embodiment to the rigidly conventional plot sequences of mainstream cinema. The temporal space opened up by *I probably want perfection* clashes with normative expectations about character development and action. In a long twelve-minute sequence, everything and nothing happens, and the still figure of the transvestite testifies to the violent consequences of being out of time, out of sync, or out of place. Chalkley's work, like Neshat's, is most often viewed in the space of the gallery rather than in a cinema, and viewers may be expected to watch the tape for a while, wander off, and then return to enter into Chalkley's nightmare world at a new point without necessarily "missing" anything. While a film like *Boys Don't Cry* is motored to a certain extent by suspense, by the development of a central love relationship, by the mounting sense of doom, Chalkley's video depends on viewers' ability and desire to read the image track against and through the monotone of the voice track. The split voice, in combination with the ominously and persistently still image, forces viewers to recognize the different registers within which processes of differentiation take place. It also reminds us that difficult narratives sometimes require difficult forms— forms that unsettle, disturb, and render turbulent the forms of knowing on which we usually rely.

To make sense of the different uses made of subcultural material in the mass media and artistic avant-garde contexts, we can turn to Crow's brilliant essay "Modernism and Mass Culture in the Visual Arts" (Crow 1996). Crow connects elitist avant-garde cultures in modernism to resistant subcultures. He claims that subcultural productions, before they are overwhelmed and absorbed by the culture industry, mark out original and inventive uses of leisure in a society within which leisure is usually tied to profit maximization and normalization. While subcultural challenges to the culture industry tend to come in brief but effervescent bursts, their forms may be adopted by an artistic avant-garde and kept alive elsewhere. Crow writes that "in their selective appropriation from fringe mass culture, advanced artists search out areas of social practice that retain some vivid life in an increasingly administered and rationalized society." The avant-garde thus provides, according to Crow, "a necessary brokerage between high and low" culture (35). This important essay brings subcultural theory and theories of the avant-garde into the same space rather than seeing one as the antithesis of the other. I follow up on this productive move by building on Crow's observation that the subculture is not exhausted by its exploitation:

> Exploitation by the culture industry serves at the same time to stimulate and complicate those strivings in such a way that they continually outrun and surpass its programming. The expansion of the cultural economy continually creates new fringe areas, and young and more extreme members of assimilated subcultures will regroup with new recruits at still more marginal positions. So the process begins again. (35)

We can interpret Crow's description of this process of resistance and incorporation as a model for understanding the ways in which queer subcultural production can live on, often separate from the subculture, in "difficult," experimental, or highly abstract artworks, thereby merging the function of the avant-garde and the practices of the subculture. In what follows, I trace images of resistant gendering from the spectacular images of subcultural life made by transgender photographer Del LaGrace Volcano, to the collage paintings by JA Nicholls, to the abstract large-scale paintings of Linda Besemer. Arguing that these relays between subculture and avant-garde create a powerful venue of political postmodernism, I look at aesthetic practices shared by both avant-garde and subcultural artists, and aimed at representing new logics of embodiment and space. These new logics resonate in particular and even peculiar ways with the spectacle of transgenderism.

Bodies with New Organs

Tracking an art practice that Neshat calls turbulent and I label as a transgender aesthetic, I want to examine the framing of bodily ambiguity from the highly figural and representational to the impossibly abstract. Looking at Saville's epic-scale oil paintings of scarred and surgically altered female bodies from her collection *Territories,* I consider the ways in which this work stretches the epistemology of transgender embodiment from sex reassignment surgeries to the complex project of bodily transformation in general. But I will also consider Hesse's fetishistic latex sculptures from the 1960s that seem to detach organs from bodies altogether, and create technotopic erotics from new configurations of flesh, decay, seriality, and randomness as their forms shift and change over time.[4] And while Volcano's work leads us through a spectacular parade of shape-shifting portraits to convey the instability of even the most deliberately performed gender identity, Besemer's colorful abstractions—her circles, lines, and strokes—will articulate, like Hesse, the formal qualities of perverse and abject gendering. Nicholls's work, like Besemer's, turns to the abstract to represent ambiguity apart from identity, and both Nicholls and Besemer seem to build on the work of the earlier "queer" art practices of Hannah Hoch, Louise Bourgeois, Hesse, and others to place themselves within a discernible genealogy of queer artistic production. Finally, the *Tissue Culture and Art Project* from Perth, Australia, represents "semi-living" objects (some of which the artists refer to as "wetware") as a futuristic vision of in-betweenness, a state between life and death, animate and inanimate, organic and synthetic. Not every artist discussed here sets out to represent transgenderism and yet each project attempts to capture ambiguous states of being that can be summarized as transgender. Much of this artwork conceptualizes embodiment in Butlerian terms as a repetitive series of gestures that in these instances, depict identity as process, mutation, invention, and reconstruction.

Like a sly pun on the meaning of "inversion," Saville's painting of transgender photographer Volcano turns the body inside out, upside down, and forces the viewer to contemplate the image of a man trapped *outside* a woman's body. First you see the genitals, splayed out like a slab of meat on the butcher's block, and then, as your eye travels up the scary and distorted landscape of an ostensibly female body, you come face-to-face with the ruddy and bearded visage of the model, and inevitably, you must now travel back down the pink slopes of breast and belly to see if this head belongs to this vagina. The body is just barely draped over the platform, half on and half off, the head slumped and lifeless, one breast endlessly falling to earth, pulled downward by gravity, and the other breast seemingly moving in some other direction. Body parts hang and droop, smudge and blur, into an approximation of wholeness. The model looks uncomfortable, the viewer shares in his discomfort, and the artist deliberately frames the whole as a study in body dysphoria by calling the picture of the man with a vagina simply *Matrix*, meaning, of course, womb.

In his essay "On Being a Jenny Saville Painting," transgender photographer Volcano discusses the strange "out of body experience" that he had while posing for another artist as a woman. As Saville took pictures of what Volcano calls his "naked and corpulent hybridity," he feared that her photographs and then the final painting might "dislocate and/or diminish my transgendered maleness" (Volcano 1999, 25). Having carefully created and sustained his own "mutant maleness," Volcano feels threatened by the sheer excess of the Saville portrait, its curves and crevices, its gynecological, intrusive gaze. And yet, Volcano's mutant maleness does indeed survive the painting—and it even becomes the very point of the painting, highlighting the drama of a disidentification that can only ever be imperfectly realized. The imperfection of the body is precisely what Saville is drawn to; and in its flawed balance between maleness and femaleness, Volcano's body offers a map of the loss and longing that tinges all *transsexual* attempts to "come home" to the body. But that same map locates the *transgender* body as a paradigm for the impossibility of bodily comfort. Saville's transgender portrait of Volcano, of course, is no more or less grotesque than her other paintings of rearranged female flesh. Whether her female subjects have been surgically altered or simply captured at a particularly undignified angle, female flesh in these paintings just looks excessive and somehow hypernatural. For Saville, femaleness resides in the flesh, but comes apart at the seams, bleeds over the edges of the body, and makes us unsure as to the limits of skin or self. Saville's all-too-fleshly subjects come to be defined by the distortion of the body, its inability to carry the heft of social identity. In many ways, Saville wields her paintbrush as surgeons may manipulate their scalpels. Indeed, her gallery catalog includes an interview with a plastic surgeon whose operating room Saville would visit while completing her paintings (Weintraub 1999, 27). The surgeon comments on the similarities between his manipulations of flesh and Saville's, and calls them both sculptors of human tissue. What the plastic surgeon does not comment on is the obvious difference between his aesthetic project and Saville's. He admits that he works on "youthening" the human face, yet he fails to notice that Saville paints the same subjects not in "before" and "after" modes but in the in-between stages—the transgender stages—of bodily alteration. Saville paints the bloated and bruised face rather than the rearranged and aquiline nose. She captures the intractability of the flesh and its transformation nonetheless; she freeze-frames the catastrophic consequences of surgical intervention, its aftermath rather than its outcome. In this way, her paintbrush is a scalpel digging into messy flesh rather than a suturing device that smoothes over and masks the evidence of intervention. Identity in Saville's paintings of bodies lies in between, and it is captured as a crease in the flesh, an unhealed wound, a scab, a pimple, signs of the skin's rupture. And her painterly gesture, in the end, consists in a refusal to put the unsightly bodies back together again in a pleasingly symmetrical arrangement.

The surgeon and the painter both consider themselves to be sculpting flesh, albeit for different purposes—the surgeon to approach perfection; the painter to disturb it—but both still insist on using the body as the ground or canvas for their new creations. An Australian art research group named SymbioticA has dispensed with the body altogether by making flesh sculptures separate from human bodies. In its *Tissue Culture and Art Project,* the group uses recent medical research into human tissue growth for artistic rather than medical purposes. SymbioticA describes its sculptures as "still in the realm of the symbolic gesture representing a new class of object/being. These objects are partly artificially constructed and partly grown/born. They consist of both synthetic materials and living biological matter from complex organisms."[5]

While medical researchers have to justify their interest in tissue growth by demonstrating the potential for their research to improve the quality of human life, the *Tissue Culture and Art Project* creates a complex set of ethical problems by growing tissue "sculptures" for art's sake. The goal is to create "semi-living objects" and to produce a "new artistic palette."[6] The group does provide an environmental justification for its research, arguing that semi-living objects shift processes of production from manufacturing to growth and therefore "could reduce the environmental problems associated with manufacturing." But mostly the group is interested in creating a "new breed of things," and a new set of relations between humans and inanimate as well as semi-living objects.

Like the transgender person who may desire body modifications without desiring sex reassignment, the tissue sculptures produce spare body parts with no practical use and they eschew the logic of the perfectible body offering instead the body, as mutant form. One project in particular by this group participates in a transgender aesthetic. The *Art(ificial) Womb* project imagines an external womb as a laboratory, and in SymbioticA's version of the womb, the artists "grow modern versions of the legendary Guatemalan Worry Dolls." These dolls are handmade from degradable polymers and surgical sutures. The group describes them in the following terms:

> The dolls were sterilized and seeded with endothelial, muscle, and osteoblast cell (skin, muscle and bone tissue) that are grown over/into the polymers. The polymers degrade as the tissue grows. As a result the dolls become partially alive. . . . The process in which the natural (tissue) takes over the constructed (polymers), is not a "precise" one. New shapes and forms are created in each instance, depending upon many variants such as the type of cells, the rhythm of the polymer degradation and the environment inside the artificial womb (bioreactor). It means that each doll transformation cannot be fully predicted and it is unique to itself. Our "next sex" is still in the realm of a dialogue with nature rather than a complete control over it. Our dolls are not clones but rather unique.[7]

Putting aside for a moment the symbolic or psychological function of the dolls (worry dolls), these semi-living objects, grotesque little conglomerates of plastic and flesh, challenge our usual conceptions of dolls as cuddly and warm, and offer instead something that is hard and wet, but closer to being human because nearly alive. The dolls solicit our emotional investments and they soothe humanist fears over cloning by representing *unique* forms of degradation and decay. In true Frankensteinian form, they are not of woman born and their monstrosity finds expression in echoing the parts of the human (uniqueness, individuality) that humans most fear to lose through technological innovation. The SymbioticA group also creates other monstrous entities through tissue engineering: for example, it grows "unnecessary" animal organs such as pig wings, and is working on a project called *wetware* that merges material grown from fish neurons (wetware) with software and hardware devices. The unpredictability of the behavior of the semi-living objects and the potential relationships that we may form with them, through them, and to them creates a living workshop of bodily mutation and affective adaptation.

The technotopic potential of the semi-living objects has to do with the function and meaning of neo-organs and body bits once they are removed from the frame of the human body. Lifted from this frame, the body bits take on different meaning—while the worry dolls retain a human resemblance, their liveliness resides less in their replication of human form and more in their ability to mimic fleshly processes of decay. We are more used to thinking of mutation as a process that alters the whole body. Transgender photographer Volcano captures both whole body mutation and neo-organ growth in his work. Generally speaking, Volcano explores the contours and erotics of what he calls "sublime mutation" by glorifying bodies and body parts that might otherwise be read as freakish or ugly. His photographs of drag kings and female-to-male transsexuals as well as his self-portraits over the last fifteen years make use of the body as a canvas for spectacular and often highly aestheticized gender transformations. In his collection *Transgenital Landscapes,* however, Volcano specifically focuses on the technotopic project of lovingly fetishizing the testosterone-enhanced clits, the "dick-lits," of FTMs daring the viewer to laugh at or reject the hormonally managed genitalia. Here, a neo-organ is literally grown onto the body and then isolated and eroticized by the photographer, who endows the neo-organ with erotic meaning and creates new gender associations through it.

In other work in *Sublime Mutations* under the heading of "Gender Optional," Volcano performs what Prosser has cleverly called a cross between photography and autobiography: "ph/autography" (Prosser 2000; Volcano 2000). In this series, Volcano leaps from one creation to another, morphing from the sexy Delboy, to an older balding man, and finally to an "androskin" clone. As "Balding Del," Volcano looks sinister, gray, and oddly sick. This photograph belies the myth of testosterone as the wonder drug that imparts sexual energy and new life to the female-to-male transsexual. Here, the testosterone has worked its magic only into a male balding pattern, and the slight sneer on the mutant man's face hints at the "side effects" of becoming male and the new pattern of decay produced through gender transition. Reading Del's mutational self-portraits in relation to the *Tissue Culture and Art Project,* we can reconceptualize the relations between various historically located selves in terms of the ever mutating relations between the polymers and the tissue that we saw in the worry dolls series. Self, in both cases, is a dance of decay and growth. In "Androskin," gender markers are literally removed from the flesh as a platinum head leaps out from a checked background and returns the gaze with a fearful intensity. While "Androskin" refuses to suggest maleness or femaleness in any explicit way, it is not beyond gender or genderless but it does conjure the awful image of the clone that haunted the SymbioticA group's experiments with reproduction. The clone threatens the viewer with the terrifying possibility of reproduction without difference, the replication of the same, the creation of stasis.

In the same book, *Sublime Mutations,* that houses his transgender self-portraits, Volcano explores the multiple mutations of a wide range of transsubjectivities from what are now being called "transsensual femmes" (women who desire trans bodies) to "lesbian boys" and "hermaphrodykes." At the end of the book in a section titled "Simo 2000," Volcano photographs a butch who has appeared many times with Volcano in his earlier work as his hermaphrodyke double (Volcano 2000). Simo, in her solo portraits, bares a body twisted by intense scarring, the aftermath of a brutal accident. While the *Transgenital Landscapes* series shows bodies that have morphed elegantly, almost seamlessly, from female to male, bodies budding micropenises, bodies with neat surgically constructed chests, Simo's torso is contorted and twisted, a turbulent field of trauma, and it appears transformed by its new features, at once new and old. Simo emphasizes her own sense of Baconian grotesqueness in this shot by pulling her face away from the camera with her own hand, marking the ways in which her body has been knocked off its pivot. In another shot, a fetishizing close-up of the scarred belly, a line of sewn flesh proceeds around a distorted navel. The navel sits now atop the distended belly like a new genital, far more compelling, in many ways, than the micropenises—a rude protuberance that in no way mimics the phallus, but that marks this body as literally an assemblage, a rough draft, or skin and tissue pulled together around a literally de-centered self. It is in these portraits more than any others in *Sublime Mutations* that the transgender body approaches sublimity.

"Her scars are my scars," says Volcano when asked about these images, noting a kind of turbulent twinning, which links Volcano's whole but transgender body to Simo's patchwork flesh.[8] In this act of identification, Volcano refuses the traditional divide between artist and object, refuses to take up the position of the look, and allies himself firmly with the damage, trauma, scar. As Amelia Jones notes about Hannah Wilke's grueling self-portraits taken when Wilke was undergoing treatment for lymphoma, artistic acts of radical narcissism "de-objectify" the body, and allow it to express something through pain and sickness (Jones 1998). The self that pain expresses is in trauma and in doubt; but it is also in the grips of a visible process of self-negotiation that can then stand for the many ways in which the flesh roughly encounters a technology that extends, supplants, and distends it. Just as Saville's portraits of cosmetic surgeries reveled in the scars and tracked the lines of the surgeon's intrusion, so these portraits of Simo give us close-ups of the self's improvisation of wholeness. All of these representations of sutured embodiment echo a curious painting of Warhol from 1970 by Alice Neel. Painted a few years after Warhol was shot by Valerie Solanas, Neel captures perfectly Warhol's own understanding of self as a patchwork surface. But notice too how the scars and the hips make this look like a "portrait of the artist" as an old woman. The uncertainty of gender here, the transgender aspect of Warhol, is all the more pronounced for the fact that he is specifically not in drag here but captured for the first and last time, naked. Warhol hated the idea of nakedness, saying, "Nudity is a threat to my existence" (Warhol 1975, 11). Here, his nakedness both undoes him, but also makes him otherwise. Like Saville's mottled bodies and Volcano's portrait of Simo's damaged torso, the representation of the scars on Warhol's body conjures a technotopic body, a body situated in an immediate and visceral relation to the technologies — guns, scalpels, cars, paintbrushes — that have marked, hurt, changed, imprinted, and brutally reconstructed it. Remarkably, in all three instances, the impact of technological intervention is to disrupt gender stability, and so gender ambiguity becomes the sign of other more invasive alterations to the human form.

If we return once more to Saville's paintings, we notice the way Saville also literally paints trauma into and onto the raw flesh; she tattoos the skin with the demands that have been made of it and binds the flesh in its own undergarment. This painting, titled *Trace,* acknowledges how female flesh in particular is already a form of tissue engineering, a culture grown in a lab; Saville's portraits suggest, however, that we should locate femaleness not as the material with which we begin nor as the end product of medical engineering but as a stage and indeed a fleshly place of production. Saville, echoing Chalkley's eerie title, captures beautifully the body on its way to a perfection it can never achieve. And this *Trace* rhymes with the scars Volcano studies obsessively in order to remap the body's erotic potential. Of course, there is nothing so new in and of itself in the representation of the body as a form of montage, collage, assemblage, or aesthetic hybrid. Artists like Hannah Hoch, Louise Bourgeois, and Nancy Grossman have all represented the body, and often the female body at that, as a grotesque but beautiful patchwork of the bodily and the machinic, the fleshly and the metallic, the unfinished, imperfect, and incomplete. Saville, Volcano, and others draw from a vast archive of hybrid images by avant-garde artists, but they address the specific emergence of the transgender body in subcultural terms.

One artist who has proven to be particularly influential on contemporary artists grappling with the dimensions of gender ambiguity in an age of flexibility is the late Hesse; and her work can stand in here for a long tradition of work on embodiment by women that, in a way, predicted the aesthetic and physical phenomenon of transgenderism. Hesse's work, unlike that of her contemporaries, can be considered both modernist and postmodernist: on account of the materials that Hesse used to create her sculptures, her work has entered into a process of decay that has changed its meaning and context, and provided it with a new, if temporary and fleeting, moment of reception. Hesse's work, in fact, gives us access to and puts us in proximity with the primary processes of decay itself. Hesse produced a huge and eclectic body of work at a fever pitch between 1960 and 1970, but died young, tragically, at age thirty-four. She worked in cramped quarters with some extremely toxic materials like latex and fiberglass, which may or may not have contributed to her death from brain cancer. Hesse worked with these toxic materials because she loved their malleability and she experimented widely with their properties.

A retrospective of Hesse's work in 2001 at San Francisco's Museum of Modern Art displayed some pieces from her rapidly decaying collection of sculptures and installations made from latex and fiberglass. Many of the essays in the catalog that accompanied the show and much of the conversation surrounding the show concerned the relationship of the decaying work on display to the original as created and installed by the artist herself. Some commentators, critics, and curators claim that the work has degraded so much that "it is not a work of art any longer" and "it would not be right to show it" (Timpanelli 2002, 295). Others argue in the catalog that the work should be shown in its degraded condition because "it is the contemporary appearance of these works, degraded or not, that has been important and influential for younger artists" (310). Hesse herself was quite aware of the work's fragility and she told one interviewer that she felt guilty about selling works that would not last. But she also stood by her decision to use nonpermanent materials, saying, "Life doesn't last, art doesn't last. It doesn't matter."[9] While Hesse produced her sculptures a good thirty years before Saville, Volcano, and SymbioticA, and while her work must be situated on the cusp between late modernism and early postmodernism, her work becomes significant today precisely because it has aged and decayed over time, and while it may have represented modernist concerns with form and antiform in the 1960s, now it represents postmodern preoccupations with mutation, space, decay, and hybridity. Hesse predicted the evolution of the status of her sculptures over time, and she said: "I would like the work to be non-work. This means it would find its way beyond my preconceptions. . . . It is my main concern to go beyond what I know and what I can know. The formal principles are understandable and understood. It is the unknown quantity from which and where I want to go. As a thing, an object, it accedes to its non-logical self. It is something, it is nothing."[10]

Hesse's installations and sculptures resemble the semi-living objects produced three decades later by the SymbioticA collective, and they achieve the status of animation because they are actively eroding, rotting, and transforming. *Contingent* features material dipped in latex that would have glowed amber and caught the light when originally displayed, but that later became rigid and began to disintegrate. The title of the piece itself conveys the conditional and fragile status of the work. These latex works by Hesse also prefigure Saville's attempt to capture the in-betweenness of identity, which for Saville is captured in bodily trauma, but that Hesse constructs through the work of "salvage." Briony Fer in "The Work of Salvage" has called attention to this activity of salvaging in Hesse's opus, noting that she was an artist who worked with the very materials that other artists would discard after creating a sculpture. "Salvage," writes Fer, "is what binds together the two aspects of Hesse's procedure, the undoing and the layering. But it is a kind of salvage that is permanently incomplete" (Fer 2002, 85–86).

And finally, Hesse's work echoes all the other work we have looked at so far, but particularly Volcano's, in terms of her fetishistic practice of detaching organs from bodies. Hesse's work veers back and forth between the abstraction of layers and boxes to material representations of odd organic shapes—balls, breasts, and penises (often bent or in pieces) as well as intestines. In *Ringaround Rosie,* the abstract and the literal come together and form two neat circles, slightly raised from the canvas; this relief with rope coiled around it produces the effect of a cross section of embodiment and again a neo-organ, detached from any recognizable body and representing the impact of detachability itself. As Hesse said of the circles she obsessively produced, "I think that there is a time element. I think that was the sequence of change and maturation" (Nemser 1970, 8). Hesse's work, in some sense, is all about temporality, but not in a conventional way; not in terms of placing herself in a tradition or racing with time. Hesse places herself quite firmly at odds with time, tradition, and futurity. She wrote in her diaries that painting had too much to do with being placed within a tradition or art history; she avoided painting, and turned to reliefs, sculptures, and serial projects in order to escape the notion of progressive order: "Making art. 'Painting a painting.' The Art, the history, the tradition, is too much there. I want to be surprised, to find something new. I don't want to know the answer before but want an answer that can surprise."[11]

Because they change over time and reproduce the process of fleshly decay, Hesse's sculptures emphasize what is to be gained in moving away from both hyperabstract and hyperrealist images of the body in order to explore gendered subjectivity as a set of dislocated experiences. While representational art pins bodily ambiguity to this or that subject, abstract forms lose a connection to any specific subjectivity at all. Hesse steered a course between the figural and the abstract, making process itself into the form. In this way, she was able to make the provisionality of identity, subjectivity, and gender a universal or at least generalizable condition. A contemporary artist, much influenced by Hesse, who creates abstract representations of gender indeterminacy and who locates her aesthetic in the process of detachability is California-based painter Besemer. In her huge installation paintings of circles, slabs, and folds, Besemer seems at first glance to be saying little about the postmodern body, with its transitivities and traumas. The clean lines of the circles hint at perfection and a little bit more, but still bear the marks of a faint smudging effect that troubles the spiral and flirts with the flaw. Like Hesse, Besemer invests in the circle in order to trouble its symbolic representation of life cycles, progress, and development. While Hesse built the flaw into her work through her choice of material, Besemer marks the flaws on the very surfaces of her art, elevating the flaw, the queer, and the trouble to the level of form.

In her slabs, Besemer seems, again like Hesse, to have dispensed even with the canvas itself. Here we see paint layered on paint; no longer anchored to a pliant and absorbent canvas, the paint announces its own artifice, detachability, and even performativity. And by calling attention to the act of painting itself as a gesture that has left the canvas behind, Besemer rescripts the traditionally gendered relationship between figure and ground that locates the canvas as female body and the brushstroke as male genius. While for Jackson Pollack, the paint and the paintbrush represent the exertion of a phallic will, for Besemer, the paint, the canvas, the stroke, and even the brush all come apart in unnerving ways, allowing for the prosthetic essence of the brush to surface. In her paintings titled *Detachable Strokes,* we see the logical culmination of Besemer's method of peeling dried paint off of glass and mounting it directly onto the gallery wall. The sturdy thickness of the paint, its ability to stand alone, as it were, its distinctive folds as it hits the gallery floor, all suggest the plasticity of the paint and its remarkably controlled flow. Here, the paint does not spurt or splatter as in a Pollack piece; rather, like Hesse's art sculptures, it refuses to be absorbed into the softness of the canvas, and it deliberately ignores the boundary between wall and floor, plaster and wood. This paint is defined by its transferability and the way it bears the imprint of the brush, but circulates apart from the brush and makes a canvas of whatever material is at hand.

But Besemer's paint sculptures announce their affiliation with artifice through more than just their materiality; the colorfulness of the paintings also announces a gleeful refusal of the grim monochromatic palette of minimalism. In a study of the ways in which color, bright color, has been devalued in Western art, and particularly in modernism, David Batchelor writes:

> It is, I believe, no exaggeration, to say that, in the West, since Antiquity, colour has been systematically marginalized, reviled, diminished and degraded. Generations of philosophers, artists, art historians and cultural theorists of one stripe or another have kept this prejudice alive, warm, fed and groomed. As with all prejudices, its manifest form, its loathing, masks a fear: a fear of contamination and corruption by something that is unknown or appears unknowable. This loathing of colour, this fear of corruption through colour, needs a name: chromophobia. (Batchelor 2000, 22)

JA Nicholls, *in another place,* 2000, oil on canvas, 102 x 152 in. Printed by permission of the artist.

Brian Dawn Chalkley, still from *I probably want perfection in everything and a little more. Maybe that'll be my downfall.* Printed by permission of the artist.

Jenny Saville, *Matrix,* 1999, oil on canvas, 84 x 120 in. Printed by permission of the artist.

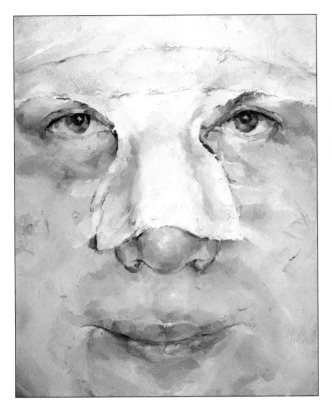

Jenny Saville, *Cindy*, 1993, oil on canvas, 22 x 18 in. Printed by permission of the artist.

Jenny Saville, *Knead*, 1994, oil on canvas, 60 x 72 in. Printed by permission of the artist.

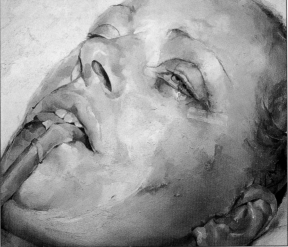

Del LaGrace Volcano, "Cooper," 1999, *The Drag King Book*. Printed by permission of the artist.

Del LaGrace Volcano, "Crevice," 2000, *Sublime Mutations.* Printed by permission of the artist.

Del LaGrace Volcano, "Delboy,"
2001, *Sublime Mutations*. Printed
by permission of the artist.

Del LaGrace Volcano, "Balding
Del," 2001, *Sublime Mutations*.
Printed by permission of the
artist.

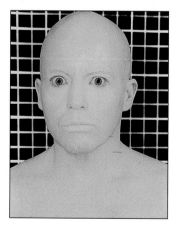

Del LaGrace Volcano, "Androskin,"
2001, *Sublime Mutations*. Printed
by permission of the artist.

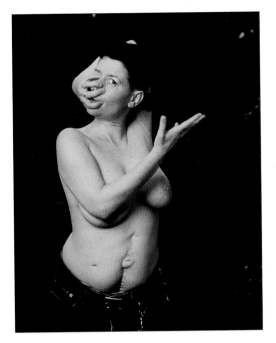

Del LaGrace Volcano, "Trauma,"
2001, *Sublime Mutations*. Printed
by permission of the artist.

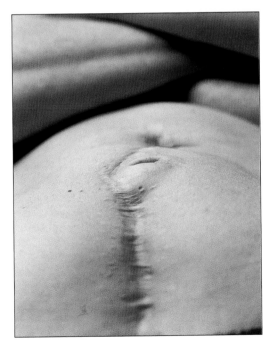

Del LaGrace Volcano, "Scar,"
2001, *Sublime Mutations*. Printed
by permission of the artist.

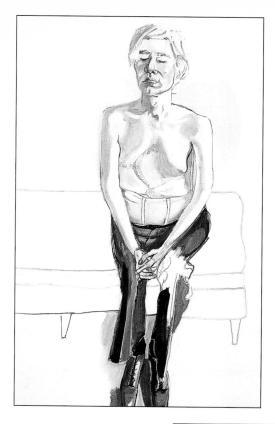

Alice Neel, *Andy Warhol,* 1970, oil on canvas, 40 x 60 in. Whitney Museum of Art.

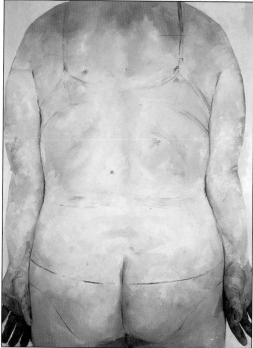

Jenny Saville, *Trace,* 1993/4, oil on canvas, 84 x 72 in. Printed by permission of the artist.

Eva Hesse, "Augment in Decay," 2002. From *Eva Hesse,* ed. Elisabeth Sussman.
Copyright The Estate of Eva Hesse Zurich/London.

Eva Hesse, *Contingent,* 1968–9,
fiberglass, latex, cheesecloth.
Copyright The Estate of Eva Hesse
Zurich/London.

88. 1965-66 sculpture photographed in Hesse's Bowery studio.

Eva Hesse, "Bowery Studio View," 1965–6, mixed media. Copyright The Estate of Eva Hesse Zurich/London.

Eva Hesse, *Ringaround Arosie*, 1965, pencil, acetone, varish, enamel, paint, ink, and cloth-covered electrical wire on papier-mâché and masonite. Copyright The Estate of Eva Hesse Zurich/London.

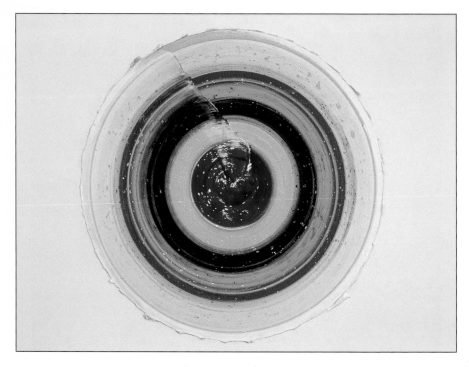

Linda Besemer, *Circle #1*, 1996, pure acrylic paint. Printed by permission of the artist.

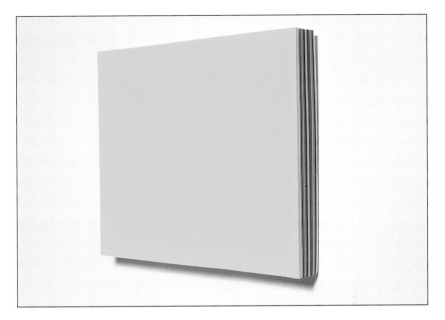

Linda Besemer, *Slab #8,* 1999, solid slab of consecutive layers of acrylic paint. Printed by permission of the artist.

Linda Besemer, *Detachable Stroke #1,* 1993, acrylic paint. Printed by permission of the artist.

Linda Besemer, *Detachable Stroke #9,* detail, 1993. Printed by permission of the artist.

Linda Besemer, *Large Zip Fold,* 2002, acrylic paint, fiberglass, aluminum. Printed by permission of the artist.

Linda Besemer, *Tall Girl,* 1994, acrylic paint. Printed by permission of the artist.

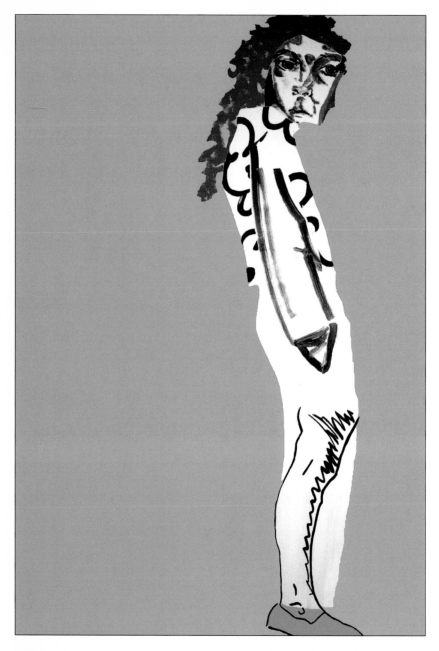

JA Nicholls, *let me be,* 2001, oil on canvas, 108 x 84 in. Printed by permission of the artist.

In the world of painting, color, as Batchelor implies, sparks irrational responses that mirror homophobic responses. If straightness (masculinity in particular) is associated with minimalism, then excess (of form, color, or content) becomes the signification of the feminine, the queer, and the monstrous. In a published conversation titled "Too Colorful" between Besemer and Batchelor that accompanies the catalog for Besemer's exhibition in 2002 at Cohan, Leslie, and Browne, the two artists discuss color, formalism, plasticity, and painting. Batchelor notes that "any art that craves respectability will have a problem with color" and that this has to do with color's relationship to language (Batchelor 2002, 20). To the extent that abstract work, in other words, is about the art practice itself and wants to avoid being subordinated to the literary, intense color must be avoided; intense color speaks, it adorns, it brings the artwork dangerously close to the feminine and decorative. Besemer confirms that she is interested in excessive and vivid color, and she associates formalism not simply with the retreat from language and ideology but with "non-narrative." Besemer says, "I was always taken by Meyer Shapiro's idea of the non-narrative. Unlike Greenberg, Shapiro did not see abstraction as a transcendent, apolitical or 'purely formalist' art form. Rather he viewed 'Abstract Expressionism' as a salient critique of a burgeoning post-war industrial culture" (20). Besemer uses color and her plastic forms to reclaim formalism for a queer artmaking practice and to adapt the nonnarrative potential of abstract art into an oppositional practice.

Besemer's attempt to find a place for her work in the tradition of abstract art acknowledges the ways in which queer artists, feminist artists, and artists of color have been left outside of art history canons. As Ann Eden Gibson notes in her history of the "other politics" of abstract expressionism, this happens subtly and overtly in art history narratives. Sometimes, marginality itself has been claimed by the canonical artists, leaving no room for "disenfranchised groups to affirm their difference" (Gibson 1997). At other times, the explicitly political nature of the work of disenfranchised artists would disqualify that work from the category of "universal." Finally, once universality has been defined in relation to the aesthetic practices of a group of elite artists, all other artists are cast as unoriginal. As Gibson summarizes it, "To the extent that the work of an artist who is not in the canon looks like that of one who is, the noncanonical artist's work is derivative. To the extent that the noncanonical work does not resemble that in the canon, the contending work is not Abstract Expressionist." With such methods of evaluation, historical narration, and aesthetic selection in play, queer traditions, as Richard

Meyer's *Outlaw Representation* has brilliantly shown, have to be excavated, restored, invented, and imagined (Meyer 2002).

In her work, Besemer uses nonnarrative abstract forms in order to circumvent the imperative on the female artist to tell stories, to narrate self, and to reveal psychology. She playfully flirts with "feminine" arts and crafts forms in her large textilelike paintings, and yet she uses her rigorously formalist compositions to comment on the folly of essentialism. Both Besemer and Batchelor embrace a return to abstraction as a way of resisting the binary opposition between abstract and conceptual art, and they turn a genre that has been historically hostile to marginalized artists into a postmodern location for artistic practices associated with color, plasticity, and repetition. Hesse and, then following her example, Besemer both invest heavily in the notion of seriality, and it is this temporal construct that marks the distinction between the art traditions tracked by conservative cultural critics like T. S. Eliot or Greenberg and Marxist critics like Jameson and Harvey, and those that must be pieced together in more haphazard and productively random ways. While conservative and Marxist critics chart art traditions and narrate a history that is properly cyclic, progressive, and yet marked by ruptures and breaks as an innovator or genius male does the work of interrupting the cycle and beginning a new one, queer and feminist art histories are produced through seriality, repetition, absurdity, and anomaly. Hesse elevated repetition to the level of structure in her work and she talked about it as obsessive. When asked why she repeats a form over and over, Hesse responded, "Because it exaggerates. If something is meaningful, maybe it's more meaningful said ten times. It's not just an aesthetic choice. If something is absurd, it's much more greatly exaggerated, absurd, if it's repeated" (Nemser 1970, 11). Repetition, after Butler's work on performativity, has taken on the status of queer method in postmodernism, and so Hesse's prescient comments about repetition and seriality outline the terms of a queer practice to come. In Besemer's work, repetition becomes performance; circles and slabs are detachable paint sculptures, and they are numbered and labeled in order to place the objects in relation without implying advancement. In their art practices, both Hesse and Besemer convey performance but not maturation, mobility but not progress, change and transformation but not rupture and newness. Besemer sees herself as quoting Hesse, not only through the repetition of forms, but also in her blurring of the boundaries between painting and sculpture. Besemer explains that "Hesse's famous 'Hang Up' and really all the floor-wall pieces have had a great impact on me. I particularly love the resin

Judd-like pieces which run the wall down to the floor. I like the symbiosis of geometric and organic forms, the translucency of the resin, and as you [Batchelor] say its 'flexibility'—particularly as it relates a condition of gravity in the pieces" (Batchelor 2002, 22).

The intersection of flexibility and seriality thus becomes a way of allowing the paint sculptures to comment on, indeed participate in, definitions of bodilyness in postmodernism—the flexibility of the paint, its plasticity, gives it a utopian sense of pliability that is captured in Besemer's "sheets" as a fold. The fold promises unlimited pliancy, but actually delivers elasticity only within a constrained and bounded space. The zip fold flows onto the floor from the wall; it seems to refuse containment altogether and yet it is held motionless by nearly invisible supports, by the fold between the wall and the floor, by gravity itself. Thus, Besemer eloquently captures the precise formal coordinates of the transgender body—pliant to a point, flexible within limits, constrained by language, articulation, and gesture. But as if to immediately refute the limits placed on form, one final detachable stroke defies even gravity. Besemer has said of her *Tall Girl* painting: "I attached and reattached my strokes to various architectural environments. . . . This painting I titled *Tall Girl* to literally describe the way the painting is too tall for the architecture."[12] The painting, she also says, represents a female who exceeds the boundaries of the structures put in place to accommodate her. *Tall Girl* slips onto the ceiling and dangles above the floor, thereby calling into question the rightness of the four walls that mark the gallery space. Here we come face-to-face with the subject, the tall girl or large woman or male-to-female transvestite, who exceeds the new architectures that baffled Jameson, and who has grown new organs and expanded the body to meet the "impossible dimensions" of postmodernism itself. Besemer's wry formalist paintings offer both a realistic look at the dimensions of flexibility and a utopian vision of genders without sexes; they beckon and seduce the viewer with the clean, precise, and pure abstractions of flesh into paint while constructing, in Besemer's words, "a recipe of 'purity' which is wholly impure" (Batchelor 2002).

"Let me be"

Nicholls's large painting *let me be* echoes the sense of excess in Besemer's *Tall Girl*. Her tall figure threatens, like Alice in Wonderland, to grow beyond the framework of the painting, to crawl off the canvas and onto the wall. S/he also threatens the viewer with the sheer size of her body, and this body also lounges against the deep empty space filling the rest of the canvas. Nicholls finds an interesting place somewhere between figural and abstract to launch a new chapter in transgender aesthetics—one in which the abstract and the figural are not binary opposites but where they inhabit the same space at the same time, letting us know what it means to live in a queer time and place. This chapter has traced a postmodern aesthetic through eccentric and extravagant representations of the body, body parts, neo-organs, and trans bodies. I have used the term technotopia, or technotopic, to refer to the spatial dimensions of this aesthetic, its preoccupation with the body as a site created through technological and aesthetic innovation. Technotopic inventions of the body resist idealizations of bodily integrity, on the one hand, and rationalizations of its disintegration, on the other; instead, they represent identity through decay, detachability, and subjectivity in terms of what Hesse referred to as "the non-logical self." The transgender form becomes the most clear and compelling representation of our contemporary state of permanent dislocation. Semi-living objects, semi-dying art pieces, and semi-coherent human bodies express and condense the set of relations that Jameson referred to as postmodern; but while he feared the loss of historicity, the waning of affect, and the decline of the masterwork, these "nonworks" remind us that political defiance in late capitalism has a powerful place, takes unexpected forms, and hides out in the seemingly superficial and ludic forms of experimentation that have been dismissed as a form of superficial body politics. Superficiality, Besemer's and Nicholls's work suggests, may not be a symptom of a diseased political culture but a marvelously flat and uninhibited repudiation of the normativity inherent in "deep" political projects.

6

Oh Behave!

Austin Powers and the Drag Kings

That ain't no woman! It's a man, man!

—Austin Powers

There has been much ink spilled in popular media and popular queer culture about the intimate relations shared between gay men and straight women. The "fag hag" role has indeed become a staple of popular film, and at least part of the explanation for how gay male culture and gay male images have so thoroughly penetrated popular film and television cultures has to do with the recognized and lived experience of bonds between "queens" and "girls."[1] New bonds on television between gay men and straight men (*Queer Eye for the Straight Guy* and *Boy Meets Boy*) only solidify a general recognition of the important contributions made by gay white men to popular culture. Still, there is no such recognition of the influence of lesbian queer culture, and there is no relationship between lesbians and straight men that parallels the bonds between "fags" and their "hags." While the structure of the dynamic between lesbians and hetero-males could change significantly in the next few decades as more and more lesbians become parents and raise sons, for the moment there seem to be no sitcoms on the horizon ready to exploit the humorous possibilities of interactions between a masculine woman and her butch guy pal or set to send five dykes to "makeover" some unsuspecting heterosexual guy or gal. This is not to say that no relations exist between the way lesbians produce and circulate cultures of masculinity and the way men do. These relations, however, are for the most part submerged, mediated, and difficult to read.

This chapter recognizes that masculinity has become a hot topic in recent years for both scholars and journalists, but that popular culture continues to protect the essential bond between masculinity and men. Any number of writers claim now to be examining a current "crisis" in masculinity, and in both the United States and England, articles appear regularly in leading newspapers asking questions about male violence, the difficulties faced by parents raising male children, and the long-term effects of changing conceptions of manliness. As another indication of the popular appeal of masculinity in the 1990s, Susan Faludi's book *Stiffed: The Betrayal of the American Man* received widespread attention, and was lauded for its attempt to address the trials and the tribulations as well as the power and the glory of contemporary manhood (Faludi 1999). In academia, there are journals and book series given over to the study of men, male bodies, and masculinities; furthermore, there are numerous new titles in the burgeoning field of "men's studies." Unfortunately, in this flurry of media interest and scholarly work on dominant maleness and its crises, almost no attention has been paid to the way that the crisis produces its own solution in terms of alternative forms of masculinity. All too often, solutions for the crisis of white male masculinity are proffered in terms of the shoring up of that same form of manhood; real solutions have to be sought out in the minority masculinities that flourish in the wake of dominant masculinity's decline.

As an example of the limited ways in which we approach the crisis of dominant masculinity in the United States, we can turn the series of school yard shootings by white boys in the 1990s—in Arkansas and Colorado most prominently—that rocked the nation and may have had some connection to the escalation of hate crimes toward gays, lesbians, and transgender people, particularly in rural areas. Much of the popular coverage of these seemingly random events asked broad questions about gun control, violence in video games, and the breakdown of the family, but few critics thought to interrogate the construction of adolescent white hetero-masculinity itself. In fact, only rarely were these violent crimes specifically attributed to white boys or white men. More often, school shootings and hate crimes are depicted as random attacks by disparate individuals. While obviously it does not make sense to simply demonize young white men as a group, we should be asking some hard questions about the forms of white masculinity that we encourage and cultivate in this society. I believe that the rise of alternative models of masculinity within gay, lesbian, and transsexual communities in this century has been part of an ongoing interrogation of models of manhood that were previously viewed as "natural," "unimpeachable," and even "inevitable." These alternative masculinities, moreover, have long histories and have spawned potent subcultures. Very little time or scholarship, however, has been devoted to recording and documenting the shape and the narratives of these subcultures. For this reason, few mainstream critics think to look to those subcultural histories when searching for answers to the problem of white male violence.

This chapter traces the strange and barely discernible influence of lesbian drag king cultures on hetero-male comic film. My contention throughout will be not that straight men learn how to parody masculinity from butch women and then take that parody to the bank; rather, I will be trying to map circuits of subcultural influence across a wide range of textual play. I take for granted Dick Hebdige's formulation in *Subculture: The Meaning of Style* of subcultures as marginalized cultures that are quickly absorbed by capitalism and then robbed of their oppositional power, but I will expand on Hebdige's influential reading of subcultures by arguing that some subcultures do not simply fade away as soon as they have been mined and plundered for material (Hebdige 1979). Furthermore, I emphasize the utility in tracking precisely when, where, and how the subculture is "beamed up" into the mainstream. Tracing the mysterious process by which, say, a performance in a queer nightclub, a genre of queer humor, or a specific mode of parody has been observed, appreciated, and then reproduced is not simple, and has much to offer future studies of the ever more complex lines of affiliation between the marginal and the dominant. One obvious way to trace the difference between the dominant and the marginal in this instance is to see who becomes rich from certain performances of male parody and who never materially benefits at all. And yet, profit is not ultimately the best gauge of success, and it may well be that by tracing a cultural phenomenon back to its source, we restore a different kind of prestige to the subculture and honor its creativity in the process.

King Comedies

Nineteen ninety-seven was a banner year for abject English masculinity films—*The Full Monty* (directed by Peter Catteneo) and *Austin Powers* (directed by Jay Roach) both took U.S. audiences by surprise. *The Full Monty,* for example, was made for only $3 million, but within a few months it had made twice that at the box office. Both of these "king comedies," as I like to call them—using king as a more precise term than camp—were built around the surprising vulnerabilities of the English male body and psyche. Indeed, the king comedy as a genre attempts to exploit not the power but the frailty of the male body for the purpose of generating laughs that come at the hero's expense. King comedies also capitalize on the humor that comes from revealing the derivative nature of dominant masculinities, and so it trades heavily in tropes of doubling, disguise, and impersonation. So while *Austin Powers* parodically reenacts a long tradition of secret agent films, raiding the coffers of sexist British humor from *Benny Hill* to the *Carry On* comedies, *The Full Monty* forces its lads to relearn masculinity the hard way—from women.

What models of masculinity do *Austin Powers* and *The Full Monty* draw on? What is their appeal to U.S. audiences in particular, and what vision of Englishness and English manliness circulate through these very different comedies? Furthermore, what cultural changes have allowed for mainstream parodies of dominant masculinity in the 1990s? What are the main features of the king comedy genre, and what kinds of subcultural histories go into this particular form of humor? Can we read kinging and king comedy as an equivalent for camp? If camp, on some level, describes an ironic relation between femaleness and the performance of femininity, can king describe the distance between maleness and the performance of masculinity in comic terms?

King comedies emerge out of specific traditions of masculine humor, but in their present incarnation they can also be linked to the recent explosion of active drag king cultures. Not surprisingly, mainstream comedies about masculinity never do articulate their indebtedness to these subcultural and queer comedic representations; accordingly, we have to re-create and actively imagine the possible routes of transmission that carry drag king humor from the queer club to the mainstream teen boy blockbuster movie. In his book *Disidentifications,* Jose E. Muñoz allows for such re-creations of routes of transmission by way of the term counterpublics: for Muñoz, counterpublics are "communities and relational chains of resistance that contest the dominant public sphere" (Muñoz 1999, 146). Counterpublics, in Muñoz's work on performances by queers of color, validate and produce minoritarian public spheres while at the same time offering a potent challenge to the white heteronormativity of majoritarian public spheres. Drag king culture, I believe, constitutes just such a counterpublic space where white and heteronormative masculinities can be contested, and where minority masculinities can be produced, validated, fleshed out, and celebrated.

In my work on drag kings, I have tried to identify the specificity of drag king acts and distinguish them from drag queen acts by using the term kinging. As I explain in my drag king chapter of *Female Masculinity,* to king a role can involve a number of different modes of performance from earnest repetition to hyperbolic re-creation, and from quiet understatement to theatrical layering (Halberstam 1998). My hope was there, and remains here, that we can recognize a particular kind of cultural work that takes place in drag king performances that is not exactly commensurate with what we call camp and yet has similar effects. Camp has been written about widely as a critical comic style deployed by Euro-American gay male and drag queen cultures, but present in other nongay cultural forms. Esther Newton, in particular, in *Mother Camp* traces camp back to drag queen performances where specific use is made of "incongruity, theater and humor" to denaturalize gender (Newton 1979, 106). Obviously, while camp may have originated in and be particular to drag queen cultures, it also travels as a cultural style, and allows for a gay counterpublic site to influence and ironize the depiction of femininity in mainstream venues. In other words, in the same way that camp shows up in many sites that are not gay as an aesthetic mode detached from one particular identity, so we might expect kinging to exceed the boundaries of lesbian and transgender subcultures and circulate independently of the drag king act itself. In relation to the king comedies, we need not trace one-to-one instances of transmission between drag king cultures and filmmakers and producers; what we can trace, however, is a particular kingy effect within otherwise mainstream representations.

We find moments of king humor in both auteur comedy (Jerry Lewis or Woody Allen) and ensemble comedy featuring a comic duo or trio (Abbot and Costello, Laurel and Hardy, the Marx Brothers); in each case, male fragility or male stupidity has been tapped as a primary source of humor. In much male comedy, indeed, a weak or vulnerable male is paired with a more robust specimen of manhood. Sometimes—as in Laurel and Hardy, say— both forms of manhood are shown to be lacking and futile, but often—as in a Jerry Lewis and Dean Martin routine—the bumbling guy makes the straight guy less formal and the straight guy makes his idiot companion more appealing. And sometimes, it is difficult to see or appreciate the kingy effect of the classic comedy act until it is reproduced in a counterpublic sphere. So, for example, Laurel and Hardy may not immediately shout male parody, and yet, when we see Beryl Reid and Susannah York dressing up as Laurel and Hardy in *The Killing of Sister George,* the kingy effect comes to the surface. In much the same way as the image of a gay man impersonating Bette Davis makes Davis herself into a camp icon, so the image of lesbians impersonating Laurel and Hardy can transform them into king icons.

Del LaGrace Volcano, "Mo B. Dick with Muscles," 1999, *The Drag King Book*. Printed by permission of the artist.

Whereas camp reads dominant culture at a slant and mimics dominant forms of femininity to produce and ratify alternative drag femininities that revel in irony, sarcasm, inversion, and insult, kinging reads dominant male masculinity and explodes its effects through exaggeration, parody, and earnest mimicry. It may be helpful to use some images to establish some of the methods of drag king performance. In "Mo B. Dick with Muscles," Volcano's photographic method allows us to visualize the drag king technique of "de-authentication." The mirror scene is one that Volcano returns to repeatedly in his work. Here, the mirror is a clue that what you are looking at is not to be read as real, and yet the image itself of Mo B. flexing is a classic pose of authenticity. The muscle pose is complemented by the basketball T-shirt, but even as the shirt affirms maleness, seemingly it also deconstructs it because "DRAG KING" is inscribed across the back. As the viewer searches for clues as to the "authentic gender" of the body in sight, the photograph frames the project of authenticity as flawed and unproductive. Instead, Volcano revels in the proliferation of clues and red herrings all in the same location.

Another strategy favored by Volcano can be called "masculine supplementarity." Now we move from the drag king and his mirrored self to the drag king coupled with what could be a drag queen or a bio-woman in Volcano's "Tits and Tomcat." The "tits" on the "woman" here both affirm and destabilize Tomcat's masculinity. On the one hand, they allow us to see him as obviously not female, but on the other hand, his size in relation to the much larger female allows him to be read as not male. Ultimately, however, the woman's hyperfemininity *lends* the drag king any masculinity that his own image lacks and indeed supplements his masculinity. In many ways, the contrast between Mike Myers and Elizabeth Hurley as Austin Powers and Vanessa Kensington, respectively, in *Austin Powers: International Man of Mystery* depends on masculine supplementarity. He anxiously announces and emphasizes his masculinity even as she towers over him and makes visible his masculine lack. Powers's lack of sex appeal is supplemented and veiled by Vanessa's desire *nonetheless*.

Del LaGrace Volcano, "Tits and Tomcat," 1999, *The Drag King Book*. **Printed by permission of the artist.**

Del LaGrace Volcano, "The Geezers: Double the Trouble," 1999, *The Drag King Book*. Printed by permission of the artist.

Here one drag king is coupled with another in order to enhance or emphasize the realness of the drag masculinity. Doubling, as we will see, is a major trope in *Austin Powers,* and in both the dominant and the subcultural arenas, masculine doubling invokes a homoerotic aesthetic. Doubling, however, is different from cloning or impersonating—white masculinity in particular becomes more performative when it is not simply multiplied but, as we see here in "Elvis Herselvis and Elvis Herselvis Impersonator," replicated imperfectly. We might consider the Mini Me clone in *Austin Powers 2* as the mainstream version of this standard drag king move whereby a form of masculinity, which is already defined in terms of impersonation (Elvis), is impersonated. Finally, I want to name one last drag king strategy of masculine performance: indexical representation. Volcano's cover for *The Drag King Book*, a photo titled "Duke: King of the Hill" (in chapter 5), uses one of the "realness" kings as a cover and as *the* cover. Without the title that runs across his middle, viewers would not know that this masculine icon was a king—so we can refer to a strategy of indexical naming that reminds viewers or readers at various moments that they are watching or viewing a representation of a representation. Mike Myers uses precisely this mode of indexing in a clever sight gag in *Austin Powers*. In this scene, Austin walks around a room nude while Vanessa, seated in the foreground and oblivious to his presence, holds up various objects (a sausage, a magnifying glass, a pen) that simultaneously conceal and prosthetically extend his penis. In this penis concealment/replacement sequence, the naked body of the male is both on display and under construction; while the gaze of the camera at Austin's nude body should confirm at least that this body is phallic, in fact, once again it suggests that the body requires a prosthetic supplement. Like the drag king strip act that culminates in the exposure of not the female body but the dildo, this scene suggests that masculinity and indeed maleness are no less constructed on the body than in the clothing.

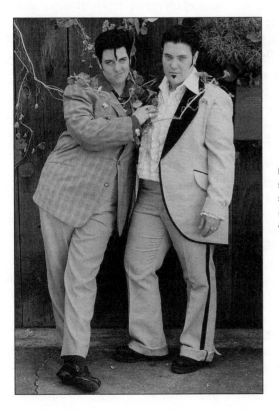

Del LaGrace Volcano, "Elvis Herselvis and Elvis Herselvis Impersonator," 1999, *The Drag King Book*. Printed by permission of the artist.

Drag king parodies of particularly white masculinity are perhaps the most popular form of drag king performance at present. In the past, male impersonation might have been much more oriented toward the production of an effect of male credibility (Storme Delaverie of the Jewel Box Revue, for example); but the most recent wave of drag king cultures has reveled in the humor of male mimicry and the power of male parody. At a drag king show nowadays, spectators will see comedic acts outnumbering sexy acts ten to one, and while certainly this has something to do with the influence of drag queen models of camp performance, it also seems to appeal to the spectators' desire for a deconstruction of maleness rather than a reconstruction of masculinity elsewhere. Much of the humor of these parodies will revolve around exposing the dated look of latter-day sex gods (like Tom Jones, Elvis, or Donny Osmond), and emphasizing the prosthetic nature of male sexual appeal by using overstuffed crotches, chest rugs, and wigs.

In my own work on female masculinity, I have tried to provide full accounts of the histories, forms, and cultures of these so-called counterfeit masculinities—masculinities that are produced subculturally, and that challenge the primacy, authenticity, and originality of dominant masculinities—and I want to continue that work here by tracking the effect of the rise of mimic genders on those bodies that still imagine themselves to be original. So while we may grant the reversal of original and copy in queer theoretical formulations of heterosexuality and homosexuality, the question I want to tackle here is how do drag king performances (copies, supposedly) influence the representation of male performativity (original, supposedly)?

Drag king shows draw large crowds of both straight and gay spectators, and they have also attracted quite a bit of media interest. Mainstream magazine articles on drag kings have commented on the altogether unusual and hilarious spectacle of ridicule directed at dominant masculinity; and yet the general interest shown in drag king theater has not translated into anything like mainstream visibility. Drag king shows and clubs may well have been a fixture in places like New York City and San Francisco for well over five years now, but there still seems to be little market beyond the lesbian club circuit for the parodies of male midlife crisis, the performances of bloated male pride, and the drag king stand-up comedy routines. The reverse sexism of the drag king shows has, not surprisingly, simply failed to sell. But while marketing people presume that mainstream audiences will not tolerate the active ridicule of male sex symbols by queer male impersonators, there is no such assumption made about the appeal of men parodying masculinity. Of course, the tolerance for male parodies of masculinity depends on a long history of male comedy within which male insufficiency is first played for laughs and then rescued from a future of constant boyhood or else explicit effeminacy by the mechanism of compulsory heterosexuality. The transition from being an inadequate, but humorous boy to becoming a sufficient and funny man is made by coding humor as either an intellectual skill (as in Woody Allen films, for example) or a mark of attractive male vulnerability (as in Jerry Lewis films). In the new king comedies, however, humor is neither a skill nor a gift; rather, it is an effective tool for exposing the constructedness of male masculinity.

Many of the king comedies in the theaters today, oddly, seem to have learned some lessons in gender trouble and even show signs of recognizing what students in cultural studies programs across the country already know so well—namely, that in Butler's influential formulation, gender functions as a "copy with no original" (Butler 1991, 21). While this phrase has become a standard academic formulation for rethinking the relations between heterosexual and homosexual embodiment and performance in the late twentieth century, we may still be a little shocked to find evidence of a self-conscious recognition of performativity in mainstream culture itself. Still, the king comedies that I am most interested in here all show dominant masculinity to be the product of repeated and scripted motions; and furthermore, they highlight the ways in which most masculinity copies and models itself on some impossible ideal that it can never replicate.

The king comedy derives much of its humor from an emphasis on small penises and a general concern with male anxiety and fragility. In this respect, it seems to call for a psychoanalytic reading. And yet while psychoanalysis has usefully detailed the forms and methods of male empowerment, only rarely does it provide tools for the examination of male vulnerability. Because of the emphasis on the drama of castration in psychoanalysis, we are left with remarkably limited and humorless ways of thinking about male vulnerability. Indeed, within a phallic economy, one either has the phallus or lacks it; one either masters castration anxiety or is mastered by it. In either case, the drama of castration is tragic rather than comic. The king comedy, however, takes castration anxiety to new levels or new depths rather, and in the process, manages to find and produce more nuanced models of male masculinity. The king comedy, for example, may build on not castration but phallic renunciation, and much of its humor may well derive from exposing the elaborate mechanisms that prop up seemingly normative masculinity.

Traditional psychoanalytic formulations of male comedy tend to read the comic male body as tainted by fallibility and femininity. The funny man, in other words, has often been marked in explicit ways as simply hysterical in all senses of the word. The comic hero, think here of Jerry Lewis, is some combination of twitches and spasms, pratfalls and stutters; he spits, trips, cries, and screams. And yet by marking the funny man as flawed and hysterical, instead of seductive and hyperbolic, say, we simply read him back into that phallic economy of having or lacking.

Psychoanalytic critics talk about masculine comedy in terms of oedipal and pre-oedipal genres. In an oedipal comedy, the overgrown boy (think here of Jim Carey or Adam Sandler) resists adult manhood and indeed seems inadequate to its demands. The plot involves the boy's accession to maturity, which is marked by the beginning of a heterosexual romance with an acceptable female love object; the love object may find the funny boy humorous but not ridiculous, and this distinction allows him access to the illusion of mastery. Pre-oedipal comedy, on the other hand, tends to avoid excessive individuation and revel in the farcical humor of undirected play—the keystone cops and Buster Keaton are some examples of this kind of comedy, which almost refuses narrative coherence.[2] The king comedies actively resist, in various ways, the narrative conditions of both oedipal and pre-oedipal comic conventions. In *Austin Powers* and *The Full Monty*, the comic heroes are struggling neither to resist adulthood nor to achieve it; on the contrary, in both films, our heroes have become men and have discovered that manhood does not allay the fear of castration—it confirms it. In fact, the comic hero in both films has to grapple with the serious limitations of male masculinity in a world where feminism has empowered women, changes in the workplace have altered dominant conceptions of masculinity, and queer models of gender seem far more compelling and much more successful than old-fashioned heterosexual models of gender polarity. Confronted by the failure of the masculine ideal, the male hero must accept economic as well as emotional disappointment and learn to live with the consequences of a shift of power, which has subtly but completely removed him from the center of the universe. While contemporary oedipal comedies like the gross-out films released in the late 1990s (*American Pie* and *Big Daddy*, for example) continue to invest in fantasies of robust and normative masculinities that have both national and racial dimensions (U.S. manhood in one, and white fatherhood in the other), the king comedies expose the anxious male posturing of these films as the aftershocks of a seismic shift that has already taken place. The humor in *The Full Monty* in particular depends on some recognition of the toll taken by postimperial decline on the psyches of white males in England in the 1980s and 1990s. And the ridiculous but lovable character of Austin Powers derives at least in part from a serious reconsideration of the waning appeal of stereotypical English masculinity in a postcolonial and multiracial Britain.

On account of the decline of empire in the second half of the twentieth century, and the rise of new ethnicities in postimperial Britain, white English masculinity offers more opportunities than its U.S. counterpart for registering widespread cultural changes in conceptions of manhood. At the beginning of the twentieth century Great Britain had achieved international dominance, but with the dissolution of the British Empire by midcentury, we can talk about the rise of U.S. military and economic hegemony. Accordingly, what can be called "Anglo-American dominant masculinity" shifted in the late twentieth century from British to U.S. cultural terrain. In fact, U.S. cultural dominance of conceptions of manhood have been so complete on both sides of the Atlantic that by the close of the century, even representations of white English masculinity, as portrayed in films such as *The Full Monty* and *Austin Powers,* return to U.S. audiences as minority masculinities.

The Full Monty

The Full Monty, starring Robert Carlyle, takes place in the aftermath of the decline of Sheffield's steel industry. At least part of the current crisis in masculinity must be explained in terms of the effects of economic restructuring in the United States and Europe. Beginning in the 1970s, the privileging of service-oriented economies over industry among Western nation-states dramatically changed our conceptions of who makes up the "working classes." The surge of labor force participation among women, the privileging of service over industrial labor, and the rise of sweated and "unorganized" labor in the heart of the metropole have all contributed to significant and radical changes in the conceptions of manliness that emerge from and are connected to definitions of the working body. Useful information about the changing relationships between men and work can be gleaned, surprisingly, using contemporary theories and studies of performativity. Eric Lott's work on Elvis impersonation, for example, uses these performances to talk about "how white working-class men currently live their whiteness" (Lott 1997). Lott sees these acts of impersonation as both the repository of a particular kind of cultural envy of black culture and black masculinities, but also the imaginative response to "post-white-male politics" and to post-Fordist era changes in the meaning of work. As he makes clear, when "work" for work-ing-class men no longer simply signifies in terms of factories and manual labor then the terms "working class" and "masculinity" shift perceptibly in meaning. Lott's attempt to map the effect of the emergence of "office styles of manhood" on male class identities provides one richly complex account of the interlocking structures connecting class to gender.

The Full Monty refers clearly to the effects of changes in the workplace on the meaning of male masculinity. The film opens with a short documentary, a public service film, that recounts the glory of Sheffield's steelworks in the early 1970s. The film begins some twenty years later when the steelworks have closed and thousands of steelworkers are unemployed. Steel, in this film, works as a metaphor for past models of masculinity—masculinities de-pendent on "hard bodies," to use Susan Jeffords's term—but the decline of the steelworks also serves as a grim reminder of the ravages of Thatcherism on British nationalized industry (Jeffords 1994). Many men in Sheffield are out of work while their girlfriends, wives, and mothers, who all work in the service industry, still have jobs. The economic disparities between the blue-collar men who are now unemployed and the blue-collar women who retain their service jobs shifts significantly and irrevocably the coordinates and meanings of gender and sexuality. When a Chippendale show comes to town, some of the local lads decide that they should try and make some money by stripping and erotic dancing. Amazingly, the process of develop-ing a show throws the men into a series of dilemmas that we almost never associate with masculinity, but have instead come to define femininity: the men worry about their bodies, their clothes, their ability to dance, and their desirability.

The film opens with a series of assaults on male privilege. The film's pro-tagonist, Gaz, is unemployed and struggling to make custody payments to his ex-wife in order to maintain a relationship with his son. Dave, his mate, has in the words of his wife "given up" and resigned himself to redundancy at work and at home. Gerald, the former boss of Gaz and Dave, cannot bring himself to tell his wife that he is out of work, so he leaves for work every morning and heads to the job center, desperately hoping to find work before she finds out that their money has run out. The conventional masculine roles of father, husband, and breadwinner are all under serious pressure as the film begins, and masculinity is defined from the outset as a category threatened on all sides by redundancy. As Gaz and Dave return home after a hard day of trying to steal scrap metal from the old factory, they encounter a long line of women waiting to be admitted to the Working Men's Club, where the Chippendale dancers are performing. Gaz sneaks into the men's bathroom through a window to survey the "women-only" scene inside. But before he has a real chance to take in the glorious scene of hundreds of women yelling and whooping at a male stripper, three women make their way toward the men's room, hoping to avoid a line for the toilet. Gaz slips into a stall and watches what transpires through a hole in the door. While Gaz here occupies the seemingly traditional male position of the voyeur or Peeping Tom, what he sees changes radically the gendered roles of spectatorship. At first, Gaz takes pleasure in watching the women transform the men's room into a women's room by applying makeup in the mirror. He watches them watching themselves. Right before his eyes, however, the scene changes abruptly from a feminine scene of display to a masculine scene of activity when one of the women hikes up her skirt and pees standing up at the urinal to the delight of her friends. Rather than conforming to simply a psychoanalytic model of either castration or female phallicism, this scene, I think, registers a refusal of several gender logics. First, it refuses to mark maleness as the place of sexualized voyeurism, and second, the scene suggests the effects of even casual invasions of male space by women. Finally, the framing of the shot—which locates a man hiding behind a door, two women in front of a mirror, and another woman at a urinal—predicts the politics of the gaze that will be elaborated in the film and will culminate in the film's final shot.

The growing redundancy of old forms of both gender relations and masculinity is underscored in *The Full Monty* by this abrupt, irreversible reconfiguration of the male gaze. In Hollywood cinema, as I discussed in chapter 4, the male gaze structures the look of the viewer, and allows for the male spectator to identify with activity in the scene and to desire the female, who is positioned as the object of his gaze/desire. The masculine woman in this scene, the woman at the urinal, restructures the male gaze by insisting that it be routed through alternative modes of masculinity. In the men's room scene, then, Gaz can peer voyeuristically at the women in the mirror only if he also looks at the woman at the urinal. His struggle, here and in other key scenes of watching and being watched, indicates how thoroughly male-female relations have been transformed by changes at the level of economy and labor practices. It would be inaccurate, however, to say that the lack of economic power exercised by the working-class men of Sheffield "castrates" them; rather, it allows them to see themselves, rather than women, as the subjects who represent and figure lack.

When Gaz reports back to his friends at the unemployment office about what he has witnessed in the men's room, their responses record unfamiliar forms of male paranoia that are inflected less by rage at women and more by a sense of the impending redundancy of heteronormative maleness once masculinity circulates through different bodies. Gaz himself suggests that "when women start pissing like us, that's it, we're finished, Dave, extincto." Another man adds, "They're turning into us." "A few years," Gaz continues, "and men won't exist, except in zoos or summat. I mean, we're not needed no more, are we? Obsolete, dinosaurs, yesterday's news." This theme of male self-deprecation reaches its nadir when Dave and Gaz find a man trying to kill himself in his car. The rescue and resuscitation of the suicidal character, Lamper, is unsentimental and yet it precipitates a strong fraternity between men in trouble. The fraternity crosses class lines when the lads recruit their former boss, Gerald, to be their dance instructor. His ballroom dance skills, once the mark of a refined and respectable masculinity, now become the basis for a new male collectivity inspired by disenchantment and exclusion, but productive of a new model of maleness centered on masculine display and vulnerability.

The dance fraternity grows in numbers when Gaz and his new friends begin auditions for their stripper troupe and they find two more members: a black man named Horse, and a gay man named Guy. *The Full Monty* hints at alternative constructions of masculinity, and associates them through these characters with race and sexuality. The character of Horse, despite his name, manages to rise above the stereotype of a black masculinity anchored by a huge phallus, and it is the gay man, generically called Guy, who assumes the role of alpha male in the group. Furthermore, when Guy begins a relationship with Lamper, their alternative versions of masculinity only persuade the other men that dominant masculinity (like the dying steel industry) is a totally bankrupt form.

The film ultimately suggests that when men and women reverse places socially, financially, and even culturally, the effects are not all bad. Women with power, we discover, do not simply behave like men; they cultivate their own relations to masculinity and femininity, and encourage the men around them to do the same. Similarly, disempowered men may easily fall into conventional concerns about impotence, but they also learn lessons in objectifi-cation. In a hilarious scene at Gerald's where the men first try stripping in front of each other, a whole array of issues come up about embodiment. When Dave confesses that he feels fat and out of shape, Gerald shoots back, "Fat is a feminist issue, you know." The men proceed to give Dave and each other advice about dieting and working out. The fact that this scene takes place in the "posh" suburban home of the former boss also recalculates the class differentials within the group as well as the relationships between men and domesticity. Just as we found women in the men's room at the Working Men's Club, so we find men at home during the day discussing body issues.

One final scene suggests how new conceptions of masculinity can and in-deed must be routed through feminism and the female body. Gaz steals a copy of *Flashdance* in order to give his dancers some sense of what good danc-ing should look like. But as the film begins, Dave peers at the screen in won-der at the film's opening scene of Jennifer Beals, dancer by night, welding by day in a factory. The spectacle of the female dancer as welder, like the image of the woman at the urinal, challenges once more the idea of woman as an object of display, but also creates the uncanny image of a female masculinity that the men must now emulate. Masculinity throughout *The Full Monty* is precisely welded together from a collectivity of minority masculinities. This film about men under pressure creates new standards for the depiction of masculinity in mainstream film and it ends by referencing the taboo repre-sentation of male nudity. In its final flourish, this British comedy reveals that minority masculinities can expose mainstream masculinity as a dangerous myth of potency, invulnerability, and violence. The final shot that should constitute the "money shot" of "the full monty," actually refuses to make the visibility of the phallus into the totality of maleness; the finale of the strip show is filmed from the back of the stage, and a freeze-frame captures the six naked men from behind and the crowd of screaming women full on. The *full monty*, then, is this shot that includes the female voyeur looking and the male body on display, and it echoes in form and content the earlier shot of the woman at the urinal. In both scenes, we only see the phallic subject from behind, and in both scenes, the gaze of the male voyeur is routed through the gaze of women. The two scenes together make up the full monty.

We can link this final shot in *The Full Monty* to the use of reaction shots in *Austin Powers*. As we will see next in *Austin Powers*, masculinity may not be learned directly from women but it is modeled on a drag king aesthetic.

Austin Powers: International Man of Mystery

In Myers's first and classic *Austin Powers* film, our hero leaves behind the shagadelic revels of 1967 and enters a thirty-year cryogenic sleep in order to pursue the nefarious Dr. Evil (also Myers) through time and space. When he awakens, various British intelligence agents and his future partner, the delectable Vanessa, welcome Austin into the 1990s. Vanessa also warns him promptly that "a lot has changed in thirty years, Austin." Undaunted, Austin responds, "As long as people are still having premarital sex with many anonymous partners while at the same time experimenting with mind-expanding drugs in a consequence-free environment, I'll be sound as a pound!" Of course, Austin finds that safe sex and enforced monogamy are only the most obvious signifiers of what has changed since the groovy 1960s in London. Confronting the brave new world to which he awakens, Austin discovers slowly that the time warp that propelled him into the future has also transformed him into a dinosaur whose particular brand of English masculinity has come and gone. Undaunted by the prospect of being the last of his kind, Austin dives into the 1990s still wearing his Union Jack Y-fronts and hoping against hope that he can still find lots of willing "birds" to shag.

In a self-conscious nod to its own time-loop conceit, *Austin Powers* tries to carry forward into the 1990s comic English masculinity from the 1960s and 1970s. Part Peter Sellers from *Casino Royale,* part Benny Hill or Frankie Howard, the character of Austin Powers is both a loving tribute to and a fond critique of the repulsive and lascivious "carry-on" heroes of 1970s British comedy. The *Carry On* comedies of the 1960s and 1970s created a comic universe on the thin—very thin—premise of the ubiquitous appeal of the randy white Englishman embodied most often in these films by Sid James. The *Carry On* comedies paired James, however, with a rather flaming counterpart, played by Kenneth Williams, whose signature line, "stop messing about," is echoed in Austin's naughty and nasal "oh behave!" While Williams spends his time in these films running from matrons and other overpowering females (mostly played by Hattie Jacques), the James character in a *Carry On* comedy usually tries to ditch his wife while constantly propositioning busty nurses and curvaceous ingenues. These two forms of masculinity are depicted as interdependent, and Williams's homoeroticism is tolerated by James while James's homophobia is actively encouraged by Williams. In *Austin Powers,* Myers brings these two carry-on masculinities into one body with interesting and queer results. Inheriting James's randy disposition,

Austin Powers and the Fembots.
Press packet for *Austin Powers.*

Austin also channels Williams through his campy overuse of double entendres. By combining these two carry-on roles, indeed, Myers exposes English masculinity as a peculiar combination of camp and compulsory heterosexuality.

While I will return later to the implications of this parody of national manhood, I want to focus here on the queerness of Austin's masculine affect and the drag king effect of his particular mode of male parody. I do so precisely because the film does not reference these sources for its humor even as it is positively meticulous in telegraphing the mainstream historical sources.[3] Austin's clothing, his fashion photography career, and his overall camp affect suggest that his imperfect masculinity owes much to gay male models of manhood; but his nonphallic, emphatically prosthetic, and endearingly cloddish attentions to women make his sexual identity look butch or kingy rather than "faggy." Furthermore, Austin's prosthetic masculinity is matched in the film by the fabulous prosthetic femininity of the "fembots," robotic killer females sent to shoot Austin. The fembots serve to locate an automated femininity that ensures that femaleness cannot be the signifier of the "natural" in the film. The drag king effect becomes more readable indeed when Myers takes his parody of English masculinity beyond camp and adds phallic renunciation to the mix. As we see in the infamous penis-enlarger scene, Myers particular genius lies in his ability to transform the rather unappealing and misogynist English comic masculinities of the 1960s into a new form of abject comic masculinity that acknowledges its debts to queer and subcultural forms.

In a film in which penis jokes come second only to jokes about flatulence, the penis-enlarger scene stands out as the ultimate acknowledgment of the failure of the phallus. I want to read this scene closely in order to demonstrate the kingy effect of both phallic renunciation and what Myers refers to as "comedy torture." In some remarks about his comedic method in *Austin Powers*, Myers speaks of the effect of taking a joke much further than it should go. Comedy torture, he says, comes from repeating something until it stops being funny and then repeating it some more until it becomes funny again.[4] That line between comic and no longer comic is of course narrow and quite precise, but repeatedly in *Austin Powers*, Myers finds exactly the right balance between repetition, overkill, torture, and comedy. In this scene, a joke that points to Austin's failed phallic masculinity, is repeated until it becomes the source of a new masculine power accessed through abjection.

In brief, the penis-enlarger scene begins when Austin goes to collect his belongings after being awakened from his long sleep and welcomed into the 1990s. Austin is handed back his kit piece by piece by a cloakroom guard who presents Austin with a crushed-velvet suit, a pair of pointy black boots ("bonjourno, boys!"), a pendant with a male symbol on it, and finally a Swedish penis enlarger. "That's not mine," Austin says to Vanessa. The officer now presents Austin with "one credit card receipt for Swedish-made penis enlarger signed by Austin Powers." Again Austin protests, "I'm telling you, baby, that's not mine!" The guard continues, "One warranty card for Swedish-made penis-enlarger pump, filled out by Austin Powers." Austin protests again, "I don't even know what this is! This sort of thing ain't my bag, baby." And then the guard clinches the scene: "One book, 'Swedish-

Made Penis Enlargers and Me: This Sort of Thing Is My Bag, Baby,' by Austin Powers."

Here, we witness the castration of Austin under the withering gaze of Vanessa. In this scene, Austin reclaims his kit, the bundle of accessories that were crucial to his sex appeal in the 1960s. The male symbol necklace and crushed-velvet suit with black pointy boots suggest the swinger, the sexy man about town, but the Swedish penis enlarger implies that the accessories are not simply the superficial markers of an invisible phallic potency; instead they cover over phallic lack. Austin is revealed by the law (represented by the officer) and in front of the desirable woman as lacking the equipment for phallic success, and as hopelessly sexist at a moment when women simply expect more. But rather than wilt or rebuild his masculinity in normative ways, Austin actually works his loser status up into an alternative mode of masculinity throughout the film. Danger may be his middle name, but his last name, Powers, speaks to the refusal of the logic of castration. This is not to say that Austin repudiates lack; instead he revels in it. This point is driven home by the rivalry between Austin and his nemesis, Dr. Evil. In a parody of conventional spy film rivalries, within which two men compete for phallic mastery, Austin and Dr. Evil are matched by equal levels of incompetence. Dr. Evil may be floating around the earth in a phallically promising spaceship called Big Boy, but when he comes down to earth, he too finds he is hopelessly and permanently out of date. The incompetence of Dr. Evil, matched only by Austin's spectacular knack for losing, ensures that this will be a film with no winners.

Furthermore, Austin's lack of phallic authority does not at all diminish his ability to attract the attention of Vanessa, his love object. The penis-enlarger scene then stands as proof that her attraction to Austin depends not at all on phallic endowment. In fact, Austin becomes attractive to her precisely because he lacks and therefore has to try harder, has to literally seduce her through laughter rather than phallic mastery. In one scene, for example, Vanessa declares her absolute abhorrence at Austin's randy attentions, telling him, "Mr. Powers, I would never have sex with you, ever! If you were the last man on earth and I was the last woman on earth, and the future of the human race depended on our having sex, simply for procreation, I still would not have sex with you!" When Austin responds quickly with "What's your point, Vanessa?" he literally refuses to understand her rejection of him, refuses phallic mastery, but also playfully turns the intensity and hyperbole of her rejection into a potential for further comic interaction.

Vanessa's responses to Austin are recorded in minute detail in this film. As if to emphasize the subtle but momentous shift in gender dynamics that this film records, the comic power of the penis-enlarger scene depends absolutely on a series of these reaction shots from Vanessa. For instance, as Austin plays out the comedy torture of repudiating and then accepting the penis enlarger as his own—as his bag, baby—Vanessa responds with a range of reactions from amused to disdainful, to amused again, to imperious, and finally to seduced. The director, Jay Roach, has commented that the film could easily have consisted of 10 percent comic action and 90 percent comic reaction shots.[5] This cinematic emphasis on the reaction shot here, as in *The Full Monty,* reverses the formula of the masculinist action film where little time is spent on reaction—the reaction shot, of course, records and actively engages the presence of an other, and in this film, it acknowledges rather than obliterates the comedic contribution made by the mostly female other to the comic success of the film. Vanessa plays earnest to Austin's superficial, knowing to his ignorant, competent to his ineptitude, and prim to his lascivious. She is not simply his opposite, nor his stooge; she is a filter for the audience's own responses and, again as in *The Full Monty,* a powerful image of female voyeurism.

In terms of his dependence on the reaction of others, his camp femininity, and his demonstrably prosthetic, presumably charming butch masculinity, Austin is marked irredeemably as queer. And with his foppish clothes and fake chest hair, his penis enlarger and off-color jokes, Austin is abject masculinity incarnate. Austin's name, however, specifies his masculinity by linking Englishness to power (his name echoes that of the Aston Martin driven by James Bond), and suggesting that white English masculinity, perhaps more than most, relies heavily on prosthetics, tricks, and bad jokes. As I contended earlier, *Austin Powers* also continuously recalls its debts to other generic traditions (the spy film or British comedy), and its hero is marked throughout as a winner from the 1960s who becomes a loser in the 1990s. Through this mechanism of the time loop, *Austin Powers* remarks on and indeed participates in the recent English nostalgia for the 1960s, which are not remembered as one step removed from the ravages of World War II and the decline of empire but instead glorified as the good old days when England had just "won the war."

By making the 1960s in *Austin Powers* into the fab world of swingers, the film participates fully in the romance of this golden age. And yet by remarking throughout on Austin's obvious repulsiveness—bad teeth being the metonym for unappealing white English masculinity—the film seems to be aware of the cultural agenda at work in harkening back to a memory of an all-white England and erasing other memories of the 1960s. While the romance with a depoliticized 1960s is somewhat understandable in the context of the anxieties generated by a multiracial and postcolonial England in the 1990s, what is the appeal of the British 1960s to U.S. audiences? Specifically through the *Austin Powers* films, U.S. audiences have invested heavily in the idea of England as a place untouched by civil rights strife and racial disharmony; *Austin Powers*'s shagadelic visions of 1960s lovefests replaces the more threatening history of a postimperial Britain torn by race riots and struggling with the pernicious anti-immigration legislation inspired by Enoch Powell's new populism. Moreover, the advertising campaigns that accompanied the second *Austin Powers* film, *The Spy Who Shagged Me,* continued to sell England to U.S. tourists as the land of the Fab Four, Carnaby Street, and Monty Python.

In 1999, U.S. audiences lapped up another version of an idyllic England—a place emptied of people of color and rich in traditional values—in yet another summer comedy: *Notting Hill.* This comedy of errors tells of a U.S. slave to celebrity (Julia Roberts) who tries to escape into the anonymity of a bustling London neighborhood. Hugh Grant reprises his role from *Four Weddings and a Funeral* here as the bumbling lover whose masculinity is understated, restrained, and quintessentially English. In *Notting Hill,* he is contrasted favorably to the muscle-bound, bad-boy, U.S. masculinity of Roberts's ex-boyfriend, played by Alec Baldwin, and Grant's appeal continues to rely on what one critic has called "the social tactics of niceness, compliance and liberal tolerance" (Rutherford 1997, 46). Grant's "nice" model of manliness aspires to represent both old-world charm and also new-world sensitivity to women's issues. And the setting in Notting Hill for the romance between the new woman and the "new" old man wipes out the racial past of Notting Hill as the site of race riots, and holds fast to the idea of England as a place that balances properly the charge of keeping alive a tradition while remaining in touch with contemporary culture. That Grant's character works in a charming old bookstore—a travel bookstore, in fact—only completes the imperial fantasy of a Great Britain whose "greatness" resides in a learned cultural tradition that must be preserved in England and imported elsewhere by any means necessary.

Mike Myers, of course, is no Hugh Grant in the sense that he deliberately pokes fun at this fantasy of English masculinity. In the first *Austin Powers* film, Myers creates a wicked parody out of the U.S. romance with white English manliness. The appeal and even charm of the first *Austin Powers* film lay precisely in its acknowledgment of a sea change in sexual mores and gender norms—a sea change, moreover, that left Austin's once dominant mode of masculine narcissism exposed to ridicule at every turn. No longer the international man of mystery from the 1960s, in the 1990s Austin becomes a lovable loser. But in the overmarketed sequel, *Austin Powers 2: The Spy Who Shagged Me,* Austin's abject masculinity is recuperated and turned into potency once more. Even before the sequel's release in summer 1999, Myers's mug appeared on numerous billboard ads selling Virgin Atlantic ("Shagatlantic, Yeah Baby!"), Heineken Beer, and other products. What, we might ask, happened between 1997 and 1999 to make *Austin Powers* into a marketing dream? How and why did the rotten-toothed antihero in need of a Swedish penis enlarger morph from dated and dateless in the first film to hip and clueless in the second?

In many ways, the second *Austin Powers* attempted to rewrite or reroute the cultural chain of transmission that begins with queer parodies of masculinity in drag king comedies, passes into subcultural visibility through extensive press coverage and more limited forms of exposure in films like *Pecker* by John Waters, and finally ends with male parodies of male masculinity consumed by mass audiences. In *The Spy Who Shagged Me,* not even the British *Carry On* comedies and spy farces occupy the position of original. Instead, the second *Austin Powers* retells the first *Austin Powers,* meticulously repeating every clever joke from the first film and thereby making those jokes seem original. The difference between these two films reveals the ways in which mainstream culture absorbs and disarms the subcultural material on which it depends. The first *Austin Powers* tried to disarm both hero and villain in the espionage set piece, but the second makes both hero and villain equally attractive and powerful. In the first film, Austin fights to save the world for free love; in the second, he saves it for multinational capitalism. The first *Austin Powers* clearly and humorously acknowledges as well as articulates a feminist critique of sexism that changes completely the constitutive forms of male masculinity. In the sequel, Austin's sexism is no longer a mark of his anachronism; it has become his comic signature.

But this is not to say that *Austin Powers 2* is totally irredeemable. Cloning and doubling in *Austin Powers 2* remain as an echo of the powerful humor of the first film. In *The Spy Who Shagged Me,* Austin clones himself through a malfunctioning time machine; at the same time, Dr. Evil, not satisfied with his legitimate offspring, his son Scott, creates a literal clone of himself in miniature. "I shall call him Mini Me," Dr. Evil says of his clone in one of the film's few highlights. The presence of the Mini Me clone self-consciously refers to the kingy effect of "repetition ad nauseum" and allows for a forceful critique of masculine authenticity. There is another evil character in *Austin Powers 2*, an obese Scotsman called Fat Bastard who is again played by Myers; the cumulative impact of having Myers in three of the main roles is to make masculinity into merely another of the film's special effects. Myers's monopolization of the film's male roles (with the exception of Mini Me, played by Verne Troyer) seems to quote Eddie Murphy's virtuoso comic performances in *The Nutty Professor*, where Murphy plays the nerdy professor, his alter ego Buddy Love, and Love's entire family (both Buddy Love and Austin Powers are also marked by grandiose allegorical names). Murphy's *Nutty Professor*, of course, was already a remake of the original version by Jerry Lewis. Lewis's film used the trope of cloning to suggest that a perfect masculinity can emerge from the combination of two extreme forms—the nerd and the cad—but in Murphy's remake, the practice of cloning becomes a fascinating meditation on racial stereotypes as fetish figures for all of black masculinity. *Austin Powers* refuses the Lewis method of resolving masculinity into a perfect whole and offers us in many ways a counterpart to Murphy's clever representation of the stereotypes of black masculinity. If Murphy tries to expose both the pleasure and the danger of racial stereotyping, Myers tries to disarm white masculinity of the power it draws from racial stereotyping. In *Austin Powers 2*, the effect of cloning allows white masculine failure and ineptitude to spread across the entire narrative, and breaks down all claims to masculine and white authenticity.

One scene explicitly registers the historical debt that seemingly authentic white masculinity owes to performative black masculinity. In this scene, Dr. Evil and Mini Me perform a rap duet that samples not only Grover Washington's "Just the Two of Us" but also Will Smith's version of the Washington original. In one comic move, Myers reveals the structure of "evil" white masculinity as homoerotic, narcissistic, and culturally derivative. The spectacle of Dr. Evil and Mini Me rapping and dancing to a romantic duet creates a drag king effect within which one form of masculinity is expressed through and layered over another kind, but also articulates the cultural debt that white hetero-masculinity owes to the gay, black, and butch masculinities that it absorbs and erases.

The scene also reminds us that significantly, *Austin Powers 2* has moved from England to the United States in location as well as in terms of the cultural archive it draws from—for example, when we first see her, Austin's love object in the second film, Felicity Shagwell, is dancing to Lenny Kravitz's remake of "American Woman"; later, when Austin and Ms. Shagwell drive off together, Austin notes that the English countryside looks an awful lot like Southern California, and references to U.S. products like Starbucks litter the script. The Americanization of king comedy—in the case of this film, self-conscious as it may be—severely diminishes the set of opportunities that the film offers for the representation of masculine abjection. In terms of its box office success, marketing tie-ins, and mainstream appeal, *Austin Powers 2* has clearly relinquished the more subculturally informed aspects of the original, opting instead to feed into the gross-out comedy market designed to fill the theater with teenage boys chortling at shit jokes. And so the king method of repetition ad nauseum meets a sorry end by reneging on its promise of non-phallic mastery and humorous seduction. By the end of *Austin Powers 2,* we are no longer in the realm of king comedy, drag king parody, subversive repetition, and masculine abjection. Austin does not have to work hard to get the girl, he is no longer bewildered by the abrupt time zone shifts, nor is he playing off an English sensibility of white male decline. Rather, he is an American imperial master of his domain and no longer a comic king; he has become instead another American king of comedy.

In this chapter, I have tried to trace the evolution of a sensibility that we can call kinging that links mainstream critiques of normative masculinity to subcultural forms of parody, tribute, and satire. While refusing to trace a one-to-one or cause-and-effect relationship between mainstream culture and queer subcultural productions, I have argued that like camp, kinging works through indirect and mediated influence. If camp can as easily be found in classic Hollywood films, 1960s drag queen performances, and contemporary fashion shows, then we should also attend to the multiple sites within which the distance between maleness and masculinity becomes visible with comic effects. I am also trying to allow for distinctions between mainstream comedies that prop up dominant masculinities and king comedies that aim at disarming them. The *Austin Powers* phenomenon illustrates for me both the power of the kinging effect and yet how short-lived the subversive ripples may be. While the first *Austin Powers* film reveled in the phallic incompetence of its comic hero, the second film reduced his masculine abjection by cloning him and transforming him into a sex machine who temporarily loses his "mojo." While the first film is marked by its cultural debt to other locations of king comedy, the second film, as sequel, turns the first *Austin Powers* into an original. The mechanism of mainstreaming can be seen in precisely the way the two films create a neat circuit of transmission that cuts out the subcultural, and even the historical, influences altogether. Significantly, then, the punch line in *Austin Powers 2* is not from a low-budget spy film, a drag king performance, or even a *Carry On* comedy but instead from the Tom Cruise blockbuster romance *Jerry Maguire*: Dr. Evil is reunited with Mini Me after a near disaster and he mimics Cruise in *Jerry Maguire*, telling his romantic partner in sign language, "You Complete Me." This gesture, hilarious as it is, unfortunately fails to parody *Jerry Maguire* and shows how far we have come from the king comedy acknowledgment that "gender is a copy with no original." This combo of Dr. Evil completed by his Mini Me clone takes the sting out of king comedy and reminds the queer spectator that once again, the joke is on us.

But as the summer's gross-out comedies give way to the winter's mawkish dramas, we can at least take comfort in our knowledge that *Austin Powers, The Full Monty,* and other king comedies have borrowed liberally from butch, nonmale, or penisless models of masculinity. They have also resigned themselves to a world in which the phallus is always fake, the penis is always too small, and the injunction to the masculine subject is not to "be" but to "behave." The work that falls to us, then, is to constantly recall the debts that the successful king comedies would rather forget—in other words, to remember that behind every good king comedy is a great drag king.

7

What's That Smell?

Queer Temporalities and Subcultural Lives

How do we read the agency of the subject when its demand for cultural and psychic and political survival makes itself known as style?
—Judith Butler, "Agencies of Style for a Liminal Subject"

In the last chapter, I examined relays of influence between dominant and minority representations of eccentric gendering. Mainstream films like *The Full Monty* and *Austin Powers* might borrow or even pilfer an aesthetics of drag and gender construction from subcultural sources, and they then tend to bury their subcultural sources in the process of transforming resistant performance into lucrative entertainment. The relationship between subcultural production and the avant-garde, however, is much more complex and interactive, as I argued in chapter 5. Here, I want to theorize queer subculture production in relation to new considerations of time and space that as I have tried to show throughout this book, make sense of the decisions that queer people make about where to live, how to live and how to recraft relationality itself.

Queer Temporalities

One of my central assertions has been that queer temporality disrupts the normative narratives of time that form the base of nearly every definition of the human in almost all of our modes of understanding, from the professions of psychoanalysis and medicine, to socioeconomic and demographic studies on which every sort of state policy is based, to our understandings of the affective and the aesthetic. In Western cultures, we chart the emergence of the adult from the dangerous and unruly period of adolescence as a desired process of maturation; and we create longevity as the most desirable future. We applaud the pursuit of long life (under any circumstances) and pathologize modes of living that show little or no concern for longevity. At a moment when so many middle-class gays and lesbians are choosing to raise children in conventional family settings, it is important to study queer life modes that offer alternatives to family time and family life. In the descriptions of subcultural life in this chapter, I explore the stretched-out adolescences of queer culture makers that disrupt conventional accounts of subculture, youth culture, adulthood, and maturity. The notion of a stretched-out adolescence, for example, challenges the conventional binary formulation of a life narrative divided by a clear break between youth and adulthood; this life narrative charts an obvious transition out of childish dependency through marriage and into adult responsibility through reproduction. Subcultural involvement, by delaying the onset of reproductive adulthood, challenges what Lauren Berlant and Michael Warner in their essay "Sex in Public' have termed the "institutions of intimacy" through which heteronormative culture secures its "metacultural intelligibility" (Berlant and Warner 1998, 553).

The Butler essay cited in the epigraph above—from a volume dedicated to the work of Stuart Hall—tackles the question of what kinds of agency can be read into forms of activity that tend to be associated with style. And building on the work by Hall and others in the classic volume on subcultures *Resistance through Rituals,* Butler puts the concept of "ritual" into motion as a practice that can either reinforce *or* disrupt cultural norms. Liminal subjects, she implies, those who are excluded from "the norms that govern the recognizability of the human," are sacrificed to maintain coherence within the category of the human, and for them, style is both the sign of their exclusion and the mode by which they survive nonetheless. The power of Butler's work, here and elsewhere, lies in her ability to show how much has been excluded, rejected, and abjected in the formation of human community, and what toll those exclusions take on particular subjects.

Punk has always been the stylized and ritualized language of the rejected; queer punk has surfaced in recent years as a potent critique of hetero- and homonormativity, and dyke punk in particular, by bands like Tribe 8 and The Haggard, inspires a reconsideration of the topic of subcultures in relation to queer cultural production and in opposition to notions of gay community. Subcultures provide a vital critique of the seemingly organic nature of "community," and they make visible the forms of unbelonging and disconnection that are necessary to the creation of community. At a time when "gay and lesbian community" is used as a rallying cry for fairly conservative social projects aimed at assimilating gays and lesbians into the mainstream of the life of the nation and the family, queer subcultures preserve the critique of heteronormativity that was always implicit in queer life. Community, generally speaking, is the term used to describe seemingly natural forms of congregation. As Sarah Thornton comments in her introduction to *The Subcultures Reader*, "Community tends to suggest a more permanent population, often aligned to a neighborhood, of which family is the key constituent part. Kinship would seem to be one of the main building blocks of community" (Thornton 1997, 2). Subcultures, however, suggest transient, extrafamilial, and oppositional modes of affiliation. The idea of community, writes Jean Luc Nancy in "The Inoperative Community," emerges out of the Christian ritual of communion and expresses a sense of something that we once had that has now been lost—a connection that was once organic and life-giving that now is moribund and redundant. Nancy calls this the "lost community" and expresses suspicion about this "belated invention": "What this community has 'lost'—the immanence and the intimacy of a communion— is lost only in the sense that such a 'loss' is constitutive of 'community' itself" (Nancy 1991, 12). The reminder that quests for community are always nostalgic attempts to return to some fantasized moment of union and unity reveals the conservative stakes in community for all kinds of political projects, and makes the reconsideration of subcultures all the more urgent.

The Ballad of a Ladyman

Sleater-Kinney's anthem "Ballad of a Ladyman" describes the allure of subcultural life for the ladyman, the freak who wants to "rock with the tough girls." They sing: "I could be demure like / girls who are soft for / boys who are fearful of / getting an earful / But I gotta rock!" The band layers Corin Tucker's shrill but tuneful vocals over the discordant and forceful guitar playing of Carrie Brownstein and the hard rhythm of Janet Weiss's percussion. This is a beat that takes no prisoners and makes no concessions to the "boys who are fearful of getting an earful." And while Sleater-Kinney are most often folded into histories of the "riot grrrl" phenomenon and girl punk, they must also be placed within a new wave of dyke subcultures. When taken separately, riot dyke bands, drag kings, and queer slam poets all seem to represent a queer edge in a larger cultural phenomenon. When considered together, they add up to a fierce and lively queer subculture that needs to be reckoned with on its own terms. This chapter tracks the significant differences between the ladymen who rock and roll, drag up, and slam their way toward new

Sleater-Kinney, *All Hands on the Bad One*, CD cover, 2000.

queer futures and the punk rockers of an earlier generation of subcultural activity. My tour of dyke subcultures takes in riot dyke punk by bands like Sleater-Kinney, The Butchies, Le Tigre, Tribe 8, The Haggard, and Bitch and Animal; drag kings like Dred, and drag king boy-band parody group Backdoor Boys; and slam poets like Alix Olson and Stacey Ann Chin. Queer subcultures are related to old-school subcultures like punk, but they also carve out new territory for a consideration of the overlap of gender, generation, class, race, community, and sexuality in relation to minority cultural production.

I have long been interested in and part of various subcultural groups. As a young person, I remember well the experience of finding punk rock in the middle of a typically horrible grammar school experience in England in the 1970s. I plunged into punk rock music, clothing, and rebellion precisely because it gave me a language with which to reject not only the high-cultural texts in the classroom but also the homophobia, gender normativity, and sexism outside it. I tried singing in a punk band called Penny Black and the Stamps for a brief two-week period, thinking that my utter lack of musical ability would finally serve me well. But alas, even punk divas scream in key, and my rebel yells were not mellifluous enough to launch my punk singing career. Instead of singing, I collected records, went to shows, dyed my hair, and fashioned butch outfits from safety pins and bondage pants. And so I learned at an early age that even if you cannot be in the band, participation at multiple levels is what subculture offers. I found myself reminiscing over my punk past when I began researching drag king cultures for a collaborative project with photographer Del LaGrace Volcano. Through my new subcultural involvement, I began to see some specific features of queer subculture as opposed to larger historical subcultures like punk rock.

After finishing my drag king book in 1999, I received calls every few months from television stations wanting me to put them in touch with drag kings for talk shows and news shows (Halberstam and Volcano 1999). Most of these shows would invite the kings on to parade around with some drag queens in front of a studio audience. At the end of the show, the audience would vote on whether each king or queen was *really* a man or *really* a woman. A few of the kings managed to circumvent the either/or format and offer up a more complex gendered self; and so, black drag king Dred took off her moustache to reveal a "woman's" face, but then took off her wig to reveal a bald pate. The audience was confused and horrified by the spectacle of indeterminacy. Josh Gamson in *Freaks Talk Back* has written about the potential for talk shows to allow the "crazies" and "queers" to talk back, but most of the time when drag kings appeared in mass public venues, the host did all the talking (Gamson 1999). Drag kings also made an appearance on HBO's *Sex and the City* and MTV's *Real Life*. On every occasion that drag kings appeared on "straight" television, they were deployed as an entertaining backdrop against which heterosexual desire was showcased and celebrated. As someone who has tirelessly promoted drag kings, as individual performers and a subculture, I found the whole process of watching the mass culture's flirtation with drag kings depressing and disheartening. But it did clarify for me what my stakes might be in promoting drag kings: after watching drag kings try to go prime time, I remain committed to archiving, celebrating, and analyzing queer subcultures before they are dismissed by mass culture, or disheartened by lack of exposure or dogged by what might be called "subcultural fatigue"—namely, the phenomenon of burnout among subcultural producers.

As the talk show phenomenon vividly illustrates, mainstream culture within postmodernism should be defined as the process by which subcultures are *both* recognized and absorbed, mostly for the profit of large media conglomerates. In other words, when television stations show an interest in a dyke subculture like drag kings, this is cause for both celebration and concern. On the one hand, the mainstream recognition and acknowledgment of a subculture has the potential to alter the contours of dominant culture

Betsy Gallagher, "Dred," 1996.
Reprinted by permission of the
artist.

(think here of the small inroads into popular notions of sex, gender, and race
made by the regular presence of black drag queen Ru Paul on cable television). But on the other hand, most of the interest directed by mainstream
media at subcultures is voyeuristic and predatory. The subculture might appear on television eventually as an illustration of the strange and perverse, or
else it will be summarily robbed of its salient features and the subcultural
form—drag, for example, will be lifted without the subcultural producers,
drag queens or kings. In an essay called "Elements of Vogue" that tracks the
results of precisely this process, José Gatti and Marco Becquer examine the
contradictory effects of the sudden visibility of Harlem drag balls and their
drag practices. In their analysis of the co-optation of gay voguing by
Madonna's hit single "Vogue" and Jenni Livingston's acclaimed independent
film *Paris Is Burning,* Gatti and Becquer show how the counterhegemonic

157

knowledge articulated in voguing meets with "the violence of the universal." Gatti and Becquer write of Madonna's video and Livingston's film that "both partake in the production of newness, a process which purports to keep us up-to-date as it continually adds on novelties to a relational system that absorbs them; both contain vogueing beneath the pluralist umbrella of hipness" (Gatti and Becquer 1997, 452). And so while the queens in *Paris Is Burning* expressed a desire for precisely the kind of fame and fortune that did eventually accrue to voguing, the fame went to Livingston and the fortune went to Madonna. The subculture itself—the gay black and Puerto Rican children of the houses of Channel, Extravaganza, and LaBeija—disappeared back into the world of sex work, HIV, and queer glamour, and within five years of the release of *Paris Is Burning*, five of the queens in the film were dead.[1]

The mainstream absorption of voguing highlights the uneven exchange between dominant-culture scavengers and subcultural artists: subcultural artists often seek out mainstream attention for their performances and productions in the hopes of gaining financial assistance for future endeavors. Subcultural activity is, of course, rarely profitable, always costly for the producers, and can be short-lived without the necessary cash infusions (in the words of Sleater-Kinney, "This music gig doesn't pay that good, but the fans are alright"). Some subcultural producers turn the subculture itself into a source of revenue, and as Angela McRobbie comments in her essay "Shut Up and Dance: Youth Culture and Changing Modes of Femininity," "Subcultures are often ways of creating job opportunities as more traditional careers disappear" (McRobbie 1994, 162). So while the subcultural producers hope for cash and a little exposure, the dominant culture scavengers are usually looking for a story and hoping for that brush with the "new" and the "hip" described so well by Gatti and Becquer. In my experiences working with drag kings, however, I found that while big media reached their "hipness quota" quickly with the addition of a few well-placed drag kings, they almost never paid for drag king services in return, and when they did pay, it was always a pittance. Obviously the payback for the subcultural participants cannot come in the form of material benefits; what seems more useful, then, in this exchange between mainstream attention and subcultural product, would be to use the encounter to force some kind of recognition on audiences that what is appealing about mainstream culture may well come from subcultures that they do not even know exist or that they have repudiated.

As George Lipsitz's work on popular music in East Los Angeles has shown in relation to ethnic minority cultures, cultural producers often function as organic intellectuals, in a Gramscian sense; as such, minority artists can produce what Lipsitz terms "a historical bloc" or a coalition of oppositional groups united around counterhegemonic ideas (Lipsitz 1997). While in Antonio Gramsci's formulation, the organic intellectual undermines the role of the traditional intellectual who serves to legitimize and authorize elite political interests, in subcultures where academics might labor side by side with artists, the historical bloc can easily describe an alliance between the minority academic and the minority subcultural producer. Where such alliances exist, academics can play a big role in the construction of queer archives and queer memory. Furthermore, queer academics can—and some should—participate in the ongoing project of recoding queer culture as well as interpreting it and circulating a sense of its multiplicity and sophistication. The more intellectual records we have of queer culture, the more we contribute to the project of claiming for the subculture the radical cultural work that either gets absorbed into or claimed by mainstream media.

Subcultures: The Queer Dance Mix

Subcultures have been an important object of study for sociology and cultural studies since the 1920s. In about the 1980s, however, work on subcultures seemed to fall out of favor as scholars began to doubt the utility of the term, and the descriptive potential of the binary opposition between subculture and dominant culture. While early work on subcultures from the Chicago school assumed a relationship between subcultures and deviance or delinquency, later work from the Birmingham University Center for Contemporary Cultural Studies characterized subcultures as class-specific "youth formations" (Hall 1975). One of the most influential texts on subcultures, *Subculture: The Meaning of Style* by Dick Hebdige, read subcultures in terms of the way they challenged hegemony through style rather than simply through overt ideological articulations. Hebdige characterized the recuperation of subcultural disorder in terms of either an economic conversion of the subculture's signs and symbols into mass culture commodities or an ideological conversion of the subcultural participant into either complete otherness or complete spectacle (Hebdige 1979). Hebdige's work has been both widely celebrated and critiqued in the two decades since its original publication, and obviously it cannot be applied in any simple way to contemporary subcultural scenes. And yet it remains an important text for thinking about how to move beyond the contextualization of subcultures in terms of relations between youth and parent cultures, and for its formulations of style and historicity.

Almost all of the early work on subcultures, including Hebdige's, presumed the dominance of males in subcultural activity and studied youth groups as the most lively producers of new cultural styles. The subcultures that I want to examine here are neither male nor necessarily young, and they are less likely to be co-opted or absorbed back into dominant culture because they were never offered membership in dominant groups in the first place. Queer lesbian subcultures have rarely been discussed in the existing literature, and they offer today a new area of study for queer scholarship as well as exciting opportunities for collaborations between queer cultural producers and queer academics. One of the reasons that theorists tend to look to subcultures for political mobilization has to do with the conflation of subculture and youth culture. Hebdige, in his essay "Youth, Surveillance, and Display," for example, understands youth subcultures to register a dissatisfaction and alienation from "parent cultures" that is both "a declaration of independence . . . and a confirmation of the fact of powerlessness" (Hebdige 1997, 404). Even though this reading provides us with a better understanding of how political protest might be registered in a youth subculture, it remains trapped in the oedipal framework that pits the subculture against the parent culture.

Queer subcultures, unlike the male-dominated youth cultures that Hebdige, Stuart Hall, and other members of the Birmingham school have written about, are not located in any easy relation to parent cultures. Much of the Birmingham school's work on subcultures (and this is partly why it fell out of favor in the early 1990s) presumed an oedipalized structure within which rebel youths reject the world of their parents, and instead create a netherworld within which to reshape and reform the legacies of an older generation. Economic, political, and social conflicts may be resolved in subcultural arenas, according to these arguments, without really effecting any grand changes at the superstructure level. Of course, such a theory of subcultures has long since been replaced by more nuanced understandings of the relations between class, youth, and mass media, and indeed in her essay "Different, Youthful, Subjectivities: Towards a Cultural Sociology of Youth," Angela McRobbie comments, "There is certainly no longer a case to be made for the traditional argument that youth culture is produced somehow in conditions of working-class purity, and that such expressions are authentic and in the first instance at least uncontaminated by an avaricious commercial culture" (McRobbie 1994, 179). But while McRobbie goes on to rethink the relations between white youth and youth of color and the meaning of femininity in postmodern youth cultures, she still presumes a heterosexual framework.

Queer subcultures illustrate vividly the limits of subcultural theories that omit consideration of sexuality and sexual styles. Queer subcultures cannot only be placed in relation to a parent culture, and they tend to form in relation to place as much as in relation to a genre of cultural expression, and ultimately, they oppose not only the hegemony of dominant culture but also the mainstreaming of gay and lesbian culture. As Michael Du Plessis and Kathleen Chapman report in an article about "Queercore," for example, "Queercore and homocore not only signaled their allegiances to post-punk subculture, but also positioned themselves as . . . distinct from lesbian and gay" (Du Plessis 1997, 65). Furthermore, queer subcultures are not simply spin-offs from some distinct youth culture like punk: as we will see in relation to riot dyke, queer music subcultures may be as likely to draw on women's music from the 1970s and early 1980s as from British punk circa 1977.

We need to alter our understandings of subcultures in several important ways in order to address the specificities of queer subcultures and queer subcultural sites. First, we need to rethink the relation between theorist and subcultural participant, recognizing that for many queers, the boundary between theorist and cultural producer might be slight or at least permeable. Second, most subcultural theories are created to describe and account for male heterosexual adolescent activity, and they are adjusted only when female heterosexual adolescent activity comes into focus. New queer subcultural theory will have to account for nonheterosexual, nonexclusively male, nonwhite, and nonadolescent subcultural production in all its specificity. Third, we need to theorize the concept of the archive, and consider new models of queer memory and queer history capable of recording and tracing subterranean scenes, fly-by-night clubs, and fleeting trends; we need, in Jose Muñoz's words, "an archive of the ephemeral" (Muñoz 1996). Finally, queer subcultures offer us an opportunity to redefine the binary of adolescence and adulthood that structures so many inquiries into subcultures. Precisely because many queers refuse and resist the heteronormative imperative of home and family, they also prolong the periods of their life devoted to subcultural participation. This challenge to the notion of the subculture as a youth formation could, on the one hand, expand the definition of subculture beyond its most banal significations of youth in crisis and, on the other hand, challenge our notion of adulthood as reproductive maturity. I want to now consider each one of these features of queer subcultural production in relation to specific lesbian subcultures.

Queer Space/Queer Time

"Hot Topic": The Death of the Expert

First then, let us consider the relations between subcultural producers and queer cultural theorists: Queer subcultures encourage blurred boundaries between archivists and producers, which is not to say that this is the only subcultural space within which the theorist and the cultural worker may be the same people.[2] Minority subcultures in general tend to be documented by former or current members of the subculture rather than by "adult" experts. Nonetheless, queer subcultures in particular are often marked by this lack of distinction between the archivist and the cultural worker. A good example of this blurring between producer and analyst would be Dr. Vaginal Davis, a drag queen, who enacts, documents, and theorizes an array of drag characters. Another would be Juanita Mohammed, Mother of the House of Mashood, a women's drag house in Manhattan. Mohammed keeps a history of the participation of women of color in the drag cultures even as she recruits new "children" to the House of Mashood. Mohammed also goes one step further and makes herself central to AIDS activism in relation to queers of color.

The queer archivist or theorist and the cultural worker may also coexist in the same friendship networks, and they may function as coconspirators. A good example of this relation would be academic Tammy Rae Carland, who at one time ran an independent record label, Mr. Lady, managed dyke punk band The Butchies, and taught at the University of North Carolina. Another one would be the relationship between New York University performance studies professor Jose Muñoz, and performance artists Carmelita Tropicana and Marga Gomez. Muñoz writes about both performers in his book *Disidentifications,* and in their joint performance piece titled *Single Wet Female,* Tropicana and Gomez have a lengthy comedic exchange about Muñoz's book and whether they are engaged in acts of disidentification in the play itself. This example shows clearly the merging, overlap, and mutual interaction between theories and performative practice. Finally, the academic and the cul-

Le Tigre, *Le Tigre,* CD cover, 1999.

tural producer may see themselves in a complementary relationship—Le Tigre, for instance, a riot dyke band, has a song called "Hot Topic" in which it names the women, academics, filmmakers, musicians, and producers who have inspired the band and whom the band wants to inspire. Le Tigre sings, "Carol Rama and Eleanor Antin / Yoko Ono and Carole Schneeman / You're getting old, that's what they'll say, but / I don't give a damn, I'm listening anyway."

More typically, cultural theorists have looked to groups of which they are not necessarily a part, most often youth subcultures, for an encapsulated expression of the experiences of a subordinated class. The youth subculture then becomes the raw material for a developed theory of cultural resistance, the semiotics of style, or some other discourse that now leaves the subculture behind. For a new generation of queer theorists—a generation moving on from the split between densely theoretical queer theory in a psychoanalytic mode, on the one hand, and strictly ethnographic queer research, on the other—new queer cultural studies feeds off of and back into subcultural production. The academic might be the archivist, a coarchivist, a full-fledged participant in the subcultural scene that the scholar writes about. But only rarely does the queer theorist stand wholly apart from the subculture, examining it with an expert's gaze.

I want to close this section with a quick discussion of one queer hip hop group from Oakland, California: Deepdickollective, which has made these subcultural forms of collaboration part of its mission. DDC, as it is known, is a "Bourgie-BohoPostPomoAfro-Homo" hip-hop group that situates itself firmly in an indie queer music scene, and characterizes its music and performances as "homohop." The members of DDC are not teenagers or "youth" in any conventional sense, and they aggressively and powerfully produce histories and cultural narratives about their own work. Like many queer subcultural producers (and I want to emphasize that there are many lines of continuity between white queer subcultures and queer subcultures of color; between, say, punk queer girls and homohop boys), they discuss the meanings of their songs, performances, and collaborations, and use both the Internet and local word-of-mouth publicity to get the message out. Also like other queer subcultural performers about whom I write, they pay tribute in their work to the pioneers who came before them (James Baldwin, Essex Hemphill) or to what they call the cultural legacy of homohop. DDC offers a great model for queer subcultural life, and moves us far from the white gay male circuit parties and nightlife that has stood in for all kinds of subcultural activity in the past. But DDC refuses to make its interventions only into queer life; it also points to the interactive, but repressed relations between queer culture and hip-hop. On its Web site, DDC reproduces a lengthy dialogue between DDC member Juba Kalamka aka Pointfivefag and Jamarhl Crawford, author of a homophobic article titled "Will You Stand Up for Hip-Hop or Bend Over?" Crawford's article, briefly stated, claims that while "homosexual integration" has affected and infected much of mainstream culture, thankfully (according to him) hip-hop is impervious to homosexual influence. Kalamka dialogues with Crawford and schools him in the meaning of homohop. At one point, Crawford tells Kalamka that he thinks DDC is great and will be extremely successful. Kalamka responds,

> Actually, we tend to think about it a little differently from that. We look at what we are doing as a function of a greater movement rather than just being a hip-hop crew. We specifically called ourselves a collective because of what it implies in a greater cultural sense in terms of a place for people to enter and exit based upon their needs rather than a band of hard and fast membership. . . . To make some money at hip-hop, a living say, would be a good thing. There's more at stake here though than star-seeking. We are all educators fighting to make space for ourselves and others.[3]

This exchange gives us a model for thinking about interactions between the subculture and the mainstream, and between new youthful groups and performers who have come before them.

Wildcat Women: Lesbian Punk and Slam Poetry

Second, queer subcultural theory should begin with those communities that never seem to surface in the commentaries on subcultures in general: namely, lesbian subcultures and subcultures of color. Cultural theory has created a hierarchy of subcultures that places English punk near the top, and then arranges mods, rockers, metalheads, club kids, DJ cultures, ravers, and rappers in some sort of descending order of importance. At the bottom of the pyramid of subcultures we will find girl fan cultures, house drag cultures, and gay sex cultures. Lesbian subcultures almost never appear at all, and so even in the documentation on balls and drag cultures, women's involvement in and relation to drag has been left out of theoretical accounts and subcultural histories. Recording the presence of lesbian subcultures can make a huge difference to the kinds of subcultural histories that get written—whether it is a history of drag that only focuses on gay men, a history of punk that only looks at white boys, or a history of girl cultures that only concentrates on heterosexual girls.

To give one example of the difference an awareness of lesbian subcultures can make, we can turn to early work in the 1970s on the participation of girls in punk subcultures. Theorists like McRobbie, Jennie Garber, and others talked about the invisibility of female subcultures and the tendency of girls to participate in coed subcultures only as girlfriends or groupies. McRobbie and Garber concluded that "girls' subcultures may have become invisible because the very term 'subculture' has acquired such strong masculine overtones" (McRobbie 1997, 114). In this essay, "Girls and Subcultures," and even in more recent work on girls and subcultures, there tends to be little recognition that some girls, usually queer ones, may in fact involve themselves in subcultures precisely because of the "strong masculine overtones" associated with the activity. And so a young queer girl interested in punk will not be put off by the masculinity of the subculture but may as easily be seduced by it. In another essay, "Settling Accounts with Subcultures," written some twelve years later and collected in McRobbie's book *Feminism and Youth Culture*, however, McRobbie articulates the failed promise of subcultural membership for young girls: "Whereas men who 'play around' with femininity are nowadays credited with some degree of power to choose, gender experimentation, sexual ambiguity and homosexuality among girls are viewed differently." McRobbie then concludes that "the possibility of escaping oppressive aspects of adolescent heterosexuality in a youth culture . . . remains more or less unavailable to girls" (McRobbie 1991, 36). It is not until the 1990s that girls begin to find in subcultural life an escape hatch from heteronormativity and its regulations.

McRobbie's work over the years has served as a critique of the masculinism of early pronouncements on subcultures; but more than this, McRobbie has returned insistently to the topic of youth cultures and gender, race, and class. Indeed, McRobbie's opus now stands as a rich, deep, and important theoretical archive on oppositional forms of culture making. In her collection of essays *Postmodernism and Popular Culture*, McRobbie models a form of intellectual practice that she calls "feminist postmodernism" and that allows her to "confront questions which otherwise remain unasked" (McRobbie 1994, 2). In the process of engaging these otherwise unasked questions, she suggests that "we also find our academic practice and our politics undergoing some degree of transformation and change" (2). McRobbie's willingness to track the transformations in her own body of work and to trace changes in her own thinking about key topics provides an excellent model for cultural theory in an ever evolving and shifting field. In one key chapter titled "Shut Up and Dance: Youth Culture and Changing Modes of Femininity," McRobbie returns to the topic of femininity and subcultures, and considers her position now as the mother of a daughter who attends raves. Commenting that we need to reorient our analyses of youth culture given "shifts in gender relations in the last decade," McRobbie examines the impact of feminism on both mass media representations of femininity and gender norms circulated by and among young girls. McRobbie concludes that girls are now operating with more flexible gender norms and that "femininity is no longer the 'other' of feminism" (173).

McRobbie does not go on to study the punk femininities within dyke cultures, yet if she did, she would find a fabulous array of feminist and queer femme performances. Guitarists like Leslie Mah of Tribe 8 as well as vocalists like Kathleen Hanna of Le Tigre and Beth Ditto of The Gossip all articulate the powerful potential of a queer femininity that served as an undercurrent to much of the riot grrrl feminism and is readable as radical style in queer punk. The recent explosion of dyke punk bands like Bitch and Animal, The Butchies, Le Tigre, The Need, The Haggard, and Tribe 8 also challenges the conventional understandings of punk as male dominated and queercore as a

largely gay male phenomenon. This explosion also makes visible the queerness that energized the riot grrrl movement even as it was assiduously ignored by mainstream media. The hardcore styles of many of these bands reminds us that punk in general, contrary to the usual accounts of the subculture, has always been a place for young girls to remake their genders. In her
excellent book on women in punk, *Pretty in Punk: Girls' Gender Resistance in a
Boys' Subculture*, Lauraine Leblanc tracks the relationship of girls to punk
rock. While some girls involved themselves in the scene through their
boyfriends, Leblanc argues that some of the really tough girls engaged in
punk had to become "virtual boys" in order to earn the respect of their male
counterparts. Although the subculture remains resolutely heterosexual in
form, Leblanc found that punk offered girls "strategies of resistance to gender norms" (Leblanc 1998, 13).

Lesbian punks are pretty much absent from Leblanc's otherwise excellent
and thorough ethnographic study of punk girls, and this may have had as
much to do with when she conducted her research as with the reluctance of
the girls she studied to identify as queer. For as the wave of riot grrrl crested
and began to recede in the mid-1990s, many of the most interesting bands
left standing were queer, female, and loud. Some of these bands, like Sleater-
Kinney, retooled femininity and made punk femininity unreliable as a
marker of heterosexuality. Sleater-Kinney modeled new femininities at the
level of musical performance as much as at the level of style. For example,
the band layers two distinctive guitars over the drums, but it omits the bass.
The bass can be read here as a "masculine" instrument in terms of its production of noise in the lower registers, but it can also be read as a stereotyp-
ically "female" instrument given that many women in rock bands have been
relegated to bass players because the "lead" guitar was presumed to be a male
role.[4] By using two guitars, Sleater-Kinney both undercut the notion of
"lead," and refuse the conventional arrangement of bass, guitar, and drums.
Other bands, like The Haggard, a hard-core group from Portland, Oregon,
produce a gender-bending sound by combining drum and guitar noise with
a butch voice overlay. The singer, Emily, produces a guttural roar that is neither a male voice nor a female one and she spews out her lyrics in an indeci-
pherable growl. This butch voice shows no concern for intelligibility or vir-
tuosity, but it produces a raw and original sound while redefining the meaning of voice, singing, and lyric.

Just as the recognition of lesbian involvement in punk subcultures
changes the way we understand both the punk phenomenon and the recent

riot dyke music trend, so lesbian involvement in slam poetry forces commentators to rethink universalizing narratives about youth cultures. While slam poetry is a nationwide phenomenon, the emergence of highly talented lesbian slam poets has changed the nature of the slam event. Two performers in particular have garnered mainstream and local attention: white lesbian Alix Olson and Jamaican-born StaceyAnn Chin. Olson was a member of the Nuyorican slam team that won the national championship in 1998. She was also the 1999 OUTWRITE slam champion after a long and thrilling slam off between herself and Chin.[5] Slam poetry is a form of competitive poetry in which poets perform three-minute poems for a panel of judges chosen from the audience; the judges rate the poems on a scale of one to ten, and the slammers move through preliminary rounds until they face-off in the finals. This necessitates each poet often memorizing and performing up to ten poems a night.

As popularized by the film *SLAM,* the slam poetry contest can easily degenerate into a macho contest of speed and fury; but it is also an offshoot of rap in terms of its rhythm and combination of spoken word with a beat. Slams therefore do attract poets of color in large numbers. Slam appeals to queer youth and queer youth of color because of the obvious connections to rap, and in places like Oakland, spoken word groups of color have been at the center of queer youth activity. Recently, queer poets of color like Chin and Sri Lankan slam poet D'Lo have made the slam a forum for very different messages about love, race, and poetry. In "Dykepoem" from her collection *Wildcat Woman,* Chin begins with the line "I killed a man today," and tells of a young black girl who fights off a rapist and justifies her sinful act: "I going to hell anyway / women who like other women go there, you know." The poem closes with a vision of prison as "a place / with only girl children inside / that place ain't no hell / sounds like heaven to me" (Chin 1998). Chin is a superb performer and regularly slams at queer people of color events all over New York City—she is as likely to appear in a nightclub as at a rally, at a conference as on the street. And while many of her poems are tough, sexy, and angry, she also infuses her work with a sense of irony and self-reflexivity. In "Don't Want to Slam," Chin writes, "I've decided / I don't want to be / a poet who just writes / for the slam anymore." The slam, she goes on to say, is just a "staged revolution," a spectacle of word pimps selling lines and rhymes for a quick "ten" from the judges. With breathtaking speed, the poem moves through a pointed critique of slamming, and makes a call for poems that tell "true histories of me and you" (Chin 1998). But the last verse shows that the slam *is* true history, *is* revolution, and may just change the world by changing the *word*. By the end of the last line, we believe her:

> I want to write
> I left my lover and
> now I want her back poems
> I miss Jamaica
> but now I'm never going back poems
> I know it's not a ten
> but it sends shivers down MY back poems
> poems that talk about life
> and love and laughter
> poems that reveal the flaws
> that make strikingly real people
> real poems
> poems that are so honest
> they slam.

Chin and Olson's slam poetry takes both lesbian feminism and women of color feminism to a new stage and a new audience, and make poetry into the language of riot and change.

Shooting Stars: Queer Archives

Third, the nature of queer subcultural activity requires a nuanced theory of archives and archiving. Work on archives and archiving is well underway, and can be found in the work of an eclectic group of queer cultural theorists including Ann Cvetkovich, Lauren Berlant, and Jose Muñoz (Cvetkovich 2003; Berlant 1997; Muñoz 1999). Ideally, an archive of queer subcultures would merge ethnographic interviews with performers and fans with research in the multiple archives that already exist online and in other unofficial sites. Queer zines, posters, guerrilla art, and other temporary artifacts would make up some of the paper archives, and descriptions of shows along with the self-understandings of cultural producers would provide supplementary materials. But the notion of an archive has to extend beyond the image of a place to collect material or hold documents, and it has to become a floating signifier for the kinds of lives implied by the paper remnants of shows, clubs, events, and meetings. The archive is not simply a repository; it is also a theory of

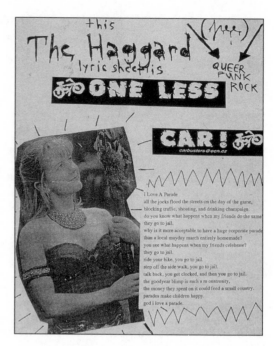

Haggard lyric sheet, 2001.

cultural relevance, a construction of collective memory, and a complex record of queer activity. In order for the archive to function it requires users, interpreters, and cultural historians to wade through the material and piece together the jigsaw puzzle of queer history in the making.

While some of the work of queer archiving certainly falls to academics, cultural producers also play a big role in constructing queer genealogies and memories. As we saw in Le Tigre's song, the lyrics to "Hot Topic" create an eclectic encyclopedia of queer cultural production through unlikely juxtapositions ("Gayatri Spivak and Angela Davis / Laurie Weeks and Dorothy Allison") and claim a new poetic logic: "Hot topic is the way that we rhyme / hot topic is the way that we rhyme." In other words, the historically situated theorists, filmmakers, and musicians rhyme with each other's work—the rhyme is located in the function and not in the words. Similarly, while many lesbian punk bands do trace their influences back to male punk or classic rock, as we saw in the last section, contrary to what one may expect, they do not completely distance themselves from or counteridentify with 1970s and 1980s "women's music." In fact, some dykecore bands see themselves as very much a part of a tradition of loud and angry women. On their CD *Are We Not*

Femme? for example, North Carolina–based band The Butchies performs a cover of feminist goddess Cris Williamson's classic song "Shooting Star." Williamson's soaring emotion-laden song becomes a tough, percussive anthem in the capable hands of The Butchies's members, who add drum rolls and screeching guitars to lift the song out of a woman-loving woman groove and into a new era. On the band's liner notes, The Butchies thank Williamson for "being radical and singing songs to girls before too many others were and for writing such a kickass song." If we look at the covers from The Butchies's CD and Williamson's CD, it would be hard to detect the connections between the two. The Butchies's CD pays obvious homage to punk concept band Devo both in terms of its title (Devo's first album was called *Are We Not Men*) and its iconography. The connection between The Butchies and Williamson, however, runs much deeper than their relation to punk bands like Devo. The Butchies appear on the cover wearing short red-leather miniskirts that do quote the red plastic flowerpot hats worn by Devo on the cover of *Are We Not Men*. Williamson, on the other hand, appears in dungarees and stands in what looks like the Joshua Tree Desert. Her album title *The Changer and the Changed* references a modality of mutuality, organic transformation, and reciprocity. The song itself, in her hands, tells of "wonderful moments on the journey through my desert." She sings of "crossing the desert for you" and seeing a shooting star, which reminds her of her lover. The spectral image of the shooting star figures quite differently in The

The Butchies, *Are We Not Femme?* CD cover, 1998.

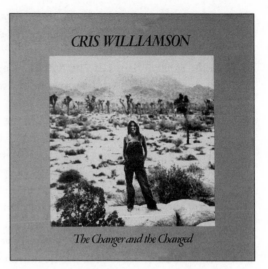

Cris Williamson, *Changer and the Changed,* LP cover, 1975.

Butchies's version, where it takes on more of the qualities of a rocket than a galactic wonder. But The Butchies cover version of Williamson's song has the tone of a tribute and not a parody by making her song relevant for a new generation of listeners.

The Butchies refuse the model of generational conflict, and build a bridge between their raucous spirit of rebellion and the quieter, acoustic world of women's music from the 1970s and 1980s. Like the new queer punk productions, women's music by Alix Dobkins, Williamson, and others was produced on independent labels (like Olivia Records) and received only scant mainstream attention. This music opened up a new phase in U.S. acoustic folk music by developing large and enthusiastic lesbian audiences for music that had previously been associated with heterosexual political culture. This reorientation of folk has had repercussions in the contemporary folk scene, where being a lesbian is often seen as a prerequisite for being a successful acoustic musician.

In her excellent essay "The Missing Link: Riot Grrrl, Feminism, Lesbian Culture," Mary Celeste Kearney also points to the continuity rather than the break between women's music and riot grrrl. But, she comments, links between earlier modes of lesbian feminism and contemporary riot grrrl productions are regularly ignored in favor of a history that makes riot grrrl the female offspring of male-dominated punk. The earlier music was made for, by, and about women, and while much of it did consist of folk-influenced ballads, there was also a hard and angry subgenre that combined lyrics about man hating with loud guitar playing (Maxine Feldman's music, for example). As Kearney observes, however, the noncommercial practices of 1970s lesbian musicians has made them less easy to identify as major influences on a new generation of "all-girl community," and so while women's music is erased as a musical influence, so lesbianism is ignored as a social context for riot grrrl. Kearney writes that "in spite of the coterminous emergence in the US of riot grrrl and queercore bands like Tribe 8, Random Violet, The Mudwimmin and Team Dresch, there have been relatively few links made by the mainstream press between lesbian feminism, queercore and riot grrrl" (Kearney 1997, 222).

Other lesbian punk or punk/folk bands see themselves as both heirs to an earlier generation of "pussy power" and pioneers of new musical genres. Bitch and Animal, for example, authors of "The Pussy Manifesto," describe their CD *What's That Smell* as "tit rock."[6] In live performances, Bitch plays an electric violin and Animal plays an array of percussion. Their songs, like those of The Butchies, are themselves archival records of lesbian subculture. One song from *What's That Smell* called "Drag King Bar" posits the drag king bar as an alternative to a rather tired mainstream lesbian scene. With Animal picking out a "yee hah" tune on the banjo, Bitch sings about a place where "all the boys were really girls and the fags whip out their pearls." Bitch tells of being picked up by one particularly bold king, and the song ends in a rous-

Bitch and Animal, *What's That Smell?* CD cover, 1999.

173

ing symphony of violin and drums. Bitch and Animal document and celebrate the emergence of a drag king scene in contemporary queer clubs, and
they blend country-influenced folk with avant-garde percussion to do so. But
their cover art and manifestos harken back to an era of women-loving-
women in their embrace of the female body; on their Web site, furthermore,
fans are encouraged to take up terms like "pussy" and "tits" with pride by
brushing off the taint of patriarchal insult. Like The Butchies's decision to
cover a Williamson song, Bitch and Animal's pussy power reaches out to an
earlier generation of women musicians refusing once and for all the oedipal
imperative to overthrow the old and bring on the new.

"I Want It That Way": A Time for Queers

Fourth, queer subcultures afford us a perfect opportunity to depart from a norma-
tive model of youth cultures as stages on the way to adulthood; this allows us to
map out different forms of adulthood, or the refusal of adulthood and new modes
of deliberate deviance. Queers participate in subcultures for far longer than
their heterosexual counterparts. At a time when heterosexual men and
women are spending their weekends, their extra cash, and all their free time
shuttling back and forth between the weddings of friends and family, urban
queers tend to spend their leisure time and money on subcultural involvement: this may take the form of intense weekend clubbing, playing in small
music bands, going to drag balls, participating in slam poetry events, or seeing performances of one kind or another in cramped and poorly ventilated
spaces. Just as homosexuality itself has been theorized by psychoanalysis as
a stage of development, a phase, that the adolescent will hopefully pass
through quickly and painlessly, so subcultural involvement has been theorized as a life stage rather than a lifelong commitment. For queers, the separation between youth and adulthood quite simply does not hold, and queer
adolescence can extend far beyond one's twenties. I want to return here to
the notion of queer time, a different mode of temporality that might arise
out of an immersion in club cultures or queer sex cultures. While obviously
heterosexual people also go to clubs and some involve themselves in sex cultures, queer urbanites, lacking the pacing and schedules that inhere to family life and reproduction, might visit clubs and participate in sex cultures well
into their forties or fifties on a regular basis.

We need to situate the critique of the adult/youth binary quite carefully
in relation to the production of queer public spheres because the idea of an

The Backstreet Boys, *Millennium,*
CD cover, 1999.

extended adolescence is not particularly new, and nor is it always and every-
where a sign of resistant subcultures. As the success of the MTV-generated
movie *Jackass* demonstrates, young white men are often encouraged to prolong their periods of adolescent fun and games long beyond their teenage
years. But while "risk" for a twenty-something white dude jackass means eat-
ing urine-soaked snow, driving a golf cart into a pond, or sticking a toy car
up his ass, risk means something quite different for the queer subcultural
producers with whom I work. The clearly faggoty overtones of a movie like
Jackass also shows what has been repressed in the representation of male homosocial bonding as a form of violent fun and flagrant rule breaking: the
queerness of subcultural life is implied in this film and then quickly buried
in flurries of homophobic othering. The phenomenon of *Jackass* (which has
made its young white male participants instantly rich) suggests the scope of
an "epistemology of youth"—the way in which a stretched-out adolescence
in one arena (young white manhood or "Jackass subjectivity") tends to be accompanied by high degrees of misogyny and homophobia, and can be contrasted with the extended adolescence of nonreproductive queer subcultural
participants that facilitates community formation and offers alternative life
narratives.

Of course, a strict binary between adolescence and adulthood has also
been racially coded, and this means that work on queer subcultures that

takes aim at the adult/youth binary can have problematic implications for people of color. As Eric Lott argues in his work "Racial Cross-Dressing and the Construction of American Whiteness," the desiring dynamics between white men and men of color often posits blackness as a state of "arrested adolescence" through which white masculinity must pass on its way to adulthood (Lott 1999). Lott quotes Leslie Fiedler's uncritical observations on the developmental narrative of white adulthood: "Born theoretically white, we are permitted to pass our childhood as imaginary Indians, our adolescence as imaginary Negroes, and only then are expected to settle down to being what we really are: white once more." Obviously in Fiedler's description of becoming "white once more," we hear the pernicious effects of racializing the divide between adulthood and childhood. While much of the resistance to this binary has come in the form of claiming the powerful space of adulthood, responsibility, and maturity for people of color, another method of opposing the racialized epistemology of youth, is to dismantle the inevitability and mutually exclusive construction of youth/maturity.

One consequence of the unproblematic assumption of the youth/adult binary can be observed in the recent popularity of queer youth groups. "Queer youth" has become a meaningful category largely as a result of outreach by social service providers. While I am arguing here that we might want to slow down the rush to adulthood insofar as adulthood has been unquestioningly associated with reproduction and the family, I am also suspicious of the rush to market queer youth as a new "at risk" group with its own special interests and needs. Queer youth sets up younger gays and lesbians not as the inheritors and benefactors of several decades of queer activism but rather as victims of homophobia who need "outreach" programs and support groups. By creating age limits for the groups and requiring people to "age out" at twenty-six or above, these programs both extend the period of youth into the mid-twenties and also make a sharp division between youth and adult, and often set up the two groups as antagonists. I would also claim that the new emphasis on queer youth, can unwittingly contribute to an erasure of queer history. At this particular historical moment, queers who came out in the 1930s, 1940s, and 1950s are fast approaching old age; these folks did not have the benefit of LGBT activism, queer activism, and so on, and their histories are important to an understanding of our present. This new emphasis on youth—again, an emphasis that arises out of an overreliance on the youth/adulthood binary—encourages young queers to think about the present and the future while ignoring the past. Not all queer youth groups organize around the category of youth such as it has been established by social service providers, however, and some groups for queer youth of color seem more likely to mark out generational differences with a set of new categorical markers like "homo-thug," "homey-sexual," or "stud."

At the same time that queers extend participation in subcultural activity long beyond their "youth," some queer subcultures also provide a critical lens through which to revisit seemingly heterosexual youth cultures. In new work on subcultures and gender/sexuality, generally speaking, there is the potential to explore the possibilities and the promise of rebellious youth genders. By focusing on the realization of tomboy desires or youthful femme aspirations in dyke punk bands and forms of queer fandom, we can see that preadult, preidentitarian girl roles offer a set of opportunities for theorizing gender, sexuality, race, and social rebellion precisely because they occupy the space of the "not-yet," the not fully realized. These girl roles are not absolutely predictive of either heterosexual or lesbian adulthoods; rather, the desires, the play, and the anguish they access allow us to theorize other relations to identity.

Gayle Wald's essay "Teenybopper Music and the Girling of Boy Bands" has also drawn our attention to the homoerotic subtext of much teen culture. Boy bands like the Backstreet Boys, Wald suggests, produce and manage anxieties about gay modes of gender performance. Boy bands perform what Wald calls "a girlish masculinity" and they channel the fantasy of perpetual youth referenced by the moniker "boy"; but they also play out socially acceptable forms of rebellion ("backstreet," for example, conjures up images of working-class youth) that can be both expressed and neatly channeled into white, middle-class heteronormativity. The phenomenon of boy bands, for me, raises a number of questions not simply about the performance of masculinity but also about what Wald refers to as the threatening aspect of the "ecstatic responses that they elicit" (Wald 2002, 25). After all, while music critics love to dismiss fandom as a passive teenybopper subculture, there is something all too powerful about a nearly hysterical audience of teen girls screaming and crying together; this activity may well have as much to say about the desire between the screamers as it says about their desire for the mythic boys. Wald argues that the phenomenon of teenybopper fans and young boy bands creates a homophobic fear of both boy fandom and homoerotic dynamics onstage between the boy performers. Yet the policing of male homosexuality, Wald continues, "creates opportunities for girls to engage in modes of consumption that have a markedly homoerotic component, although they are typically characterized in terms of (hetero-sexual) 'puppy love'" (32). Again, the notion of homoerotic bonding as a stage on the way to heterosexual maturity creates a context within which both subcultural activity and queer desire can be dismissed as temporary and nonserious. Wald's careful excavation of the sources of social scorn levied at teenyboppers and her contextualization of the boy band phenomenon within popular culture opens up new and important questions about youth cultures and femininity, and it makes possible a consideration of the queer-ness of even the most heterosexually inflected preadult activity.

I never invested much hope for queer alternatives in the performance of boy bands, I must admit, until I was present at the world premiere of New York's Backdoor Boys. When this drag king boy band took the stage as A. J., Nick, Kevin, Howie, and Brian, I saw at last the butch potential of the boy band phenomenon. The queer audience screamed as each boy was intro-duced, picked their favorites, and began the ritual ecstatic fan worship that we associate with teenage girls, but that seems to be fun at any age. The cur-rent between the stage and the packed house was electric. At least part of the appeal of the Backstreet Boys depends on the production of seemingly safe and almost unreal masculinities—the boys croon about what they would do for their girls, about being there for them, buying them flowers, giving them gifts, doing everything that other boys supposedly won't do. The boys, in short, offer themselves as a safe alternative to the misogyny and mistreat-ment that many girls find and expect in adolescent relationships. Here, in a drag king context, the space of the alternative is taken back from the realm of popular culture and revealed as proper to the subcultural space. As the Backdoor Boys went into their version of "I Want It That Way" and began to act out the barely concealed homoerotic implication of the lyric, the queer crowd went wild; the source of pleasure for the queer fans had as much to do with the acting out of the song's homo potential as with the sexual appeal of the drag kings. The Backdoor Boys's performance of "I Want It That Way" speaks to the purpose of what Wald calls "the deliberate sublimation of sex-ual explicitness" in the Backstreet Boys's lyrics and dance moves. The fan de-sire and ecstasy can only be maintained by keeping at bay the erotic relations between the boys, on the one hand, and the potentially erotic relations be-tween the screaming girls, on the other. As the boys sing together, the girls scream together, and the whole fragile edifice of heterosexuality could come tumbling down at any moment if the homosocial structures of desire are made explicit. The drag king impersonation of the faggy boy band, finally, recognizes the act as a performance of neither male heterosexuality nor gay masculinity—this is rather an intricate performance of butch masculinity, queer masculinity, that presents itself to screaming girls as a safe alternative to hetero-masculinities.

Finally, all of these representations of teen and youth genders offer us a space within which to think through the alternatives that young people create for themselves to the routine and tired options recycled by adult culture. When the Backstreet Boys croon "I want it THAT way" and the girls scream, we think for a moment that it does not have to be *this* way, and that just maybe girl and boy partial identities can be carried forward into adulthood in terms of a politics of refusal—the refusal to grow up and enter the heteronormative adulthoods implied by these concepts of progress and maturity. The boy bands in particular allow us to think of boyhood, girlhood, and even tomboyhood and riot grrrlhood not as stages to pass through but as preidentities to carry forward, inhabit, and sustain.

Generational Divides

In this next section, I want to build on an understanding of subcultural life as a place of collectivity rather than membership, and subcultural activity, as Deepdickollective see it, as educational rather than profitable. While DDC draw powerfully on Essex Hemphill, Marlon Riggs, and other queer men of color who came before them, they also quite deliberately place themselves in relation to mainstream hip-hop culture, and demand to be heard and taken seriously within this new formation: homohop. In the example with which I conclude this chapter, a set of continuities and divisions within lesbian culture and queer punk culture produces a rupture in feminist genealogy, and reveals the stakes in producing viable theories of queer time and space.

In a brilliant essay on the relations between different historical renderings of queer identity and community, "Packing History, Count(er)ing Generations," Elizabeth Freeman introduces the concept of "temporal drag." For Freeman, temporal drag works against postmodern forms of pastiche by operating as "a stubborn identification with a set of social coordinates that exceed one's own historical moment." The possibility of such contrary temporal identifications, Freeman suggests, forces us to ask, "What is the time of queer performativity?" (Freeman 2000, 2). By breaking free from a model of intergenerational dialogue that presumes conflict and the "anxiety of influence," Freeman's close reading of temporality, affect, and queer performance

points the way to an immensely subtle and complex understanding of the relations between the "now" of performance and the "then" of historical time.
I use Freeman's theoretical frame here to explore the web of influences, identifications, and disidentifications that connects the contemporary queer
dyke music scene to an earlier movement of women's music. I will focus here
on performers who seem to answer, or at least address, Freeman's question.
As I will argue, one performer, Ferron, seems located both "out of time" and
"before her time," and is somehow trapped in between different registers of
historical realness. A performer like Ferron exemplifies what Freeman describes as "the gravitational pull that 'lesbian' sometimes seems to exert on
'queer'" (2).

In contemporary dyke scenes, queer musicians have multiple opportunities to play to diverse and large audiences. Many contemporary queer performers like Tribe 8, The Butchies, and Bitch and Animal reference themes of
gender bending and sex play while also exploring their proximity to and distance from the women musicians who paved the way for an independent
dyke music scene. Most of these contemporary bands also set themselves up
against an earlier conception of white lesbian community, which included
elements of sex negativity, gender separatism, cultural feminism, and wom-
anism. But even as these bands clearly mark their difference, generically and
politically, from the women's music that preceded them, they also draw surprising lines of affiliation with an earlier moment in feminism. As we saw
earlier, The Butchies perform a cover of Williamson's classic song "Shooting
Star" by way of tribute and as a form of archiving her contribution to the history of women's music production. Recent women's music festivals like Ladyfest 2000 are also clear inheritors of lesbian feminist music festivals and
they revive an earlier model of feminism for a new generation of grrrls. Finally, Tribe 8 certainly performs a brand of sexually explicit hard-core punk,
complete with dildo-waving antics onstage, but their old-fashioned brand of
man hating comes straight out of 1970s women's music concerts. All three
bands have played the Michigan Women's Music Festival and all three have
found themselves lumped into the catchall category of "transphobic" by
camp trans protesters.

But this new tradition of dyke punk, or riot dyke, also perpetuates another
tradition of women's music—namely, the emphasis on white womanhood,
or the exclusive focus within lesbian feminism on issues of gender and sexuality, and the disinterest in a politics of race and class. At Ladyfest, the issue
of the event's racial homogeneity has been a constant irritant, but the de-

bates about the antitrans politics of the Michigan Women's Music Festival has tended to drown out other debates about race. And while white queer punk bands have upended the sex negativity of women's music and have replaced a soft acoustic sound with raucous guitars, they have done little to change its continuing legacy of racial exclusivity.

In summer 2002 in San Francisco during the annual Queer Arts Festival, the issue of race and generational conflict, political legacy, and temporal drag was staged in a dramatic fashion. That year, for the first time, musicians were included in the lineup of performances and acts. Impresario and curator Sini Anderson of Sister Spit fame decided to create a music series by pairing up older and younger queer musicians, and then splicing their performances together with an interview segment in the middle of the show. The idea, as comedian MC Elvira Kurt helpfully explained, was to put into conversation artists and audiences who might otherwise think of each other as utterly alien. The pairings included First Nation group Ulali with Kinnie Star, a Canadian self-described "mixed blood, Mohawk, hip-hop, faker, white girl" musician; Kaia Wilson of The Butchies with acoustic maverick Ferron; rhythm and blues performer Nedra Johnson with blues singer "sugar mama" Gwen Avery; Bitch and Animal with the Jewish lesbian surfer, "Pholk" singer, the Tupperware lady Phranc. Some of the pairings worked, obviously, through racial and cultural identification, some through gender styles, and others through musical styles.

It was quickly apparent that different traditions of feminism produced different intergenerational relations between and among performers. Star, for example, paid tribute to a cappella group Ulali by sampling its music on one of her most powerful songs, "Red %!" and she showed that the relationship between their music and hers, despite the extremely different styles, was not that of past and present. Star's lyrics, in English, French, and Spanish, built respectfully on the chants of Ulali, and Ulali became the foundation for her raps. Star's tribute to Ulali modeled the ways in which the old and the new can cohabit within the space of queer subculture and across feminist generations. The legacy of white feminism and lesbian feminism in particular has been much more difficult to reconcile with contemporary queer culture, and so on the evenings when white performers from different generations shared the stage, something happened that created insights into the mechanics and function of Freeman's concept of temporal drag. On the night when Wilson opened for Ferron, a fascinating contrast in styles and modes of masculinity emerged. Similarly, when Bitch and Animal opened for Phranc, the audience was confronted with a complex politics of address. In both cases, the older performers seemed to be at odds with history, out of sync, and working with a different understanding of time and rhythm where we can understand rhythm as literally a form of "keeping time" or being in time.

On the evening when Wilson paired up with Ferron, the crowd was a blend of San Francisco young punks and older queer women. Wilson, used to playing in a band, seemed out of sorts on the stage alone. She played a short acoustic set more reminiscent of Holly Near than Johnny Rotten and moved aside for the interview segment. The interviewers were Lynn Breedlove of Tribe 8 and women's music producer Barbara Price. While Breedlove tried to joke with Wilson, Price asked tough and important questions about The Butchies's punk-influenced style and its relation to earlier women's music genres. Even though her set seemed to match up perfectly with an earlier era of women's music, Wilson seemed at a loss for language to discuss the connection. When Ferron came onstage, however, the dynamics and mood changed completed. Ferron was dressed in jeans, jacket, and tie, and looked much butcher than any Butchie on the stage and certainly butcher than she had looked in her younger days. Her butch style was also a form of temporal drag given that she had steered clear of a butch persona at the height of her career in the 1980s; but now, in the heat of a butch-femme revival, she obviously felt enabled to display an open investment in her own masculinity. And still, her butch style was not the butchness of twenty-something San Franciscans; it was the butch style that she might have indulged in during the 1980s had she thought her career as a folk singer in the midst of an era of women's music could have survived it. The tie and cowboy boots looked both dignified and sad as they carried the weight of her own repressed past.

Ferron immediately took charge of the conversation and talked about how, when she began playing music in the 1970s and 1980s, there were no early influences, no women who had laid the way for her, no histories that she had to reject or to which she could lay claim. She said, "For me there were no influences, it was empty out there and all I got back was a resounding echo. When you want to still an echo," she added, "you have to go to the source. So I decided to just rely on myself." She marveled at Wilson's sense of having musical styles from which to choose, and announced herself to be of the past and yet without a past. This created a vertiginous temporal space by placing her outside of both her own and queer time. Her dynamic with Wilson and Melissa York from The Butchies was fatherly rather than nurturing, and in true paternal style, she commended York on her drumming, describing it as "restrained and therefore all the more powerful." When Ferron took the stage a few moments after the interview ended, the theater experienced a surge of some combination of nostalgia and anticipation. Ferron, unlike Phranc, who had played a few evenings earlier to an uninterested crowd of Bitch and Animal supporters, was able to lift herself out of the past and touch down meaningfully in the present.

In her essay on temporal drag, Freeman argues that Butler's rendering of gender as a copy with no original, unwittingly forecloses the possibility that "prior signs" might have purchase over "whatever looks newer." Freeman writes, "To reduce all embodied performance to the status of copies with no originals is to ignore the interesting threat that the genuine *past*-ness of the past sometimes makes to the political present" (2). Ferron's performance presented an original with no copy—she was neither the historical template that younger performers imitated or rejected nor the representative of an earlier era. In the time of women's music, Ferron was as much of an anomaly as she was in this moment of queer punk. And so Ferron, in the context of this evening's pairing of her with a much younger and much less butch musician from The Butchies, took on the glow of authenticity and originality, and created an interesting relay of sentiment and affect between herself and the young audience.

Shadows on a Dime

Ferron's songs have always been about time passing, about her place in time, her sense of her career in music as "moving forward by holding back." I want to end with a closer look at one of her most famous songs, "Shadows on a Dime," to track the performances and performers who lie somewhere in between the "then" of historical time and the "now" of performance, the temporal drag and lag that allows some pieces of history to simply fall away and remain lost to narrative. Ferron represents what can be lost even for white lesbians in the relentless urge to universalize white lesbian culture and represent it as historically continuous. In "Shadows on a Dime," Ferron tells an origin story somewhat at odds with the lesbian feminist myths of women's community. She tells the autobiographical story of a young singer who leaves her factory job in a depressed industrial town to look for fame and fortune in the big city. As she begins her story, she also begins relentlessly to mark time—"Fifteen years ago I worked the line"—and she understands her life

Ferron, *Testimony,* LP cover, 1980.

stages as before and after she began to sing, suggesting a different form of development: coming-of-age here is literally a coming to voice. And she remembers her community as not lesbians but female factory workers, and
music is an escape from not simply hard labor but a life reduced to "doing
time." Musical time by comparison—"Ten years have worn this guitar
down"—is about "having time," and while old women die from the hard
work in the factory, Ferron's guitar marks time's passing more gently and it
"resonates with age." But Ferron also brings the past into the present by
promising that she won't forget about the factory and, by implication, the
class politics that it engenders; and this memory will install an uncertainty
in the present about a successful future: "Can I give you what you want to
see? Can we do it one more time?" Her class background, like her barely concealed butchness, leaves her outside of both the queer musical communities
in contemporary San Francisco and the women's music communities of the
1980s.

As the song builds, it progresses without recourse to a chorus and it is plot-
ted as a spiral rather than a cycle; the singer enters "dream time" and begins
to address her newly formed audience—"I sing to you to feed the dream."
This dreamscape allows for queer time, a time of eros that is represented in
the next verse by a lost lover—"Five years have blazed since she warmed my
side"—but that is actually the romantic relationship between Ferron and the

listener. Finally, dream time opens up into heterotopic space as Ferron references the motor of the song's narrative, a train that takes her from her rural working-class past to an as yet unknown queer urban future. The train represents time as movement through space, and locates subjectivity as both local and distant: "This window makes a perfect frame." In the song's last verse, we are in a tentative and even fatigued space of the now: "And now a tired conductor passes by." Even in this fleeting present, other temporalities crowd the stage; generational time enters as the conductor tells Ferron, "I have a daughter as old as you." And yet Ferron identifies not with his daughter but with a younger version of him: "I imagine him with his hair jet black." The time of his past (the younger conductor with whom Ferron identifies) and his future (his daughter) are abruptly compressed by the time of queer performativity as he announces that "the New York train stops here."

At the Brava Theater that night, the time of queer performativity was this heterotopic space crammed with overlapping temporalities for both audience and performer. Ferron represented authenticity (old butch versus new butch), copy (she comes belatedly into a butchness that she could not express in the time of women's music), a past in queer music history that is not the history of women's music, and an uncanny present of a singer whose time has come even as she remains out of time and whose audience has arrived but too late to see her in her time. When Ferron launched into the opening verse of "Shadows on a Dime" that night, the audience sat up, caught for a moment by another rhythm and pulled "forward by holding back." The bond between audience and performer was palpable and, dare I say, real. Ferron got as far as Santa Cruz—"I left my soul in Santa Cruz"— then fumbled for the words: "I ached all night / Next day I lost my. . . ." What did I lose? she asked the audience—"my shoes." She picked up pace again: "It's so optional what you may or may not lose / in this pattern we call time." But that was it, she lost the words after that, she couldn't remember what came next, and this young audience, unlike her other audiences in Santa Cruz and Michigan, could not help by calling out the words for her to sing. She strummed a few more bars and then fell silent.

In any project on queer temporality, one has to grapple with the meaning of intergenerational dialogue outside the frameworks of conflict or mandatory continuity. Today's young punky performers connect easily with their multigenerational audiences. But the older performers create an affective vortex by pulling new audiences to a place they neither remember nor know through history, and by simultaneously taking older audiences back to that place between the time of lesbian and the time of queer. Ferron surmounts the problem of her audience's conflicting time frames by articulating herself as her own best audience and refusing the empty lure of mainstream success: "But I don't forget about the factory / I don't expect this ride to always be / Can I give them what they want to see / Let me do it twice—The second time for me." And she invites those who do listen to enter that strange space behind the window of a train, and to look out from behind the music onto the urban landscape of a queer time in which fame, fortune, and success will always be as fleeting as "shadows on a dime." The song ends abruptly in the middle of a thought leaving her and us, the audience, stranded in a past that no longer exists, waiting for the future recognition that we now know will never come.

Queer Times

In his powerful study of a disappearing sexual subculture in New York City, *Times Square Red, Times Square Blue,* queer legend Samuel Delany describes queer subterranean worlds as "a complex of interlocking systems and subsystems" (xviii). The unimaginably precious meaning of these systems are of no consequence to the city planner who sees only ugliness and filth where Delaney sees a distillation of the promise of radical democracy. The porn theaters that Delany visits and learns from offer him and other men, he claims, one of the last opportunities in urban America for "interclass contact and communication conducted in a mode of good will" (Delany 1999, 111). Counterpublics, as his book shows, are spaces created and altered by certain subcultures for their own uses. Since lesbians and women in general partake so little in public sex cultures, we, much more than gay men, need to develop and protect counterpublics for subcultural uses. In the Bay Area—San Francisco and Oakland in particular—there is a long history of subcultural activity; counterpublics abound here, and new bands, spoken word artists, and performers appear weekly at different shows in different venues. These counterpublics have survived the dot.com explosion and the latest recession, the yuppies and the businesspeople; they have also survived so far the new patriotism of a post-9-11 culture and the new homonormativity of the recent lesbian baby boom. To return to Butler's question from "Agencies of Style for a Liminal Subject," "What sorts of style signal the crisis of survival?" (2000, 36), we can now answer that the crisis of survival is being played out nightly in a club near you. The radical styles crafted in queer punk bands, slam poetry events, and drag king boy bands do not express some mythically pure form of agency or will but rather model other modes of being and becoming that scramble our understandings of place, time, development, action, and transformation.

In this chapter, I have tried to chart a different epistemology of youth and seniority for queers, and an altered understanding of temporal movement and generational interaction. According to Ferron's haunting song, "We move forward fast by holding back." I want to hold on to the complex temporal pattern of her song in order to disrupt simple models of continuity and linear understandings of cultural influence. We may well be touched by the tribute paid by The Butchies to Williamson or by Tribe 8 to Joan Jett, but the echo of Ulali in Star's music reminds us that these tributes tell only part of the story of second-wave feminism, 1970s women's culture, and lesbian subcultures. The project of subcultural historiography demands that we look at the silences, the gaps, and the ruptures in the spaces of performance, and that we use them to tell disorderly narratives. A queer history of subcultures, armed with a queer sense of temporality, tracks the activity of community building, traces the contours of collectivity, and follows the eccentric careers of those pioneers who fall outside the neat models of narrative history—the Ferrons and Phrancs, but also the Joan Armatradings—and who still need to find a place in the winding, twisting story of queer subcultural lives.

In their foundational introduction to their anthology *The Politics of Culture in the Shadow of Capital*, Lisa Lowe and David Lloyd offer a more broad-based understanding of the implications of alternative temporalities. Lowe and Lloyd articulate a critique of modernity that resonates in what they label "the excavation and connection of alternative histories and their different temporalities that cannot be contained by the progressive narrative of Western developmentalism" (Lowe and Lloyd 1997, 5). In Lowe and Lloyd's anthology, the alternative political cultures in question are global in nature and mostly situated out of the West. But their call for "affirmative inventories of the survival of alternatives" can also be engaged in the very belly of the beast. Lowe and Lloyd instruct us in the methods for seeking out alternative lives in capitalism, and their introduction provides a theoretical map of capital's shadows. Ferron, like Deepdickollective and other subcultural groups, understands herself to be engaged in a collective project that is rewarded not by capital or visibility, not by the market, but by an affective connection with those people who will eventually be the vessels of memory for all she now forgets. And like Lowe and Lloyd, Ferron looks not to the dime but to its shadows.

Notes

Notes to Chapter 1

1 Thanks to Glen Mimura for the phrase "epistemology of youth."

Notes to Chapter 2

1 For more on the erasure of Philip and the downplaying of the racial narrative, see the debates about *Boys Don't Cry* in *Screen*, particularly the essay by Jennifer Devere Brody (2002).

2 I found out later that the filmmakers, Muska and Olafsdottir, had been present at an earlier screening of the film in Seattle where similar concerns had been raised and no satisfactory answers had been provided by the two directors. In some ways, I was fielding questions meant for Muska and Olafsdottir, but in other ways, I was being positioned as another "outsider" who seemed not to be able to comprehend the complexities of small-town life in the Midwest. I tried to correspond with Muska and Olafsdottir about this particular set of reactions to their work, but to no avail. They did not want to talk about the question of "condescension" at all and had no insights to offer about these readings of *The Brandon Teena Story*.

3 Alan Sinfield usefully defines the "metropolitan" for use in queer studies in his essay "The Production of Gay and the Return of Power." He remarks on the interactive definitions of metropolitan and nonmetropolitan, and defines metropolitan sexualities as those that take place in the "global centers of capital" and the "principal cities in a nation state" (21). He qualifies this homogenizing notion of the metropolitan, however, by noting that "subordinated groups living at or near the centres of capital and specifically non-white minorities, may be in some aspects non-metropolitan; a Filipino living in New York may share some ideas and attitudes with people living in the Philippines" (21).

4 See Johannes Fabian, *Time and the Other*. Fabian writes that "the temporal discourse of anthropology as it was formed decisively under the paradigm of evolutionism rested on a conception of Time that was not only secularized and naturalized but also thoroughly spatialized" (16).

5 For more on the overlap between deviance and race in the racial imaginary, see Roderick A. Ferguson, *Aberrations in Black: Toward a Queer of Color Critique* (2003).

6 This notion of rural queers being stuck in one place resonates with Gayatri Gopinath's theorizations of the meaning of queerness for those who "stay put" in postcolonial contexts rather than leaving a remote area for a seemingly liberated metropolis. See the chapter on queer South Asian diasporic literature in Gopinath's *Queer Diasporas and South Asian Public Culture* (Durham, NC: Duke University Press, forthcoming).

7 I recognize of course that "urban/rural" is not a "real" binary; it is rather a locational rubric that supports and sustains the conventional depiction of queer life as urban.

8 In "Qualities of Desire," Lisa Rofel has brilliantly pointed to the structuring contradiction in Altman's work that causes him to "assert cultural diversity and the need to respect it while also recuperating identification in a monumentalist history of gay identity, and, conversely, to further gay rights yet, in pursuing this goal, to elide diversity, articulation and alliance with radical cultural difference, thereby occluding the fault lines of power that emerge in global gay discourses and practices" (Rofel 1999, 451–474).

Altman has also been criticized by North American diasporic critics like Martin Manalansan (1997), Jacqui Alexander (1998), and Gayatri Gopinath (1995) for ignoring the alternative sexual economies in different, particularly Third World, places and for assuming that Euro-American models of sexual identity are both desirable and desired.

9 For more on the tendency of Western queer anthropologists to produce unidimensional models of Euro-American queer subjects in order to emphasize the otherness of non-Western queers, see Gayatri Gopinath, "Homo-Economics: Queer Sexualities in a Transnational Frame" (1998).

10 Lisa Duggan also gives several full accounts of passing women in North America in the late nineteenth and early twentieth century.

11 The *Ebony* article she cites is from November 10, 1954 (Wilson 2000).

Notes to Chapter 3

1 In an interview with Butler, Rubin says of her ethnographic research on the San Francisco gay male leather scene: "When I started this project I was interested in the whole question of sexual ethnogenesis. I wanted to understand better how sexual communities form" (Rubin 1994, 62–100).

2 See Don Williamson, "Interview with Little Jimmy Scott," http://visionx.ian/jazz/iviews/JScott.html (accessed January 2000).

3 See http://www.guggenheim.org/BRANDON.

4 For more on the politics of naming in the case of Brandon, see Jacob Hale, "Consuming the Living, Dis(Re)Membering the Dead in the Butch/FTM Borderlands."

Notes to Chapter 4

1 For an excellent discussion of the political contradictions of *The Crying Game,* see Shantanu Dutta Ahmed, "'I Thought You Knew!' Performing the Penis, the Phallus, and Otherness in Neil Jordan's *The Crying Game*" (1998).
2 The most sophisticated account of this narrative trajectory in cinema occurs in Teresa De Lauretis, *Alice Doesn't: Feminism, Semiotics, Cinema* (1984).
3 See Straayer's chapter "Redressing the Natural: The Temporary Transvestite Film" (Straayer 1996).
4 Patricia White has argued in "Girls Still Cry" (2001) that the gaze in *Boys Don't Cry* is Lana's all along. I think in the first two-thirds of the film, the gaze is shared between Lana and Brandon, but I agree with White that the film's ending transfers the gaze from Brandon to Lana's with some unpredictable consequences.
5 Interview by Terry Gross on *Fresh Air*, PBS Radio, March 15, 2001.
6 In the review copy of the film I saw, *Boys Don't Cry* was dedicated "To Brandon Teena and Lisa Lambert." This dedication seems to have been removed later on, possibly because it so overtly referenced Philip's erasure.
7 Unless otherwise attributed, all quotes from directors Howard and Dodge are taken from the press kit for *By Hook or by Crook,* http://www.steakhaus.com/bhobc/.

Notes to Chapter 5

1 Greenberg's essay originally appeared in *Partisan Review* 6 no. 5 (Fall 1939).
2 Francis Frascina uses this important letter by Engels to argue that "elements of the superstructure have a relative autonomy, so it is clear, for example, that ideas can be determinants on modes of production and activities, and have a revolutionary potential" (Frascina 2000, 41).
3 For an excellent account of the rise of abstract expressionism and its relation to U.S. hegemony post–World War II, see Serge Guilbaut, *How New York Stole the Idea of Modern Art* (1983).
4 Obviously, the concept of bodies with new organs draws on Giles Deleuze and Felix Guattari's rendering of the "body without organs" in their *Anti-Oedipus* (1983). For Deleuze and Guattari, the body without organs is a way of resisting the surface/depth binary model of human identity within which the concept of depth allows us to equate the "human" with psychic complexity, interiority, oedipal systems, and the unconscious.
5 See "Tissue Culture and Art(ificial) Womb," http://www.tca.uwa.edu.au/ars/text .html.
6 See "Short Manifesto," http://www.tca.uwa.edu.au/atGlance/manifesto.html.
7 See "Art(ificial) Wombs and the Next Sex," http://www.tca.uwa.edu.au/ars/text .html.
8 Interview with the author.

9 Quoted in Lucy Lippard, *Eva Hesse* (1976).
10 Ibid.
11 Ibid.
12 Linda Besemer, "Lecture Notes," shared with the author by Besemer.

Notes to Chapter 6

1 New shows on television like *Queer Eye for the Straight Guy* try to extend the influence of gay men beyond straight women and into the hallowed bastion of hetero-masculinity.
2 For more oedipal and pre-oedipal comedy, see Andrew S. Horton, Introduction to *Comedy, Cinema, Theory* (1991).
3 There are even Web sites listing the multiple references to other spy films, British comedies, and Bond spoofs in the *Austin Powers* films. On one Web site — www.frankwu.com/AP2.html — every joke has been meticulously (obsessively? anally?) traced back to its source. Thanks to Lauren Berlant for this reference.
4 Quoted in *Austin Powers: International Man of Mystery*, DVD (New York: New Line Cinema, 1997).
5 Ibid.

Notes to Chapter 7

1 For an article on the fate of the queens and children featured in *Paris Is Burning*, see Jesse Green, "Paris Has Burned" (1993). Green documents the death of Angie Extravaganza and Kim Pendarvis, among others. Drag queens are interviewed for the article, and Green reports on the anger that many in the ball world feel about Livingston's film. Green reminds us that "the film's critical and financial success should not therefore be taken for the success of its subjects." While Livingston became a filmmaker as a consequence of the circulation of *Paris Is Burning*, the film's subjects continued to live in poverty.
2 Paul Gilroy, for example, was a disc jockey while working on black expressive cultures; and nowadays, many public intellectuals straddle the worlds of cultural production and theory. Josh Kun, for example, writes about Rock en Espanol and hosts a radio show. Patrick Johnson is a theorist of black performance art and he himself performs in a one-man show. See Johnson, *Appropriating Blackness* (2003).
3 This exchange was recorded on an earlier version of their Web site, http://www .deepdickollective.com.
4 For a great article on feminism and rock music, see Gayle Wald, "Just a Girl? Rock Music, Feminism, and the Cultural Construction of Female Youth" (1998).
5 For Alix Olson's poetry, see *Only the Starving Favor Peace* (1998).
6 Online www.bitchandanimal.com.

Bibliography

Adorno, T., and Max Horkheimer. "The Culture Industry." In *The Cultural Studies Reader*, edited by S. During, 31–41. New York: Routledge, 1993.

Ahmed, S. D. "'I Thought You Knew!' Performing the Penis, the Phallus, and Otherness in Neil Jordan's *The Crying Game*." *Film Criticism* 23, no. 1 (1998): 61–73.

Alexander, J. "Imperial Desire/Sexual Utopias: White Gay Capital and Transnational Capital." In *Talking Visions: Multicultural Feminism in a Transnational Age*, edited by E. Shohat, 281–306. Cambridge: MIT Press, 1998.

Altman, D. "The Globalization of Sexual Identities." In *Global Sex*. Chicago: University of Chicago Press, 2001.

Baldwin, J. *Evidence of Things Not Seen*. New York: Henry Holt, 1995.

Barber, S. M., and D. L. Clark. "Queer Moments: The Performative Temporalities of Eve Kosofsky Sedgwick." In *Regarding Sedgwick: Essays on Queer Culture and Critical Theory*, edited by S. M. Barber and D. L. Clark. New York: Routledge, 2002.

Barrett, L. *Blackness and Value: Seeing Double*. Cambridge: Cambridge University Press, 1999.

Batchelor, D. *Chromophobia*. London: Reaktion Books, 2000.

Batchelor, D., and L. Batchelor. "Too Colorful: A Conversation." In *Linda Besemer*, 19–22. Los Angeles: Angles Gallery, 2002.

Baudelaire, Charles Pierre. *Painter of Modern Life and Other Essays*. New York: Da Capo Press, 1990.

Baudrillard, J. (1990). "Transsexuality." In *The Transparency of Evil: Essays on Extreme Phenomena*, translated by James Benedict, 20–25. New York: Verso, 1990.

Bell, D. "Eroticizing the Rural." In *De-Centering Sexualities: Politics and Representations beyond the Metropolis*, edited by R. Phillips, D. Watt, and D. E. Shuttleton, 83–101. London: Routledge, 2000.

Berlant, L. *The Queen of America Goes to Washington City: Essays on Sex and Citizenship*. Durham, NC: Duke University Press, 1997.

Berlant, L., and M. Warner. "Sex in Public." *Critical Inquiry* 24, no. 2 (1998): 547–66.

Bersani, L. *Homos*. Cambridge, MA: Harvard University Press, 1996.

Boellstorff, T. "The Perfect Path: Gay Men, Marriage, Indonesia." *GLQ* 5, no. 4 (1999): 475–510.

Bornstein, K. *My Gender Workbook: How to Become a Real Man, a Real Woman, the Real You, or Something Else Entirely.* New York: Routledge, 1998.

Breedlove, L. *Godspeed.* New York: St. Martin's Press, 2002.

Brody, J. D. "Boyz Do Cry: Screening History's White Lies." *Screen* 43, no. 1 (2002): 91–96.

Browning, F. *A Queer Geography of Desire.* New York: Noonday Press, 1996.

Butler, J. "Agencies of Style for a Liminal Subject." In *Without Guarantees: In Honor of Stuart Hall,* edited by P. Gilroy, L. Grossberg, and A. McRobbie, 30–37. New York: Verso, 2000.

———. *Bodies That Matter: On the Discursive Limits of Sex.* New York: Routledge, 1993.

———. *Gender Trouble: Feminism and the Subversion of Identity.* New York: Routledge, 1990.

———. "Imitation and Gender Insubordination." In *inside/out: Lesbian Theories, Gay Theories,* edited by D. Fuss, 13–31. New York: Routledge, 1991.

Capote, T. *In Cold Blood.* New York: Vintage, 1963.

Carson, A. *Economy of the Unlost.* Princeton: Princeton University Press, 1999.

Cather, W. *Lucy Gayheart.* New York: Knopf, 1935.

———. *My Antonia.* New York: Broadview Press, 2003.

Chauncey, G. "Christian Brotherhood or Sexual Perversion? Homosexual Identities and the Construction of Sexual Boundaries in the World War I Era." In *Hidden from History: Reclaiming the Gay and Lesbian Past,* edited by M. Vicinus, G. Chauncey, and M. B. Duberman, 294–317. New York: Meridian, 1989.

Chin, S. *Wildcat Woman: Poetry.* New York: Self-published, 1998.

Clark, T. J. "Clement Greenberg's Theory of Art." In *Pollock and After: The Critical Debate,* edited by F. Frascina, 102–12. London: Routledge, 2000.

Clifford, J. "Taking Identity Politics Seriously: The Contradictory, Stony Ground." In *Without Guarantees: In Honor of Stuart Hall,* edited by S. Hall, P. Gilroy, L. Grossberg, and A. McRobbie, 94-112. New York: Verso, 2000.

Cohen, C. J. *The Boundaries of Blackness: AIDS and the Breakdown of Black Politics.* Chicago: University of Chicago Press, 1999.

Cott, N. *The Bonds of Womanhood: "Woman's Sphere" in New England, 1780–1835.* New Haven, CT: Yale University Press, 1977.

Crow, T. "Modernism and Mass Culture in the Visual Arts." In *Modern Art in the Common Culture.* New Haven, CT: Yale University Press, 1996.

Cunningham, M. *The Hours.* New York: Picador, 1998.

Cvetkovich, A. *An Archive of Feelings: Trauma, Sexuality and Lesbian Public Cultures.* Durham, NC: Duke University Press, 2003.

Dahl, L. *Morning Glory: A Biography of Mary Lou Williams.* Berkeley: University of California Press, 2001.

Danto, A. C. "Shirin Neshat." *Bomb* 73 (2000): 64.

Delany, S. *Times Square Red, Times Square Blue.* New York: New York University Press, 1999.

De Lauretis, T. *Alice Doesn't: Feminism, Semiotics, Cinema.* Bloomington: Indiana University Press, 1984.

Deleuze, G., and F. Guattari. *Anti-Oedipus: Capitalism and Schizophrenia.* Minneapolis: University of Minnesota Press, 1983.

Dinshaw, C. *Getting Medieval: Sexualities and Communities, Pre- and Postmodern.* Durham, NC: Duke University Press, 1999.

Doane, M. A. "Film and the Masquerade: Theorizing the Female Spectator" (1982). In *Issues in Feminist Film Criticism,* edited by P. Erens, 41–57. Bloomington: Indiana University Press, 1990.

Donham, D. "Freeing South Africa: The 'Modernization' of Male-Male Sexuality in Soweto." *Cultural Anthropology* 13, no. 1 (1998): 3–21.

Doty, M. *Heaven's Coast.* New York: Harper, 1996.

———. *Sapphic Slashers: Sex, Violence, and American Modernity.* Durham, NC: Duke University Press, 2000.

Duggan, L. *The Twilight of Equality: Neo-Liberalism, Cultural Politics and the Attack on Democracy.* Boston: Beacon Press, 2003.

Dunne, J. G. "The Humboldt Murders." *New Yorker* (January 1997): 45–62.

Du Plessis, M., and K. Chapman. "Queercore: The Distinct Identities of a Subculture." *College Literature* 24, no. 1 (1997): 45–58.

Edelman, L. "The Future Is Kid Stuff: Queer Theory, Disidentification, and the Death Drive." *Narrative* 6 (1998): 18–30.

Engels, F. "Letter from Engels to W. Borgius." In *Karl Marx and Friedrich Engels: Selected Works III,* 502–3. London: Lawrence and Wishart, 1894.

Fabian, J. *Time and the Other: How Anthropology Makes Its Object.* New York: Columbia University Press, 2002.

Faludi, S. *Stiffed: The Betrayal of the American Man.* New York: Morrow, 1999.

Fellows, W. *Farm Boys: Lives of Gay Men from the Rural Midwest.* Madison: University of Wisconsin Press, 2001.

Felski, R. "Fin de Siecle, Fin de Sexe: Transsexuality, Postmodernism, and the Death of History." *New Literary History* 27, no. 2 (1996): 337–49.

Fer, B. "The Work of Salvage: Eva Hesse's Latex Works." In *Eva Hesse,* edited by E. Sussman, 85–86. San Francisco: San Francisco Museum of Modern Art, 2002.

Ferguson, R. *Aberrations in Black: Toward a Queer of Color Critique.* Minneapolis: University of Minnesota Press, 2003.

Florida, R. *The Rise of the Creative Class and How It's Transforming Work, Leisure, Community, and Everyday Life.* New York: Basic Books, 2002.

Foucault, M. "Friendship as a Way of Life." In *Foucault Live: Collected Interviews, 1961–1984,* edited by S. Lotringer, 204–12. New York: Semiotext(e), 1996.

———. *The History of Sexuality.* New York: Vintage, 1980.

———. "Of Other Spaces." Translated by Jay Miskowiec. *Diacritics* 16, no. 1 (1986): 22–27.

Frascina, F., ed. Introduction to *Pollack and After: The Critical Debate,* 1–28. London: Routledge, 2000.

Freeman, E. "Packing History, Count(er)ing Generations." *New Literary History* 31, no. 4 (2000): 1–18.

Gamson, J. *Freaks Talk Back: Tabloid Talk Shows and Sexual Nonconformity.* Chicago: University of Chicago Press, 1999.

Gatti, J., and M. Becquer. "Elements of Vogue." In *The Subcultures Reader,* edited by K. Gelder and S. Thornton, 445–53. London: Routledge, 1997.

Gever, M., P. Parmar, and J. Greyson, eds. *Queer Looks: Perspectives on Lesbian and Gay Film and Video.* New York: Routledge, 1993.

Gibson, A. E. *Abstract Expressionism: Other Politics.* New Haven, CT: Yale University Press, 1997.

Gibson-Graham, J. K. *The End of Capitalism (as We Knew It).* Malden, MA: Blackwell, 1996.

Gilroy, P. *The Black Atlantic: Modernity and Double Consciousness.* Cambridge, MA: Harvard University Press, 1993.

Gopinath, G. "Bombay, UK, Yuba City: Bhangra Music and the Engendering of Diaspora." *Diaspora* 4, no. 3 (1995): 303–22.

———. "Homo-Economics: Queer Sexualities in a Transnational Frame." In *Burning down the House: Recycling Domesticity,* edited by R. M. George, 102–24. Boulder, CO: Westview Press, 1998.

Gordon, A. *Ghostly Matters: Haunting and the Sociological Imagination.* Minneapolis: University of Minnesota Press, 1997.

Green, J. "Paris Has Burned." *New York Times,* April 18, 1993, 1.

Greenberg, C. "Avant-Garde and Kitsch" (1939). In *Pollock and After: The Critical Debate,* edited by F. Frascina, 71–86. London: Routledge, 2000.

Guilbaut, S. *How New York Stole the Idea of Modern Art: Abstract Expressionism, Freedom, and the Cold War.* Chicago: University of Chicago Press, 1983.

Gunn, T. *The Man with Night Sweats.* Boston: Faber and Faber, 1993.

Halberstam, J. "Butch Kids at Sundance: An Interview with Silas Howard and Harry Dodge." *Girlfriends* (2002): 27–28.

———. *Female Masculinity.* Durham, NC: Duke University Press, 1998.

Halberstam, J., and Del LaGrace Volcano. *The Drag King Book.* London: Serpent's Tail, 1999.

Hale, J. "Consuming the Living, Dis(Re)Membering the Dead in the Butch/FTM Borderlands." *GLQ* 4, no. 2 (1998): 311–48.

Hall, S. "The Global and the Local: Globalization and Ethnicity." In *Dangerous Liaisons: Gender, Nation, and Postcolonial Perspectives,* edited by Ann McClintock et al., 173–87. Minneapolis: University of Minnesota Press, 1997.

Hall, S., and T. Jefferson, eds. *Resistance through Rituals: Youth Subcultures in Post-War Britain.* London: Routledge, 1975.

Harvey, D. *The Condition of Postmodernity.* Oxford: Blackwell, 1990.

Hausman, B. *Changing Sex: Transsexualism, Technology, and the Idea of Gender.* Durham, NC: Duke University Press, 1995.

Hebdige, D. "Posing . . . Threats, Striking . . . Poses: Youth, Surveillance, and Display." In *The Subcultures Reader,* edited by K. Gelder and S. Thornton, 393–405. London: Routledge, 1997.

————. *Subculture: The Meaning of Style.* London: Methuen, 1979.

Hietala, T. *Manifest Design: American Exceptionalism and Empire.* Ithaca, NY: Cornell University Press, 2003.

hooks, b. *Black Looks: Race and Representation.* Boston: South End Press, 1992.

Horton, A. S., ed. *Comedy, Cinema, Theory.* Berkeley: University of California Press, 1991.

Howard, J. *Men like That: A Southern Queer History.* Chicago: University of Chicago Press, 1999.

Jagose, A. *Inconsequence: Lesbian Representation and the Logic of Sequence.* Ithaca, NY: Cornell University Press, 2002.

Jameson, F. *Postmodernism, or the Cultural Logic of Late Capitalism.* Durham, NC: Duke University Press, 1997.

Jeffords, S. *Hard Bodies: Hollywood Masculinity in the Reagan Era.* New Brunswick, NJ: Rutgers University Press, 1994.

Johnson, P. *Appropriating Blackness: Performance and the Politics of Authenticity.* Durham, NC: Duke University Press, 2003.

Jones, A. *All S/he Wanted.* New York: Pocket Books, 1996.

————. *Body Art: Performing the Subject.* Minneapolis: University of Minnesota Press, 1998.

Kay, J. *Trumpet.* New York: Pantheon, 1998.

Kearney, M. C. "The Missing Link: Riot Grrrl, Feminism, Lesbian Culture." In *Sexing the Groove: Popular Music and Gender,* edited by S. Whiteley, 207–29. London: Routledge, 1997.

Leblanc, L. *Pretty in Punk: Girls' Gender Resistance in a Boys' Subculture.* New Brunswick, NJ: Rutgers University Press, 1998.

Lieberman, R. C. *Shifting the Color Line: Race and the American Welfare State.* Cambridge, MA: Harvard University Press, 1998.

Lippard, L. *Eva Hesse.* New York: New York University Press, 1976.

Lipsitz, G. "Cruising around the Historical Bloc: Postmodernism and Popular Music in East LA." In *The Subcultures Reader,* edited by K. Gelder and S. Thornton, 350–59. London: Routledge, 1997.

————. *The Possessive Investment in Whiteness: How White People Profit from Identity Politics.* Philadelphia: Temple University Press, 1998.

Loffreda, B. *Losing Matt Shepard.* New York: Columbia University Press, 2002.

Lott, E. "All the King's Men: Elvis Impersonators and White Working-Class Masculinity." In *Race and the Subject of Masculinities,* edited by B. Stephanoupolos, 192–230. Durham, NC: Duke University Press, 1997.

————. "Racial Cross-Dressing and the Construction of American Whiteness." In *The Cultural Studies Reader,* edited by S. During, 241–55. London: Routledge, 1999.

Lowe, L. *Immigrant Acts: On Asian American Cultural Politics.* Durham, NC: Duke University Press, 1996.

Lowe, L., and D. Lloyd. Introduction to *The Politics of Culture in the Shadow of Capital,* 1–32. Durham, NC: Duke University Press, 1997.

Manalansan, M. "In the Shadow of Stonewall: Examining Gay Transnational Politics and the Diasporic Dilemma." In *The Politics of Culture in the Shadow of Capital,* edited by L. Lowe and D. Lloyd, 485–505. Durham, NC: Duke University Press, 1997.

Martin, B. "Sexualities without Genders and Other Queer Utopias." *Diacritics* 24, nos. 2–3 (1994): 104–21.

Martin, E. *Flexible Bodies.* Boston: Beacon Press, 1995.

Massey, D. "The Political Place of Locality Studies. In *Space, Place, and Gender,* 125–45. Minneapolis: University of Minnesota Press, 1994.

McHugh, K. *American Domesticity: From How-To Manual to Hollywood Drama.* New York: Oxford University Press, 1999.

McRobbie, A. "Girls and Subcultures" (1975). In *The Subcultures Reader,* edited by K. Gelder and S. Thornton, 112–20. London: Routledge, 1997.

———. *Postmodernism and Popular Culture.* London: Routledge, 1994.

———. "Settling Accounts with Subcultures: A Feminist Critique." In *Feminism and Youth Culture,* 26–43. New York: Routledge, 1991.

Merck, M. "Figuring out Warhol." In *Pop Out: Queer Warhol,* edited by J. Doyle, J. Flatley, and J. E. Muñoz, 224–37. Durham, NC: Duke University Press, 1996.

Meyer, R. *Outlaw Representation: Censorship and Homosexuality in Twentieth-Century American Art.* Oxford: Oxford University Press, 2002.

Middlebrook, D. W. *Suits Me: The Double Life of Billy Tipton.* Boston: Houghton Mifflin, 1998.

Minkowitz, D. "Gender Offender: Never More." *Village Voice,* April 19, 1994, 30.

Mirzoeff, N. *An Introduction to Visual Culture.* London: Routledge, 1999.

———. "The Subject of Visual Culture." In *The Visual Culture Reader,* 3–28. New York: Routledge, 2002.

Morris, R. "Three Genders and Four Sexualities: Redressing the Discourses on Sex and Gender in Contemporary Thailand." *Positions* 2, no. 1 (1994): 15–43.

Mulvey, L. "Visual Pleasure and Narrative Cinema" (1975). In *Issues in Feminist Film Criticism,* edited by P. Erens, 28–40. Bloomington: Indiana University Press, 1990.

Muñoz, J. E. *Disidentifications: Queers of Color and the Performance of Politics.* Minneapolis: University of Minnesota Press, 1999.

———. "Ephemera as Evidence: Introductory Notes to Queer Acts." *Women and Performance: A Journal of Feminist Theory* 8:2, no. 16 (1996): 5–18.

Myles, E. *Chelsea Girls.* Santa Rosa, CA: Black Sparrow Press, 1994.

Nancy, J. L. "The Inoperative Community." In *The Inoperative Community,* edited by P. Connor, 1–43. Minneapolis: University of Minnesota Press, 1991.

Nemser, C. "A Interview with Eva Hesse." *Art Forum* 7, no. 9 (1970): 59–63.

Newitz, A., and M. Wray, eds., *White Trash: Race and Class in America.* New York: Routledge, 1996.

Newton, E. *Mother Camp: Female Impersonators in America.* Chicago: University of Chicago Press, 1979.

Olson, A. *Only the Starving Favor Peace.* Brooklyn, NY: Feed the Fire Productions, 1998.

Ong, A. *Flexible Citizenship: The Cultural Logics of Transnationality.* Durham, NC: Duke University Press, 1999.

Phillips, R., D. Watt, and D. E. Shuttleton, eds. Introduction to *De-Centering Sexualities: Politics and Representations beyond the Metropolis.* London: Routledge, 2000.

Pile, S. "Introduction: Opposition, Political Identities, and Spaces of Resistance." In *Geographies of Resistance,* edited by M. Keith, 1–32. London: Routledge, 1997.

Prosser, J. "The Art of Ph/Autography: Del LaGrace Volcano." In *Sublime Mutations,* by Del LaGrace Volcano, 6–11. Berlin: Konkursbuchverlag, 2000.

———. *Second Skins: The Body Narratives of Transsexuality.* New York: Columbia University Press, 1998.

Reid-Pharr, R. *Black Gay Man: Essays.* Foreword by Samuel R. Delany. New York: New York University Press, 2001.

Ridgeway, J. *Blood in the Face: The Ku Klux Klan, Aryan Nations, Nazi Skinheads, and the Rise of a New White Culture.* New York: Thunder's Mouth Press, 1995.

Roach, J. *Cities of the Dead: Circum-Atlantic Performance.* New York: Columbia University Press, 1996.

Rofel, L. "Qualities of Desire: Imagining Gay Identities in China." *GLQ* 5, no. 4 (1999): 451–74.

Rubin, G. "Sexual Traffic." Interview by Judith Butler. *differences* 6, nos. 2–3 (1994): 62–100.

———. "Thinking Sex: Notes for a Radical Theory of the Politics of Sexuality." In *Pleasure and Danger: Exploring Female Sexuality,* edited by C. Vance, 267–319. Boston: Routledge, 1984.

Rubin, H. "Do You Believe in Gender." *Sojourner* 21, no. 6 (1996): 7–8.

———. *Self-Made Men: Identity, Embodiment and Recognition among Transsexual Men.* Nashville: Vanderbilt University Press, 2003.

Rutherford, J. *Forever England: Reflections on Race, Masculinity, and Empire.* London: Lawrence and Wishart, 1997.

Scott, J. C. *Domination and the Arts of Resistance: Hidden Transcripts.* New Haven, CT: Yale University Press, 1990.

Sedgwick, E. K. *Between Men: English Literature and Male Homosocial Desire.* New York: Columbia University Press, 1986.

———. *Epistemology of the Closet.* Berkeley: University of California Press, 1990.

Seltzer, M. *Serial Killers: Death and Life in America's Wound Culture.* New York: Routledge, 1998.

Silverman, K. "Suture." In *The Subject of Semiotics.* New York: Oxford University Press, 1983.

Sinfield, A. "The Production of Gay and the Return of Power." In *De-Centering Sexualities: Politics and Representations beyond the Metropolis,* edited by R. Phillips, D. Watt, and D. E. Shuttleton, 21–36. London: Routledge, 2000.

Smith, D. *The Illusionist.* New York: Scribner, 1997.

Smith-Rosenberg, C. *Disorderly Conduct: Visions of Gender in Victorian American.* New York: Knopf, 1985.

199

Soja, E. *Postmodern Geographies: The Reassertion of Space in Critical Social Theory.* New York: Verso, 1989.

Stewart, K. *Space on the Side of the Road: Cultural Poetics in an "Other" America.* Princeton: Princeton University Press, 1996.

Straayer, C. *Deviant Eyes, Deviant Bodies: Re-Orientations in Film and Video.* New York: Columbia University Press, 1996.

Stryker, S. "My Words to Victor Frankenstein above the Village of Chamounix: Performing Transgender Rage." *GLQ* 1, no. 3 (1994): 237–54.

Summerscale, K. *The Queen of Whale Cay: The Eccentric Story of Joe Carstairs, Fastest Woman on Water.* New York: Viking, 1997.

Terry, J. *An American Obsession: Science, Medicine, and the Place of Homosexuality in Modern Society.* Chicago: University of Chicago Press, 1999.

Thornton, S. Introduction to *The Subcultures Reader,* edited by K. Gelder and S. Thornton. New York: Routledge, 1997.

Timpanelli, G. "Uncertain Mandate: A Roundtable Discussion on Conservation Issues." In *Eva Hesse,* edited by E. Sussman, 98–106. San Francisco: San Francisco Museum of Modern Art, 2002.

Todd, J. M., and E. Spearing. *Counterfeit Ladies: The Life and Death of Mal Cutpurse: The Case of Mary Carleton.* New York: New York University Press, 1994.

Tsing, A. "Conclusion: The Global Situation." In *The Anthropology of Globalization: A Reader,* edited by J. X. Inda, 453–86. Oxford: Blackwell, 2002.

Tucker, S. *Swing Shift: "All-Girl" Bands of the 1940s.* Durham, NC: Duke University Press, 2001.

Valentine, D. "'I Know What I Am': The Category of 'Transgender' in the Construction of Contemporary U.S. Conceptions of Sexuality and Gender." PhD diss., New York University, 2000.

Volcano, D. L. "On Being a Jenny Saville Painting." In *Jenny Saville: Territories,* 24–25. New York: Gagosian Gallery, 1999.

———. *Sublime Mutations.* Berlin: Konkursbuchverlag, 2000.

———. "Transgenital Landscapes" in *Sublime Mutations* (Berlin: BHB Distribution, 2001).

Volk, P. "A Stranger Whose Magic Is to Feed the Starving." *New York Times,* November 12, 1997, B7.

Wald, G. "'I Want It That Way': Teenybopper Music and the Girling of Boy Bands." *Genders* 35 (2002): 1–39.

———. "Just a Girl? Rock Music, Feminism, and the Cultural Construction of Female Youth." *Signs: Journal of Women in Culture and Society* 23, no. 3 (1998): 585–610.

Warhol, A. *The Philosophy of Andy Warhol (From A to B and Back Again).* New York: Harcourt, Brace, 1975.

Weintraub, B. M. "Surgical Practice." In *Jenny Saville: Territories,* 26—27. New York: Gagosian Gallery, 1999.

Weston, K. "Get Thee to a Big City: Sexual Imaginary and the Great Gay Migration." *GLQ* 2, no. 3 (1995): 253–78.

White, P. "Girls Still Cry." *Screen* 42, no. 3 (2001): 122–28.

Wilson, A. R. "Getting Your Kicks on Route 66: Stories of Gay and Lesbian Life in Rural America, c. 1950s–1970s." In *De-Centering Sexualities: Politics and Representations beyond the Metropolis,* edited by R. Phillips, D. Watt, and D. E. Shuttleton, 199–216. London: Routledge, 2000.

Woolf, V. *Mrs. Dalloway.* London: Penguin, 1996.

Index

sex workers, 21
sex/gender systems, 37–38, 40–42, 50, 83–85, 87, 89, 90
"Shadows on a Dime" (Ferron), 183–86
Shepard, Matthew, 16, 32, 44, 46
"Shooting Star" (Williamson), 171, 180
shot/reverse shot, 86, 88–89, 105, 106, 107
"Shut Up and Dance: Youth Cultures and Changing Modes of Femininity" (McRobbie), 158, 166
Silverman, Kaja, 88
"Simo 2000" (Volcano), 115
Simonides, 74–75
Sinfield, Alan, 38, 189n3
Single Wet Female (Tropicana and Gomez), 162
Sixth Sense, The (Shyamalan), 76
Slab # 8 (Besemer). *See* insert between pages 120 and 121
slam poetry, 168–69
Sleater-Kinney (band), 154–59, 167
small town/rural environments: anonymity/privacy and, 27; class and, 27–33; gay life and, 35–36; imaginaries of, 27; lesbian writers on, 42; masculinities in, 29–30; medical discourse and, 40–41; migration from, 27, 33–34, 35–36, 37, 42, 70, 183–84; passing in, 43, 70; poverty and, 39; race and, 27–30, 28–31, 42; rural/urban binary and, 15, 30–32, 36, 190n7; sex/gender systems of, 39; "staying put," 27; staying put and, 33–34; transnational sexualities, 38–39; violence and, 14–15; whiteness and, 27–33, 41; white power movements and, 29–30; women in, 33; youth in, 32
Smith, Dinitia, 61, 62–64, 65, 66–67, 70–71
Soja, Edward, 5, 10, 11
Southern Comfort (Hill), 78
space/spatiality, 5–6, 11–12, 12–15, 189n4
Spearing, Elizabeth and Janet Todd, 72
spectatorship, 107–8, 139, 141, 146. *See also* transgender look, the
stabilization, 55
Stanwyck, Barbara, 85
Star, Kinnie, 181, 187
"staying put," 27, 190n6
Stewart, Kathleen, 33–34
Stiffed: The Betrayal of the American Men (Faludi), 126
Straayer, Chris, 86
style, 153
subcultural lives: avant-garde, 103, 109–10, 152; drag, 162; drag houses, 157–58; drag kings, 127, 128–35, 156–57, 174, 178–79; lesbian, 154–55, 160, 165–67; the main-

stream and, 127, 156–59; queers of color and, 168–69; youth, 159–62, 174, 177
Subculture: The Meaning of Style (Hebdige), 127, 159–60
Subcultures Reader, The (Thornton), 153
subcultures: adolescence/adulthood binary and, 174–77; alternative masculinities, 126–27; archives and, 169–74; community and, 153–54; counterpublics and, 186; dominant cultures and, 159–60; drag king, 37, 51, 127, 130–31, 134, 151, 156, 162; drag queen, 51, 128–29; gay and lesbian mainstream culture and, 160–61; girls and, 177; heteronormativity and, 152–54; historiography of, 187; kinging and, 128–29; mainstream absorption of, 148, 157–59; nonreproductive, 174–75; oedipal structures of, 160–61; producers of, 162–65; psychoanalysis and, 174; public sex and, 186; queers of color in, 162, 163–64; race and, 134, 175–76; resistance, 102, 109–10; slam poetry, 168–69; television/mass culture and, 156–59; theories of, 159–62, 162–65; transgender body and, 117; urban, 174
"Subject of Visual Culture, The" (Mirzoeff), 97
Sublime Mutations (Volcano), 114–15
Suits Me: The Double Life of Billy Tipton (Middlebrook), 56–59
Summerscale, Kate, 57
Swank, Hilary, 90, 93
SymbioticA, 110, 112–14

"Taking Identity Politics Seriously" (Clifford), 20
Tall Girl (Besemer), 123. *See also* insert between pages 120 and 121
Taxi Driver (Scorcese), 95–96
technotopics, 15, 101, 103, 124
Teena, Brandon, 15, 16, 23, 28, 44, 48, 54, 61, 64–69
"Teenybopper Music and the Girling of Boy Bands" (Wald), 177–78
temporal drag, 179–80, 183
temporal identifications, 179–80
Terminator 2: Judgment Day (Cameron), 76
Territories (Saville), 110
theory of archives, 169–70
"Thinking Sex" (Rubin), 35
Thornton, Sarah, 153
Time and the Other (Fabian), 25, 189n4
"Time of Plague" (Gunn), 2
time/space, 7–8, 10, 11, 15, 77, 87–88
time/temporalities, 6; alternatives, 187; dream time, 184–85; historiography and, 11; of

About the Author

Photo by Del LaGrace Volcano.

Judith Halberstam is Professor of English at the University of Southern California, in Los Angeles. She is the author of *Skin Shows: Gothic Horror and the Technology of Monsters* and *Female Masculinity,* and coauthor with Del LaGrace Volcano of *The Drag King Book.*